'Do universities have a public purpose beyond contributing to economic growth, new technologies, and the job skills of graduates? Could this purpose lie in supporting democracy not only prosperity, in nurturing understanding not only technical competence, and in preparing citizens not just workers? Morgan White doesn't just offer his answers to these questions but helps all of us think better about them – and about what democratic societies will lose if universities are transformed beyond recognition.'

Craig Calhoun, Director, London School of Economics and Political Science, UK

'Sociologically informed, philosophically insightful, and politically pertinent, *Towards a Political Theory of the University* provides a masterful critique of the problems and prospects of the university today. Morgan White brings a penetrating reading of Jürgen Habermas' philosophy to the understanding of the contemporary university, showing how the erosion of communicative reason and the colonization of the lifeworld have affected the institution in ways that are deeply corrosive for any wider culture of deliberative democracy. This is a book that should be read by anyone concerned with the future of higher education and the political culture it sustains.'

Paul Standish, Professor, UCL Institute of Education, UK

'Morgan White places the university at the heart of democratic politics. Against the popularist rhetoric of both the political left and right, he affirms the prime importance of the university as a space of public reason. Without such civic spaces, he argues, democracy is not only impoverished but seriously at risk. *Towards a Political Theory of the University* should be read by academics, policy makers, politicians and all those with a commitment to open debate and inquiry.'

Jon Nixon, Honorary Professor, The Education University of Hong Kong, Hong Kong

Towards a Political Theory of the University

Towards a Political Theory of the University argues that state and market forces threaten to diminish the legitimacy, authority and fundamental purposes of higher education systems. The political role of higher education has been insufficiently addressed by academics in recent decades. By applying Habermas' theory of communicative action, this book seeks to reconnect educational and political theory and provide an analysis of the university which complements the recent focus on the intersections between political philosophy and legal theory.

In this book, White argues that there is considerable overlap between crises in democracy and in universities. Yet while crises in democracy are often attributed to the inability of political institutions to adapt to the pace of social and cultural change, this diagnosis wilfully ignores the effects of privatisation on public institutions. Under present political conditions, the university is regarded in instrumental and economic terms, which not only diminishes its functions of developing and sustaining culture but also removes its democratic capabilities. This book explores these issues in depth and presents some of the practical problems associated with turning an independent higher education system into a state-dominated and then, subsequently, marketised system.

This book bridges political and educational theory in an original and comprehensive way and makes an important contribution to the debate over the role of the university in a democracy. As such, it will appeal to researchers, academics and postgraduate students in the fields of the philosophy of education, higher education and political and educational theory. With its implications for policy and practice, it will also be of interest to policy-makers.

Morgan White has been a tutor in Philosophy of Education at University of Cambridge, UK and a lecturer in Education at Liverpool Hope University, UK. He received his PhD from University of Manchester, UK, and has a particular interest in the public role of higher education, social justice, deliberative democracy and tensions with instrumental learning.

New Directions in the Philosophy of Education Series
Series Editors
Michael A. Peters, *University of Waikato, New Zealand;
University of Illinois, USA*
Gert Biesta, *Brunel University, UK*

For a full list of titles in this series, please visit www.routledge.com

This book series is devoted to the exploration of new directions in the philosophy of education. After the linguistic turn, the cultural turn and the historical turn, where might we go? Does the future promise a digital turn with a greater return to connectionism, biology and biopolitics based on new understandings of system theory and knowledge ecologies? Does it foreshadow a genuinely alternative radical global turn based on a new openness and interconnectedness? Does it leave humanism behind or will it reengage with the question of the human in new and unprecedented ways? How should philosophy of education reflect new forces of globalisation? How can it become less Anglo-centric and develop a greater sensitivity to other traditions, languages, and forms of thinking and writing, including those that are not rooted in the canon of Western philosophy but in other traditions that share the 'love of wisdom' that characterizes the wide diversity within Western philosophy itself? Can this be done through a turn to intercultural philosophy? To indigenous forms of philosophy and philosophizing? Does it need a post-Wittgensteinian philosophy of education? A postpostmodern philosophy? Or should it perhaps leave the whole construction of 'post'-positions behind?

In addition to the question of the intellectual resources for the future of philosophy of education, what are the issues and concerns that philosophers of education should engage with? How should they position themselves? What is their specific contribution? What kind of intellectual and strategic alliances should they pursue? Should philosophy of education become more global, and if so, what would the shape of that be? Should it become more cosmopolitan or perhaps more decentred? Perhaps most importantly in the digital age, the time of the global knowledge economy that reprofiles education as privatised human capital and simultaneously in terms of an historic openness, is there a philosophy of education that grows out of education itself, out of the concerns for new forms of teaching, studying, learning and speaking that can provide comment on ethical and epistemological configurations of economics and politics of knowledge? Can and should this imply a reconnection with questions of democracy and justice?

This series comprises texts that explore, identify and articulate new directions in the philosophy of education. It aims to build bridges, both geographically and temporally: bridges across different traditions and practices and bridges towards a different future for philosophy of education.

In this series

Educational Philosophy for a Post-secular Age
David Lewin

Towards a Political Theory of the University
Public reason, democracy and higher education
Morgan White

Towards a Political Theory of the University

Public reason, democracy and higher education

Morgan White

LONDON AND NEW YORK

First published 2017
by Routledge

2 Park Square, Milton Park, Abingdon, Oxfordshire OX14 4RN
711 Third Avenue, New York, NY 10017

Routledge is an imprint of the Taylor & Francis Group, an informa business

First issued in paperback 2018

Copyright © 2017 Morgan White

The right of Morgan White to be identified as author of this work has been asserted by him in accordance with sections 77 and 78 of the Copyright, Designs and Patents Act 1988.

All rights reserved. No part of this book may be reprinted or reproduced or utilised in any form or by any electronic, mechanical, or other means, now known or hereafter invented, including photocopying and recording, or in any information storage or retrieval system, without permission in writing from the publishers.

Notice:
Product or corporate names may be trademarks or registered trademarks, and are used only for identification and explanation without intent to infringe.

British Library Cataloguing in Publication Data
A catalogue record for this book is available from the British Library

Library of Congress Cataloging in Publication Data
A catalog record has been requested for this book

ISBN: 978-1-138-95216-4 (hbk)
ISBN: 978-1-138-61026-2 (pbk)

Typeset in Bembo
by Apex CoVantage, LLC

Contents

Acknowledgements		ix
Introduction		1
1	The university and the public sphere	9
2	Higher education and economies of worth	21
3	The role of the university in a democracy	35
4	Academic authority, trust and reliance	49
5	Higher education and citizenship	63
6	The ivory tower and public life	78
7	The corruption of democracy and education	92
8	Implications for policy and practice	115
9	Towards a modern democratic society	133
10	Concluding remarks: Communicative rationality and the cultural impoverishment of the university	147
Bibliography		179
Index		187

Acknowledgements

This book has been in the pipeline for too long and, consequently, the debts of gratitude in some cases go back many years and are rather overdue. Thanks to my editors at Routledge, Heidi Lowther, Leslie Rotsky and Thomas Storr, for their patience and diligence. For their support, I am grateful to Maurizio Passerin d'Entreves, Dave Lewin, Joey McKay, Aideen Hunter, Paul Standish, Jon Nixon and Roger Brown. I would also like to thank Joan and Ian Hughes, Ronnie and Suzanne White and Vic White, my parents, step-parents and brother, for their help and advice. I am thankful to Dan and Sophie Jones, for their interest in the work and for getting me out of a couple of nasty scrapes along the way. For all her help over the final year of writing this book, I am incredibly grateful to Inessa Melnikova. Here's to the ideas of love, loyalty and an aim for E.M. Forster's aristocracy of the sensitive, considerate and plucky.

Introduction

I have written *about* the political philosophy of universities and higher education. The argument is not so much to do with issues of distributive justice, but about how public policies and institutions shape people and culture and so change the contours of democracy. I think the argument is an urgent one because in many ways it is being made too late – once a tradition is gone it can rarely be recaptured: universities and higher education provide a public benefit by enriching democracy through a process of civilisation. Maybe it is not too late for other countries to heed the warning, and maybe it is *not* too late for policy-makers in Britain to reconsider their market system. Markets are highly differentiated but they do tend to require aggressive sales techniques, especially, perhaps, at the lower end of the market. If people within universities are rewarded through self-promotion, through 'entrepreneurial' activities, and the hierarchy stretches too far, then the capacity for civilising begins to break down. I think this is a seminal form of corruption that then engenders subsequent corrosion of civility in other institutions. Education is such a porous concept that it has come to serve as an ideal political tool: offering up the possibility of meritocracy, or social mobility, or elitism, or increased productivity, or social justice, or effective role allocation, or the development of good character. Much like the term 'democracy', education is all things to all politicians, while those students, teachers, researchers and managers are buffeted from pillar to post. Its porous character enables policy-makers and vested interests (some of whom may also be policy-makers) to equivocate over the category of good to which education most properly belongs. For instance, empirical research on earning differentials between graduates and non-graduates has supported the claim that higher education mostly benefits the individual graduate and, as such, must be a private good. If higher education is a private investment good, then it follows that individual graduates should bear the costs. 'Why should dinner ladies pay for the degrees of university graduates?' was the politician's populist refrain when justifying the introduction of tuition fees in England. But already in this story there is sleight of hand. Public goods are not defined as goods which don't confer any benefit on the private individual. Think of some paradigm example of a public good (even on Paul Samuelson's classic, narrow definition), non-excludable and non-rivalrous, like a street lamp. When the street lamp lights up the darkened alley it obviously brings me benefit as I amble home late at night, but this is not to say that the street lamp becomes a private good. This book is an attempt to shed some light on higher education and universities and what has happened to the academic ethic in recent decades. In around 1769 Denis Diderot wrote a short story called 'Regrets on my Old Dressing Gown'. The story is simple. A man gets a fancy new dressing gown. He's very pleased with it. But his new dressing gown starts to make his other possessions look rather shabby. So he replaces all his old things with shiny new things. Then he gets some more new stuff. This is not Calvino's fable about the mountain of waste that is hidden in plain sight of conspicuous consumption, but rather that before he knows what's happened, the dressing gown's owner has a whole new group of friends round at his house looking at his newly acquired works of art and it begins to dawn on him that he no longer knows anybody and he has become a different person.

Universities face a similar situation, but it is probably most visible to those with the quietest voices, in precarious employment at less prestigious institutions. So enamoured with status and rankings, new research findings, prestige and reputation, universities have lost sight of their public purposes. They produce new knowledge (for the public), they protect old knowledge (for future publics), they develop understanding in students who go on to constitute the public (see Marginson, 2006).

The argument of this book, like the street lamp, is meant as a kind of public good. No doubt, though, many will regard the argument as elitist, or inapplicable to particular disciplines. In a certain sense the argument is elitist, but it is also democratic, and we should be capable of holding on to those two ideas simultaneously. The claim that the old university system merely functioned as a large subsidy for the middle classes is too broad brushed. University students come from a wide range of backgrounds, and this has been increasingly so since the 1970s. Now, in tertiary education in countries like England or Australia, potential students from working class families may find it easier to get in to universities, but will probably not benefit in the same ways and to the same extent as previous generations. Partly, this is a product of the massive expansion of systems of higher education in post-industrial nations, but as the expansion has continued, the power of universities to act as institutions that support upward social mobility has faltered.

Universities have been around for a long time, some predate many nation states, though most are thoroughly modern and their numbers have multiplied in modern times. They are institutions which collect together people with diverse interests, knowledge and skills in an attempt to develop, preserve and transmit cultural and scientific understanding. In part, universities did this through pursuing 'higher' education that sought to go deeper and cultivate in students and academics an intellectual desire towards developing understanding further by increased specialisation and connecting differentiated ideas. Empirically, of course, not all education that goes on in universities will encourage such intellectual autonomy, and there are, no doubt, brilliant teachers in schools and colleges who do manage to cultivate it. However, the concepts of 'higher education institution' and 'university' are often used interchangeably. There is a certain irony involved in this because one large part of the argument I want to make is that universities are increasingly abdicating their responsibility to cultivate higher education. The university was a contemplative reserve army of experts, with the epistemic authority to advise governments and produce technical research of use to medicine, industry, commerce and education. 'The university' provided an alternative site of authority, it prepared people for work in professions and educated those who would go on to become managers in industry, schools, civil servants and government ministers. But as universities expanded to serve the requirements of the knowledge economy, democratic states have struggled to maintain their relations with the ivory towers. Public services fell under the spell of an accountability agenda that saw the concepts of state and public all too easily elide.

The altered relations between the state, the public and universities perhaps ought to have led to a greater political-philosophical focus, but instead political philosophy has been curiously shy, by and large, of investigating the relationships between education and democracy. Axel Honneth recently wrote that:

> Not only democratic theory but politics itself seems to have lost interest in the only kind of institution that is suited to constantly regenerate, albeit tentatively and with great effort, the fragile preconditions of a people's democratic decision-making.
>
> (Honneth, 2015, p. 29)

I think that Honneth has this half-right, for politics seems to be very much interested in using education as an economic tool, not so much as a democratic institution. This is a concern at a time of crude populist politics and culture, when slow economic growth, more precarious employment patterns, growing inequality and issues of generational injustice are causing new political cleavages and an inward orientation. If education is to be liberating, then genuine educational institutions should give serious consideration to the effects of decades of functionalist education policies. Universities should hold a position of educational authority over schools and colleges and ought to use this authority to set right a system in the hands of an elective dictatorship. The universities' authority, however, has been effectively neutered by an academic atmosphere where it would be politically imprudent to criticise those who hold the purse strings.

Plato, Aristotle, Rousseau, Kant, Bentham, J.S. Mill, Durkheim, Dewey and Oakeshott all regarded questions of education as necessarily connected with questions of politics. Yet, political theory seems somehow to have largely lost interest in education. Or, perhaps, political theory has only tended in recent times to focus on distributive questions involving education. This is odd given that political theory has a tradition of exploring the ways in which the design of institutions helps shape ways of thinking and modes of behaviour of those affected by the institutions. Axel Honneth suggests this is down to a loss of faith in the ability of schools and educational institutions to generate the sorts of dispositions required in democracy. These dispositions come, not through schooling, but from the substantive ethical attitudes generated in broader society, according at least to the Böckenförde theorem, which proposes that democracies depend on moral attitudes that come from tradition-based ethical communities (Honneth, 2015). Yet, recently there has been a revival of work on character education, virtue ethics and virtue epistemology that points towards the importance of educational institutions in generating the normative attitudes that foster democratic norms (see, for example, Arthur, 2010).

More than a generation ago, Jürgen Habermas suggested that universities must transmit technically exploitable knowledge but should do so alongside the interpretation and development of cultural tradition and forming the political consciousness of students (Habermas, 1987, pp. 1–3). Some forty years later, it seems that the purposes of universities are being reduced to the first of these goals while students (and academics) are also technically exploited. The idea of the university was once the institutionalised form of a realm for free inquiry and the rational exchange of ideas engaged in the collaborative pursuit of knowledge and understanding. Doubtless, this still goes on, but there is a palpable sense that the normative foundations of the university's idea have shifted.

The concepts of the unrestricted communication community or the ideal speech situation are important to the idea of deliberative democracy. The notion of the 'ideal speech situation' involves unrestricted communication in discourse between participants free from disparities in power. This heuristic device was intended, by Habermas, to act as a yardstick against which to measure real, concrete instances of dialogue. The idea comes, originally, from C.S. Peirce, where the ideal communication community is based around an idealised understanding of scientific progress. Peirce pointed out that scientists work within a community rather than individually. In this scientific community, teams of scientists make discoveries and propose new theories. The ideas and discoveries are discussed and criticised by other teams of scientists in order to come to a provisionally settled understanding of scientific laws. The reality of this process will tend to be distorted by a lack of information, or resources, or hierarchies of power within the scientific community. Actual agreement on what constitutes science is therefore contrasted with an ideal community of scientists where communication is undistorted. The central elements of this idea are just as applicable to scholarship in the arts, humanities and social sciences. We could argue, for instance, that the sort of undistorted communication Peirce imagined also serves as a model for teaching in seminars (see, for example, Barthes, 1989), where students participate together in deliberation and the seminar leader's role is to enable a seminar with epistemic value.

The problem, however, with the ideal speech situation is that it is too often mistaken as a model for real deliberation. David Estlund (2008) argues that this should not be its role. Instead, the ideal deliberative model functions as a template against which to judge real deliberation, but real deliberation in the public sphere should itself be divided into formal and informal publics. Different modes of real deliberation are appropriate in the formal and informal political realms: narrow civility is suited to formal politics, wide civility is required in informal politics. Estlund is concerned to point out that 'wide mirroring' of the ideal deliberative model is inappropriate to informal political discourse, outside of the state – legislature, executive and judiciary. The difficulty with this claim is that it is not clear whether a public institution like a university in a democracy belongs to formal or informal politics. I try to argue that universities are institutions that mediate between the formal and informal public realms and, as such, they are places that cultivate both narrow and wide modes of civility in order to cultivate the authority to act appropriately in different contexts.

Universities are often referred to, especially in policy language, as Higher Education Institutions (HEIs). But we ought to beware that administrative and policy speak conflate the concepts. Higher education sometimes takes place in universities, but not all education at university takes a higher form. Whether higher education always takes place in universities at the undergraduate level is one of the educational issues that I try to examine. I am certain that higher education still takes place sometimes, but it will depend on the academics and the students; it rests not only on consequences (graduate employment, etc.) if at all, or on the 'inputs' from teachers but on the relations between them and the subject matter and the discipline involved. This means higher education is relational, and the relations deepen through a process of teaching and learning. Instrumentalists will tend to see these as inputs and outputs, but this is absurd. Teachers learn as they teach because preparation is logically prior to teaching. In this regard teachers are also students. *Studere*, to diligently apply, becomes increasingly difficult when the space to think and contemplate is closed down, but teachers are often the ones studying hardest, and students, of course, are teachers too (Barthes, 1989).

This book is about universities in general, and the general idea of what it means to be a university and what makes universities and higher education valuable. Stefan Collini attacked the utilitarian purposes of universities by arguing that after economic benefits are gained we need still to consider what we want to do with those gains (Collini, 2012). The argument in my book takes a slightly different tack by trying to consider how universities should contribute to the spirit in which we live together, and like concerns raised by Christopher Newfield (2008) or Martha Nussbaum (1997 & 2010) or John Holmwood (2011) or Joanna Williams (2013). But I also hope that my argument touches on a broader point than just analysis of the idea of universities: that meaningful democracy requires strong public institutions that do not merely feed into the democratic state, but can also help support a state founded on public reason. Some people may object to an 'essentialist' line of inquiry that imposes one particular view of the university tied to a particular purpose, but the purpose in mind here is open and democratic. The university is essentially open and democratic because it is an institution oriented towards scientific inquiry and scholarship. This is a mode that takes the long view, that values projects without obvious financial returns and is sufficiently brave to commit to a self-confidence in its scholarly ethic.

The structure of the argument returns again and again to the place for rational-critical discourse in universities. In chapter 1 I explore the idea of the public sphere in relation to universities and higher education and the changing nature of the principle of publicity. I argue that public reason takes on a one-dimensional character in circumstances where consensus is sought on the grounds of economic self-interest. In chapter 2 I try to look closer at the idea of 'economies of worth' and a sociological theory of justification that manages, in my view, to miss an important aspect of higher education and relating to liberation and appeals to equality through knowledge. I then try to show how the role universities have in sustaining a democratic culture is not open to the possibility of privatisation. This, however, hinges on a particular view of the democratic state which is more open to information from citizens and institutions. On this view democracy concerns public trust. Chapter 3 is about universities in a democracy. I demonstrate that models of higher education funding grounded on the idea of human capital depend on a morally neutral conception of higher education, rather than one committed to developing public trust through reason. Chapter 4 examines the concept of epistemic authority in relation to democracy and the marketisation of higher education. I examine the concept of student partnership, which is often intended to help reduce the tension between educational relations and the producer-consumer relations of the market. I try to show how asserting relations of partnership on teachers and students actually serves to prevent the development of students with authority to act and may even generate distrust. If higher education has a role in supporting the legitimacy of democratic states, then this does not bode well for the future of democratic politics. Chapter 5 looks at the relationship between citizenship and higher education in more detail and proposes that we should think of citizenship and education in republican rather than liberal terms. In chapter 6 I propose a stronger connection between higher education and work, rather than labour. Chapter 7 considers the idea of cultural impoverishment in education in democratic societies. I examine the idea of the market communicating information through the price mechanism and the effects of policy attempts to recreate the price mechanism in other forms in a bureaucratically imposed market structure. The argument is that claims to efficiency gains in universities lose validity given the change in our understandings of the purposes of universities. Chapter 8 looks into the policy changes in British and English university governance and argues that an instrumentalist understanding of knowledge generates qualification inflation and overbearing concerns for status in institutions and individuals. Finally, in chapter 9, I connect university education with the expansion of the welfare state and social rights in order to show that higher education in instrumentalised universities places insufficient emphasis on rational-critical discourse to support democracy. In chapter 10 I set about explaining and attempting to apply Habermas' theory of communicative action to universities in order to show how recent policy changes have altered the cultures of higher education and universities in a way that has been damaging for democracy.

The story that emerges might be dismissed as a jeremiad, a lament for a past institution that never really existed. This is not the intention here. Rather, I want to reassert the public worth of universities and higher education and insist that universities contain the potential for generating legitimate authority in democratic states. It should be possible to design policies that pay much more attention to the public qualities of public institutions. Indeed, this is what we ought to focus on if public institutions are really to be held accountable *qua* public institutions. For public institutions must make a contribution to democracy.

Some readers may well wonder which universities this book address itself to. My discussion revolves around British universities, especially universities and higher education policies and practices in England. This is not meant to be a parochial exercise, though it might come across that way. The policy experiment in attempting to transform universities into a system and then turning that system into a market is a direction of change that can be seen in many countries, especially given that universities are so often regarded as engines of growth in post-industrial societies. England is undoubtedly at the forefront of this policy experiment, so while I talk about the situation in the UK or England, I intend it as a warning to anyone interested in how those policies are working. Moreover, universities exist in a global context. Scholarship and research is international, and British universities are influential and expanding into other markets in other countries as they recruit overseas students and establish campuses abroad to cater for demand for their brand. Indeed, universities are at great pains to point out how they transcend their local context. Many would do well to consider their local roles more carefully, but such considerations rarely feature in concerns about ranking in international league tables or in developing a high-status brand. The tension is stretched between the ideas of academics and students as equal participants in argument versus the idea of status ranking that is used to sell the institution.

This book is mostly about universities in democratic societies, where the state imposes targets to ensure accountability – its analysis tends towards the UK, especially England, but also applies to the USA, Australia, New Zealand, Canada. The problems are most acute where voices can least be heard: among junior academics in lower-ranking institutions. However, it is misleading to think about this in straightforward empirical terms. For the central idea involved here is that in a global system of universities and higher education, all universities are at risk from uncivilising tendencies, though the tendencies are much more marked at some (lower) levels in various hierarchies and in some (more marketised or more bureaucratised) national systems.

Some readers may worry that the argument I present sounds worryingly elitist. At times it may sound as though I am too critical of the expansion of universities and higher education, and astute critics may well point out that the universities of the twentieth century operated as a heavy subsidy for the middle classes. The subsidy point is doubtlessly true, but I do not see the argument as elitist, although that term holds many meanings. A democratic politics requires education fit for democracy, not an education that is itself democratic. Universities need to be educationally elite, for their role is fundamentally political as an alternative site of authority to the state. This becomes increasingly important in a populist culture where elected politicians, educated at the same few universities, keep their focus on the next election cycle.

Chapter 1

The university and the public sphere

Democracy is always already in crisis because democratic politics is always a matter of ongoing deliberation that is never settled once and for all. The democratic will necessarily balances on the blade of the knife. And yet, in the real world democratic politics are populist, they are corrupted, they are technocratic and this has been an echoing refrain through the twentieth and into the twenty-first century. Even though political crisis is inevitable, there is surely merit in the claim that control over democratic politics has drifted away from ordinary citizens. The idea of the university also seems to be in constant crisis. There are ongoing concerns about levels of tuition fees for students, modes of funding, managerialism and bureaucracy supplanting an academic ethic, issues surrounding freedom of speech and academic freedom, grade inflation and over-expansion, the role of higher education in social mobility, the value of pure theoretical research; the list goes on and on. I think the crises in democracy and in universities overlap considerably. The seeds of the plant that might resolve the democratic crisis are most likely to be found in our public institutions, but decision-making in universities has also drifted away from the people who study within them. The language of democracy is all too often used to cloak tyrannical regimes in the robes of legitimacy. Think of how Vaclav Havel takes apart the idea of the Prague greengrocer who puts a 'Workers of the world unite' sign in his window. Similarly, the language of the university, of higher learning, of research and scholarship can cloak academic institutions which have little interest in their public capacities yet proclaim programmes of civic engagement.

Problems with contemporary democracy

Writers like Arendt, Lijphart and Touraine have all argued that, fundamentally, democracy allows us to live together, and this seems increasingly difficult as society becomes ever more complex and differentiated. The public approves the idea of democracy but despises the reality of politics, just as academics might appeal to a love of the idea of the university while feeling their hopes dashed on the rocks of the realities of some aspects of the job.

Perhaps a central problem with democracy is that we have lost our political imagination and that ability to maintain an optimism of the will in the face of intellectual pessimism. How, Habermas has asked, do we cultivate a collective political imagination in the face of the exhaustion of utopian energies? There seems endless disagreement about what constitutes the limit of free speech, but in an era when so many voices can speak through social media we ought to draw attention to a public medium for talking. What use, Arendt says, is free speech if nobody will listen? It seems that if our political culture is a cacophony of different interests screaming into a virtual void of comments, likes, tweets and blogs then what we need to reassert is the equivalent cultural environment of the intellectual salon, where such ill-mannered discourse could not be countenanced. We need to foster the art of listening and resurrect institutions that impose conditions which enable rational discourse. Crises in democracy are often attributed to the idea that political institutions cannot adapt to the pace of social and cultural change. This diagnosis, however, seems to willfully ignore the ways in which our public institutions are being transformed into private institutions which have lost their democratic capacities.

Democracy is often said to depend on understanding and accepting the compromise between participating and being a subject. Now, however, the public is no longer deferential in the way it once was and wants to participate as skeptical, critical citizens. Skepticism, of course, is healthy but cynicism is corrosive. Zygmunt Bauman's notion of 'liquid modernity', for instance, stresses how strong social anchors and institutions have changed, like church, jobs for life and universities. In their place now we have the precariate, photoshopped images and brand management. The result is a cultural anomie that feeds a sense of legitimation crisis that affects some groups more than others. Inequality is disrupting a sense of political belonging. The young and the poor are less likely to vote compared with the old and wealthy, and this points towards a need for political education for the sake of democracy. Instead of an attempt to resolve this situation, however, public services are being moved towards those who do engage with voting. Ontological insecurity feeds narcissism and we are left with a political system that puts off anyone concerned about their own self-image. The vacuum is filled by anti-political demagogues who promise simple populist answers to intractable problems.

The democratic process is messy and ongoing, but populism wants simple quick fixes which tend to generate antipathy towards some minority that can be readily blamed. Populism is an expression of public frustration at a lack of perceived required change, and the more public institutions seem resistant to offer this change, the more likely politicians are to tap in to populist sentiment. The charge is often that democratic institutions have not kept pace with social change, but this obscures the role of the imposition of market frameworks on public institutions. Markets tend towards providing goods that consumers demand, what they want rather than what they need.

Mainstream parties have offered the market mechanism as a panacea for all problems. But the market needs the counterweight of democratic politics. Trust itself has become commodified, e.g. through customer loyalty cards where consumer data is purchased in exchange for 'points'. Market values have become imbued within ourselves in an atomised civic culture, and democratic elections have become exercises in selling policy bundles to the electorate. However, political participation is not consumption of a package of policies and the public is not a market. Indeed, economic behaviour often tends towards irrationality. David Marquand, describing Thorstein Veblen's critique of the leisure class, explains that:

> In modern societies 'good repute' depended on 'pecuniary strength'; and 'pecuniary strength' could be demonstrated only by 'leisure and a conspicuous consumption of goods'. Economic behaviour was not rational, as conventional economic theory assumed, and still assumes. It was governed by bizarre rituals of emulation reminiscent . . . of the mating displays of peacocks. . . . Like their American predecessors a century ago, today's 'celebs' are Mammon's most glittering acolytes and Mammon worship's most successful missionaries.
>
> (Marquand, 2015, p. 5)

In the face of growing inequality and celebrity culture, the public demands more from politicians, but democracy has hived off many of its institutions in an attempt to depoliticise democracy. This is an abdication of responsibility for the world because people will struggle to re-engage with democracy when politics itself has become enfeebled. The capacity to act politically has been diminished. Action is increasingly supplanted by reputation management. Cribb and Gewirtz describe the 'hollowed-out' university as one where academic substance has been transformed into organisational surface:

> It is not just that some academics choose to present their work and careers in ultra-packaged passages of hype and are, on occasions, seemingly comfortable to sell themselves as 'assets' and drive hard bargains in the careers marketplace. But it is also, and much more routinely, that the merits of academics are increasingly spoken of, not only by managers but by themselves, in terms which derive directly from the reputational drivers of the university.
>
> (Cribb and Gewirtz, 2013, p. 344)

To the extent that academics identify themselves as 4* researchers, or engage in the 'miniaturisation' of knowledge (May, 2001) in order that research issues become small and manageable in order to ensure publication, they turn away from what Alessandro Ferrara calls the 'democratic horizon' (Ferrara, 2014). This issue is also raised in relation to academic freedom, where Jon Elster has argued that freedom to think has become undermined by tendencies towards obscurantism in academic work (Elster, 2015, p. 82). Elster's argument is that academic conservatism leads to a lack of freedom if scholarship is pushed towards existing conventions and there exists a timidity about making an attempt to engage in original thought because of risks to career progression. If the quality of academic work is gauged on some metric such as numbers of citations, then voice is not free but tuned to prevailing orthodoxy.

This might be mistaken for an over supply of democracy: too much voice, free speech, openness, transparency, but the wrong sort of self-seeking rather than public spirited action. There are many ways of engaging politically, but the cacophony of information and resulting complexity makes analysis and action all but impossible, or at least, overwhelming. Noise replaces thoughtfulness. The noisiest tend to be those with the greatest interests and resources, rather than the better argument. The result is legitimation crisis for academics and citizens. The presence of more opinions should not be mistaken for democracy and such cacophony does not generate the calm conditions for rationality.

In this frenzy of opinions there is a lost capacity for listening. Listening is a public virtue for deliberative democrats. Hannah Arendt refers to the public sphere as a realm of appearances:

> Compared with the reality which comes from being seen and heard, even the greatest forces of intimate life – the passions of the heart, the thoughts of the mind, the delights of the senses – lead an uncertain, shadowy kind of existence unless and until they are transformed, deprivatized and deindividualized, as it were, into a shape to fit them for public appearance.
> (Arendt, 1998, p. 50)

Deliberative democracy requires deliberative manners. We need a calm conversation rather than a shouting match. Adversarial politics sees listening as weak, flip-flopping, etc. We need space for contemplation but we also require an ethos that allows us to see and to listen, rather than one that encourages us to package ourselves as high-grade assets that add institutional value. A conversation is catatelic, but technocratic, professional politics are about pushing through agendas to generate decisions and effective policies. Nicholas Mirzoeff points out that in our visual culture ontology is increasingly presented as a matter of performance symbolised by voguing (the dance) where the goal is to present realness and avoid being 'read' as fake, despite using exaggerated movements: 'You wanted to simply appear to be what you appeared to be. In short, for your performance to succeed so well that it becomes invisible as a performance' (Mirzoeff, 2015, p. 58). If the space of appearances comprises individuals struggling to be seen and heard but not to look and listen, then the potential for rationality contained in the space collapses. Think, for example, of the scientists encouraged to focus on publishing groundbreaking research findings and neglecting attempts to test and falsify their colleagues' work. Fetishizing the new undermines a fundamentally important aspect of the scientific community by encouraging individualist incentives (Moriarty, 2011, p. 71).

Democracy requires political literacy among engaged citizens, rather than different literacies which talk past each other. Normative learning is a lost possibility in such complex conditions. Political education, in the limited, empirical sense of understanding how the system works, ends up leading to disengagement. We need, instead, to encourage democratic literacy and critical skepticism to rebuild a civic culture whereby engaged citizens no longer feel overwhelmed in conditions of complexity.

This may well involve a need to increase the quality of politicians and improved quality in public service broadcasting. Above all, however, a re-enchantment of democracy requires publicly oriented education. Publicly oriented higher education feeds into all these. Think, for instance, how media figures like journalists but also celebrities, politicians and civil servants are increasingly brought in to universities, sometimes as occasional lecturers but also as heads of colleges.

But we need to alter the culture of universities and go beyond, for instance, universities sponsoring a few academy schools or recruiting well-known names to the staff. Who will vote for radical policies required to address pressing problems that will require self-sacrifice? This concern cannot be addressed through marketing campaigns to attract funds and students. The overarching issue is about making the public responsible for itself.

The public sphere seems still to be undergoing structural transformation, though in a deeply concerning direction. New forms of technology created new social media, newspapers are read online, television viewed on demand and on computer screens and tablets, lectures are read on mobile phones. It is tempting to regard the switch from print media, to TV broadcasting, to the internet as a structural transformation of the public sphere, and we can be sure that one is involved, but we should be careful to distinguish the locus of publics from transformations in the public sphere.

The public sphere involves relations between persons. In other words, it is a political rather than a social relation involved between actors within it, and the difference is attitudinal rather than substantive (Benhabib, 2003, p. 148). Something is public when it is open to all, but, like a public building, this need not mean the doors are thrown open to everybody. Rather, a public building might house an institution that belongs to the public realm (Habermas, 1989, p. 2), like the offices of town planners. For Arendt, the public sphere is relational: the spaces between people constitute our common world – our 'inter-est', which binds us together (Arendt, 1998, p. 182).

Now, the concept of the public sphere is unhelpfully porous. Too often the concept of the public sphere – that site where speaker and hearer meet under a principle of rational-critical publicity – is confused with civil society more broadly or particular fractions of the public. When Habermas first published *The Structural Transformation of the Public Sphere* he was keen to point out that there existed a moment in history, pre-revolutionary French bourgeois society, when the public sphere contained emancipatory potential. The salons of the Eighteenth Century Enlightenment briefly provided a moment within which unconstrained communicative rationality held sway and discourse was guided through the force of the better argument. Bourgeois intellectual society held latent within it a moment with emancipatory potential.

Some of Habermas' earliest critics were quick to point out that this portrayal of the public sphere overlooked the role of 'subaltern publics'. There are, for writers like Oskar Negt and Alexander Kluge, and Nancy Fraser, less visible groups contributing towards social change through their struggles for recognition. Candidate groups include workers' movements, the women's movement or the black civil rights movement.

The force of the criticism was that Habermas' focus on intellectualism served to privilege a particular form of (masculine or bourgeois) rationalism in argumentation. Proletarian counterpublics, Negt and Kluge argued, involved much more learning from experience rather than bourgeois reason. Fraser argued that subordinated social groups found it advantageous to establish alternative publics.

Craig Calhoun points out that the idea of counterpublics can be misleading. Analysts, keen to tell the story of subaltern groups, over-emphasise the extent to which they formed parallel publics to a dominant bourgeois public sphere as part of some deliberate political strategy. More likely it was a second-best alternative to participating in the 'primary public sphere'. Radical intellectuals of the eighteenth century often found themselves outside of the public sphere and setting up counterpublics because they had been deliberately expelled by elites (Calhoun, 2012, p. 159).

The structural transformation of the public sphere

Habermas' influential study of the structural transformation of the public sphere forms the bedrock for understanding his sociological and philosophical theories of communicative action and discourse ethics. At the heart of his immanent critique of the public sphere is the idea that moments containing emancipatory potential occasionally spring forth. This early book (written in 1962 but not translated into English until 1989) traces the category of the public through a theoretically heavy historical analysis:

> We are dealing here with categories of Greek origin transmitted to us bearing a Roman stamp. In the fully developed Greek city-state the sphere of the *polis*, which was common (*koine*) to the free citizens, was strictly separated from the sphere of the *oikos*; in the sphere of the *oikos*, each individual is in his own realm (*idia*). The public life, *bios politikos*, went on in the market place (*agora*), but of course this did not mean that it occurred necessarily only in this specific locale. The public sphere was constituted in discussion (*lexis*), which could also assume the forms of consultation and of sitting in

the court of law, as well as in common action (*praxis*), be it the waging of war or competition in athletic games.

(Habermas, 1989, p. 3)

The private sphere of the *oikos* was obscure but status over the private sphere determined membership of the *polis*. Citizens with property and slaves could therefore enter the realm of freedom and permanence where issues took shape, and the best gained the immortality of fame. Necessity belonged to the *oikos* while the polis provided the place for honourable distinction where 'citizens indeed interacted as equals with equals (*homoioi*), but each did his best to excel (*aristoiein*)' (Habermas, 1989, p. 4).

Of course, through different historical epochs the meaning of the category of the public was subject to change. For example, the English monarch of the Middle Ages enjoyed 'publicness'. His kingship was represented, or staged, publicly, before his public, as a higher power with an aura of *arete*, endowed with his authority.

This dramaturgical presentation of publicness survives in the titles, insignia, dress and demeanour associated with the university, where the vice-chancellors, the professors and, nowadays, senior managers of (perhaps especially) lower-ranked institutions have a tendency to present a traditional representation of the institution that harks back to such mediaeval hierarchy. Look to how keen universities are to establish their traditional heritage, making a case for their historical rootedness, their longevity and their proximity to the mediaeval university. The fetish for rankings and league tables among universities is important to bear in mind, of course. When we hear talk that the idea of the university is broken from the bottom end of the hierarchy, we do not wait long for a dismissal of such an overblown claim from the top tier. It seems an obvious point to make that both claims might be partially true, though voices from the lower echelons might be drowned out by those from higher ranked institutions.

The meaning of public did not remain stable. Indeed, the story of the transformation of the public sphere is one of struggle for recognition between state and society. The basis for the bourgeois public sphere which contained the potential for communicative reason rested on the separation of state and society (Habermas, 1989, p. 142), while the principle of publicity – rational-critical public debate – formed the bridge between politics and morality, as Kant noted in the appendix to *Perpetual Peace* (Habermas, 1989, pp. 102–117).

It is this Kantian principle of publicity, of the public use of reason, the convergence of politics with morality, which was to ground the just democratic legal order and the method of enlightenment. The public use of reason was first and foremost for Kant, a matter of the conflict of the faculties: the higher faculties of theology, law and medicine with the lower faculty of philosophy where knowledge was based on pure reason. However, this conflict was not restricted to the academy: 'The public sphere was realized not in the republic of scholars alone but in the public use of reason by all who were adept at it' (Habermas, 1989, p. 105).

The structural transformation of the university

The 'principle of publicity' that holds sway in our universities and the lack of protection of action (which requires an ethos involving promising and forgiveness) only undermines the public good which lies dormant as a latent potential. John Berger wrote in *Ways of Seeing* (1972) about how publicity images confront us constantly. This is even more true today when our work and leisure is so often through a screen on some device or computer. Berger writes that, 'Publicity images . . . must be continually renewed and made up-to-date. Yet they never speak of the present. Often they refer to the past and always they speak of the future' (Berger, 1972, p. 130). The publicity images pass us by: the publicity is dynamic, the actor is static; the logic of publicity implies choice and freedom, but the language of publicity proposes

> to each of us that we transform ourselves, or our lives, by buying something more. This more, it proposes, will make us in some way richer – even though we will be poorer by having spent our money. Publicity persuades us of such a transformation by showing us people who have apparently been transformed and are, as a result, enviable. The state of being envied is what constitutes glamour. And publicity is the process of manufacturing glamour.
> (Berger, 1972, p. 131)

Publicity, in this sense, is about generating envy in the potential consumer, envy of the consumer's future possible self, transformed by the product, and the object of envy of others. The contemporary principle of publicity glamourizes and focuses attention on competition between rivals, rather than focus falling on the beloved.[1]

So much of the landscape universities inhabit concerns publicity and envy and their interaction with the market because competition is intended to bring about inequality. Universities attract very bright students through the glamour of star academics, the offer of the promise of educational transformation through a higher education experience; they compete for higher places in league tables, nationally and internationally; they compete to hire Nobel laureates, to attract overseas students paying high fees, for externally funded research centres; they generate a language of aspiration – 'feel dissatisfied prior to your Oxford PPE degree?', build student halls of residence modeled on hotels (the rain shower fitted in the en-suite as standard). The implicit message of much publicity, of course, is that buying the product makes us more loveable, so it comes, perhaps, as little surprise to see more frequent concern about 'laddish' sexist campus culture among students. Universities hold out the promise of a greater sense of efficacy in an increasingly fractured labour market, agendas about widening participation take on the form of the Cinderella. The guiding idea is that hierarchy is consciously developed in order to stimulate motivation among the serried ranks (meaning with no spaces between) of foot soldier academics.

Hierarchy, envy, shame and publicity in this form have to defer endlessly to the promised future. According to Berger credibility can only be maintained because publicity appeals to fantasy rather than reality. The contemporary university is a glamourized university with (enough) new buildings, a contemporary swimming pool or leisure centre, some successful sports teams and some renowned academics. Berger explains that:

> Glamour cannot exist without personal social envy being a common and widespread emotion. The industrial society which has moved towards democracy and then stopped half way is the ideal society for generating such an emotion. . . . The gap between what publicity actually offers and the future it promises, corresponds with the gap between what the spectator-buyer [the student] feels himself to be and what he would like to be. The two gaps become one; and instead of the single gap being bridged by action or lived experience, it is filled with glamorous day-dreams.
> (Berger, 1972, p. 148)

Education generally, and university education most of all, has become a matter of personal publicity and glamour in a market culture. For Berger, publicity excludes the present and so renders rational-critical action more difficult.

The Kantian principle of publicity transforms into the variety described by Berger through what Habermas terms a 'colonization of the lifeworld'. The traditional academic lifeworld becomes rationalised and this brings initial gains. The rules generated, however, become entrenched and systematised and these systems then begin to react back upon the academic lifeworld (Habermas, 1987, on this general idea see pp. 285–294). A public university, then, is one which prioritises the Kantian principle of rational-critical discourse.

Craig Calhoun points out that the idea of a vibrant public sphere in our universities is under serious threat through diminished status for the liberal arts, higher costs, radical changes in sources of funding (away from the state and shifted onto the private individual), increased scale, fragmentation and inequality (Calhoun, 2009, pp. 561–562). Calhoun traces the history of the New School for Social Research, founded in 1919, where the public mission of the academic institution was regarded as central to its mission. Here, free inquiry of competent scholars was regarded as fundamental to grasping social conditions, which was in turn a prerequisite for changing and improving public policy (Calhoun, 2009, p. 565). John Dewey, as one of the founders of the New School and first president of the American Association of University Professors, argued (in this organisation's Declaration of Principles of Academic Freedom of 1915) that academic freedom was about more than free speech and due process for academic employees.

> As a professional right, academic freedom depended on the existence of a community of scholars distinctively competent to judge the quality of its

members' contributions. The right inhered in the community of the competent; this is what required that boards of trustees and university presidents respect the judgement of the appropriate scholarly community.
(Calhoun, 2009, p. 571)

Academics require autonomy from managerial intervention because they are 'obligated to carry out their work in a sufficiently public way for it to be judged by the relevant professional community and for it to live up to the public trust placed in the profession as a whole' (Calhoun, 2009, p. 571). Academic freedom, therefore, required both intermural and extramural autonomy. Engagement with the broad public outside its walls and the clash of ideas within enables the dialectical development of ideas through argumentation, much as Mill argued in *On Liberty* as he warned of the pressing possibility of the tyranny of convention to limit freedom and human flourishing (Mill, 2006). The guiding idea behind the foundation of the New School for Social Research was that dissent was valued in order to support intellectual life in a democratic society.

Democracy, technocracy and accountability

Jeremy Waldron recently drew a distinction between forensic accountability and agent accountability. The former concerns the liability of a person (or institution) to have his (or its) actions assessed by a tribunal on the basis of some established norm; the latter concerns the duty owed by an agent to his principal where the principal may demand from the agent an account of work done on the principal's behalf (Waldron, 2014, pp. 1–2). The imposition of a contestable market structure within which universities must compete for revenue (most obviously in England, Australia and North America) is an attempt to render institutions accountable for their activities. There are forensic and agent accountability elements involved here. For example, course validation exercises or the UK's Research Excellence Framework might be regarded as tribunals intended to assess the extent to which a course of study or a university's research projects meet norms of good academic quality. Exercises intended to produce proxies for price signals in a market, such as the publication of student satisfaction survey results, however, ought not to be regarded as an instance of forensic accountability, since the 'tribunal' lacks expertise to judge the established norms. There is a more fundamental problem still: forensic accountability may distort the established norm it is intended to assess. In terms of agent accountability, an old problem arises over the identity of the principal and the agent. From a technocratic perspective, the state regards itself as the principal acting on behalf of the public's interest. Yet, from a republican[2] perspective, the university may represent the public in asking the state to account for its actions. Is the work of the university the business of the state acting on behalf of society, or does the business of the state and society form the basis of the work of (at least some important parts of) universities? There are, as Waldron puts it, multitudes of principals in a modern complex democracy.

In the complexity of mass, modern democracy, where the news media are being rapidly transformed by freely available information online, the traditional news agencies are struggling to develop business models that allow the high quality journalism required for agent accountability, replacing this with cheap 'click-bait' articles intended to attract readers and advertising revenue. At the same time, large fiscal deficits have led to governments imposing cuts to the state and transferring the burden of debt on to individuals. This has been made easier by a form of 'consumer-accountability' employed by the state over institutions funded by government spending:

> This sense of accountability is used sometimes in business – with firms regarding themselves as 'accountable' to their customers. It is also sometimes used in government – with entities like hospitals, police forces, and inspectorates being 'accountable' to those whom they serve or supervise. Though consumer-accountability may involve elements of forensic-accountability and elements of agent-accountability, it need not. It may convey little more than a sense that it is a rather good idea – perhaps as a matter of management, perhaps as a matter of marketing – for an organization to be seen to be taking people's preferences into account, irrespective of the basis on which this sense is founded.
>
> (Waldron, 2014, p. 29)

Such consumer-accountability, of course, says almost nothing about accountability in a democratic sense. If students give their courses a high satisfaction rating it does not give the public an account of what happened on the courses, but it does provide universities with another statistic to use in its marketing campaign for new students.

Public attitudes

The public sphere is not a collection of publics, rather it contains an attitude of relating to one another as equals and engaging in deliberation in good faith where arguments are settled through the force of reason. The ethos of universities, at the normative level, ought to exhibit precisely this attitude, within and without its walls. Academic freedom of inquiry necessarily involves this Kantian spirit of rational-critical inquiry, but also demands a duty to openness and transparency and to live up to the norms of the relevant academic community within which such inquiry takes place. A democratic role for universities, in terms of teaching, research and holding corporations and governments to account is vitally important in an era of consumer-accountability where states conform to a principle of staged publicity and institutions that could help bind people together and support democracy. Instead, states and putatively public institutions conform to a principle of publicity as glamour in order to attract greater market shares.

Thinking, knowing and judging

What sort of attitude or ethos is it that education should try to generate in order that people enter into deliberation in the appropriate spirit? Two associated questions are raised here:

1 Imposing a spirit of a particular sort runs against developing autonomy – so, how do you justify the paternalism of the educator (especially when thinking of HE and adults)? Is it based on superior knowledge, or some other authority? What happens to that authority if it is based on an expectation that somehow you (the academic) can help me (the student) to get a career?
2 Substantively, what is this public attitude or political orientation? Is it a commitment to the common good? A limited self-interest? Toleration of otherness? Something like good manners? A spirit of solidarity, fraternity? A promise to be dispassionate, non-ideological? To be reasonable?

The answer to the first question (justifying paternalism) overlaps with the answer to the second. If educators are concerned with inculcating an attitude that sustains a democratic community, then paternalism is justified. However, a marketised (higher) education that promotes individualism and self-interest cannot sustain the required public attitude and therefore the authority of the educator cannot be justified.

The publication of Rawls' *Political Liberalism* (2005) led to a shift in political philosophy away from discussion of patterned conceptions of distributive justice and towards the sort of discourse to which liberal democracy ought to be predisposed. However, the liberal answers generated from within a Rawlsian perspective point towards a 'thin' state neutrality that serves to direct attention away from educational issues (Jakobsen and Lysaker, 2015, p. 13).

In place of the idea of increased earnings potential, a higher education funding system ought to focus on the possibility of generating public reason through an appeal to the principle of publicity within the democratic horizon rather than an overlapping consensus on the level of the private good of earnings potential.

Notes

1 See Kant's distinction between jealousy and envy. Consider also recent ideas on inflamed *amour-propre*.
2 Waldron finds it strange that modern republican political theorists like Skinner and Pettit adopt a narrow understanding of republicanism where freedom is about non-domination. 'Republicanism is the frank acknowledgement that the business conducted by government is the public business of the realm and everyone in it' (Waldron, 2014, p. 10).

Chapter 2

Higher education and economies of worth

Competition, privatisation and the public

Academics in the fields of social, political and educational theory have recently turned their attention to the situation in contemporary higher education institutions (see Calhoun, 2006, 2009 and Holmwood, 2011, for instance). Concern about a 'decline of the public' has led some writers to point to a structural transformation of the university, shifting away from an institution oriented towards the public and turning instead towards a private good. Such concerns have been raised against a background context in countries like the USA, Australia and the UK of rapidly increasing tuition fees, intentions by the state to sell the student loan book, grade inflation, increased 'transparency' attached to 'key information sets', league table positions, bureaucratised research assessment and higher education as a form of social prestige.

Policies of privatisation encouraging competitive behaviour intended to make universities more efficient in terms of lower costs and higher value 'outputs' are destroying the public value of higher education. A structural transformation of the university leads to a crisis of legitimacy. Universities have a vital role to play in a democracy; any democratic state has a responsibility to recognise this role.

On justification: Economies of worth

Critical social sciences and political thought explore the nature of social coordination and the nature of decision-making, but they often do so from different angles. For example, while work by Dewey, Arendt and Habermas give us a normative perspective on public institutions and practices, this needs to be complemented by another view. More theoretically inclined sociology like, for instance, the work of Pierre Bourdieu, focuses on the ways in which language tends to reproduce inequality in rather subtle ways. Working in the tradition of Bourdieu, in *On Justification: Economies of Worth* (2006), Luc Boltanski and Laurent Thévenot explore the issue of how agreements are reached. This work seeks to build sociological theory upon a basis borrowed from moral philosophy, but developed from empirical research. They write that,

> Justifiable acts are our focus: we shall draw out all the possible consequences from the fact that people need to justify their actions. In other words, people do not ordinarily seek to invent false pretexts after the fact so as to cover up some secret motive, the way one comes up with an alibi; rather they seek to carry out their actions in such a way that these can withstand the test of justification.
> (Boltanski and Thévenot, 2006, p. 37)

We ought, perhaps, to be skeptical of the logical priority of such straightforward justification in all instances. Many aspects of recent policy decisions, for instance, taken around English higher education seem to exhibit the logic of the alibi. The unsustainable English student loans system involved in the *Students at the Heart of the System* (BIS, 2011, Cm 8122) White Paper was justified by the Browne Report. Focusing at the level of our politicians who so often have no plans for tax rises and spending cuts, we ought to be wary of the justifications that may arise (O'Neil, 2012).[1] However, the richness of Boltanski's and Thévenot's theory makes it a compelling starting point for exploring contemporary higher education, which certainly appears to me as a public institution where processes of justification in public policy formation don't seem to fit easily with the self-understandings of many academics.[2] Boltanski and Thévenot propose a plurality of models of social coexistence. This accounts for competent, autonomous social actors capable of choosing between different modes of social order. However, Boltanski and Thévenot also argue that social actors generally only become conscious of the models of order they employ to coordinate their aims in situations where their lifeworldly flow of practices break down, where the actor suddenly becomes something like the Schutzian stranger in a situation where she previously felt rather at home. Boltanski and Thévenot argue that the study of these crisis moments is imperative if we are to understand the structures of social integration. These moments of crisis give us insight into the normative beliefs that enable the coordination of acting participants. A breakdown in the normative order provides a fissure through which we might see how participants reflect on conflicting conceptions of order. The third move in Boltanski's and Thévenot's theory is to propose that we grasp such 'unnatural' moments, in which we discursively examine our previously accepted conceptions of order, as the hinges of social reproduction: social life is characterized by an 'imperative to justify', which in the face of regularly occurring crises compels the members of society to reciprocally uncover their latent conceptions of order and justify them to each other. These stations of discursive justification represent the conscious, reflexive side of social reproduction, which makes explicit what was once implicit in the flow of routine lifeworld interactions: partners in communication are forced to offer arguments and justifications for why a problematic segment of their lifeworld should be solved within the horizon of one model of order rather than another (Honneth, 2012b, p. 37).

The six 'polities' of justification

Boltanski and Thévenot seek to develop a descriptive sociological theory of society which takes into account the interpretive authority of individual social agents but also delineates the various systems of interpretation that these agents draw upon. Social actors coordinate their actions by drawing on models of moral order, different 'economies of worth', which justify the ways they interact. One of the crucial elements of their theory is their emphasis on plurality. Boltanski and Thévenot argue that empirical research shows there are six basic categories of justification that apply in situations of (non-violent) conflict. Luc Boltanski has later been keen to emphasise that *On Justification* is not misread as a general social theory that applies always and everywhere, but only in particular 'regimes of action' where equivalences play a role (Bausure, 2011, p. 363). The polities of justification are employed in non-violent political disagreement. Now, we see this in the conflict between academics, university managers and higher education policy-makers in terms of a self-understanding of the university. What their form of analysis lacks, however, is a structural element that would enable a clearer view of moments of crisis. This is why Habermas' dual perspective, from system and lifeworld, is a superior social and political theory.

Boltanski and Thévenot provide first the 'inspired polity' based upon St. Augustine's thought. Here, the notion of the common good and *charity* are foregrounded. This inspired polity stresses grace and saintliness, though these are all too easily confused with pride, vanity and folly. In the 'domestic polity' the guiding philosophy comes from Bossuet, who argued for aristocracy, absolutism and the divine right of kings, where hierarchy reigns above even the king. The 'polity of fame' draws on Hobbes, where 'the construction of worth is tied to the constitution of conventional signs that condense and display the power generated by the esteem people have for one another, and thus make it possible to weigh persons against one another and to calculate their respective value' (Boltanski and Thévenot, 2006, p. 99). In the polity of fame a person's worth (or price) equates with her power. It is not absolute, for it depends on the esteem of others. The 'civic polity' (drawing on Rousseau) proposes a disembodied sovereign generated by the convergence of human wills (Boltanski and Thévenot, 2006, p. 108) which aim beyond self-interest at the level of the general will or common interest. The 'industrial polity' draws on Saint-Simon's functional notion of society as an organised machine or organism where morality is a system of functional rules that ensure harmony at the level of the social system. Here bankers are the general agents of industry, and what the nation needs is not government but administration (Boltanski and Thévenot, 2006, p. 121). Money is the lifeblood of the body politic. Society functions like a great factory. Industrial worth is judged by experts, and politics becomes a science of production. The 'market polity' tends towards social concord. Reference to a single principle can 'transform the furious heat of interpersonal confrontations into a general welfare that guarantees a peaceful society' (Boltanski and Thévenot, 2006, p. 43). Disagreements are resolved through a coordinating process that relies upon a common identification of market goods and a common evaluation of these goods in terms of prices. The market polity stresses competition between agents in a market bond where scarcity tends to raise the price of a good.

Now, we could take Boltanski's and Thévenot's framework of polities and try to examine the extent to which universities conform to each of the six different approaches to justification. For instance, to what extent does higher education exist within a mix of industrial, market, inspired, fame, domestic and civic worlds? We could try to spot imbalances, in much the same way as Michael Walzer does in *Spheres of Justice* (1983). Axel Honneth takes a different tack. He argues that Boltanski's and Thévenot's economies of worth are founded on an implicit principle of achievement. 'In "modern" society, all conceptions of a legitimate social order are, without exception, determined by the following principle: achievements considered to be especially valuable are to be honoured by being accorded a higher status or "worth"' (Honneth, 2012b, p. 103). For instance, if you make more sacrifices to the common good, you should be rewarded with higher status. But not all social arrangements conform to this pattern. David Miller's *Principles of Social Justice* (2001), for example, shows there are a variety of principles (achievement, but also need and equality) which we appeal to in different ways in different situations. Honneth explains that the real deficit in Boltanski's and Thévenot's list of forms of justification is that they are *economies* of worth. As such, these economies ignore 'an entire class of works in political philosophy that continue to be influential today. No mention is made of Kant's political republicanism, nor of John Locke's classical liberalism' (Honneth, 2012b, p. 107). The character of the *polis* is missing from Boltanski's and Thévenot's list of polities. This is important because it is just such a misrecognition that Honneth seeks to identify as a source of change in his theory of recognition. We see this in his idea of reification as forgetfulness of recognition. Recognition and empathetic engagement have a necessary priority over cognition and understanding social facts (Honneth, 2012a, p. 52). Reification is not simply epistemic, but a form of behaviour, which, to be sure, we can see in Boltanski's and Thévenot's focus on achievement, but also in the extent to which universities and higher education come to be wrapped up in such achievement.

Closed and open economies of higher education

Paul Standish explored and compared the notions of restricted and unrestricted approaches to teaching. He terms closed economies as those concerned with exchange and satisfaction, quality assurance, risk management and instrumental attitudes to learning, while open economies relate more to dynamic change, transformation and intellectual excitement. Standish defends a more open economy against the narrow closed variety, but also points towards the way in which open economies close down. We can see this at the level of the macroeconomy: open systems, in times of crisis, have a tendency to move towards a state of autarky as policy-makers put in place trade barriers to protect domestic employment levels. Similarly, we can consider the gift relationship, whereby gift giving can descend into a sort of exchange. As when the appearance of a gift given obscures the reality of self-interest, such as the interest to buy oneself a place in civic life.

The point is that there exists a paradox in the gift relationship because, empirically, gifts can never be indubitably pure. Whatever the nature of the giver's real intentions, in making his gift, these are screened out once we view his actions through the lens of a closed economy of exchange. In the closed economy there are more or less clearly defined property rights, duties to be discharged, credits and debits, contracts are formed and enforced and targets are established and met or missed. The closed economy is characterized by measurement, contract and accountability. Standish, however, points to an alternative economy where obligations deepen the more we are called to them. This alternative economy is, he says, anathema to modern thought. Just as we can imagine a responsible parent providing good food and decent clothing for his child, or the dutiful citizen who obeys the law, votes in elections and pays her taxes, so too we can conceive of the

> diligent teacher whose class has been assiduously prepared for their Standard Achievement Tests, who now goes home content that she has done her job efficiently and effectively. Star professors in universities, notching up the esteem indicators of citations, research grants, keynotes and appearances on TV in preparation for the forthcoming Research Assessment Exercise, take smug satisfaction in the stars they gain. And the wised-up student who, having identified the performance criteria, has picked off her assignments, meeting their requirements in full, is now ready to close her books on this module and this course, the latest addition to her learning portfolio. But we can imagine, can we not, also that each of these might become moral grotesques, whose characteristic vice is perhaps hubris? Is there not something virtuous about the parent (the citizen, the teacher, the student, the lover . . .) who feels that she has never done enough. . . . Is not the person who does not see things like this in danger of getting the whole thing wrong – and precisely missing the point of citizenship, parenthood, love or education? Is there not something morally repugnant about the parent who thinks she has done enough? Might we not expect a lover of learning to exceed the currency of star ratings and CVs?
>
> (Standish, 2005, p. 59)

Of course, this mass system of higher education is only massive in terms of its relative size, historically speaking. For the types of students, academics, the universities and the subjects they offer and study are also highly differentiated. But they are different in depth, as well as form, becoming what critics of the demise of the public university object to: the 'hollowing-out' or flattening of the subject of study (Holmwood, 2012).[3] A student of economics who has chosen this area of specialism because she has been told that economics graduates earn higher average income than others adopts an instrumental rationality that is blind to the deepening of intellectual interest that, perhaps, explains (among other things) why some students tend to earn higher incomes than others.

Rather than the state representing the public, the state bureaucracy has split off from the public. Therefore, when it claims to act in the interests of the public, there must be a need to transform either the public or the state bureaucracy. The pressure for prestige and status is pushing British universities into different interest group factions, lobbying from different perspectives. We have the Russell Group, 94 Group, Million+ and for-profit providers (BPP and Pearson). The university, therefore, can no longer bridge the space between public and state because the university, in understanding itself in economic terms, is blind to its public value. We can, perhaps, see this if we consider the idea of privatisation of universities.

The case against privatisation

The narrow exchange-value conception of higher education faces an inevitable legitimation crisis, despite the policy environment that supports it. To explain this, let's turn to a recent account of privatisation that seeks to question the assumption that decisions taken over the desirability, or otherwise, of the privatisation of a public function turn on the issue of capability.

Dorfman and Harel argue that some goods are inherently public goods and their functions cannot be executed successfully by private entities. The execution of the task entails that public officials perform the public task: 'private actors would inevitably fail in performing these tasks. The privatisation of the execution of these decisions would undermine the very possibility of providing their consequent goods' (Dorfman and Harel, 2013, p. 68). Their argument follows a broadly Hobbesian pattern (though we can identify hints of Bossuet as well) insofar as they regard the sovereign state as one natural body, where the joints are the magistrates and other officers of execution, and the nerves are the offices of reward and punishment. Such a unified conception of the state renders this argument clearer, but then becomes problematic. On Dorfman's and Harel's view, legitimate state action requires that the sovereign's officers must act as the sovereign (in a public way) and not as an individual private person. In the process of privatisation, the state decides and brokers the execution of a good, allowing it to be contracted out to some third party (Dorfman and Harel, 2013, p. 72).[4]

In contrast to an instrumental approach towards privatisation, which posits the idea that public acts can be performed by anyone, and it is merely a matter of establishing whether private or public bodies perform the acts better, Dorfman and Harel distinguish actions *of* the state from actions *for* the state. The former rests upon a fidelity of deference, whereby the contracted provider follows the orders of the state; the latter rests upon fidelity by reason, whereby the contracted provider makes judgements on behalf of the state. Dorfman and Harel claim that fidelity by reason, which allows agents to make interpretive judgements on behalf of the state, is inappropriate for certain public functions. So, the legitimacy of criminal punishment, for instance, hinges on punishment being carried out in the name of the polity (punishment is done by the state), rather than punishment being carried out on behalf of the state (Dorfman and Harel, 2013, pp. 76–77).

Fidelity of deference boils down to following the state's orders in providing the good. Fidelity of reason concerns agents using their judgement in providing the public good. Agents who provide a public good via fidelity of deference suppress their judgement and concede to the judgements made by their superiors. The superiors also suppress their judgement, and this suppression of judgement moves up the chain of command until the authority of the state is reached.[5] But the state cannot simply make private agents perform a public task, since the private agent cannot adopt the perspective of the state. This is because tasks (such as 'provide a higher education' or 'provide scholarly research') will necessarily involve underspecified guidance from the state, which means the private agent cannot attribute the relevant actions involved in the provision of the good to the state. This suggests that fidelity of deference cannot be the source of legitimacy in the privatised provision of public goods. However, Dorfman and Harel believe that the fidelity of deference can be reconstructed in order to enable public actions in the name of the state (and this is where their analysis starts to become more relevant for the discussion of universities under conditions of fiscal austerity).

> [D]eference [to the state] requires the existence of a practice. . . . The deferring agent defers to a community of practice to which he or she belongs – a community that collectively determines what the public interest dictates – and takes this determination as a baseline against which to measure what fidelity of deference requires in each particular case.
> (Dorfman and Harel, 2013, p. 81)

So, for a private agent to provide a public good we require a distinctive practice and an institutional form of that practice, which brings together political and bureaucratic functions such that the agent is open to political guidance and intervention.

The execution of public functions requires a framework for 'formulating, articulating, and shaping a shared perspective' (Dorfman and Harel, 2013, p. 82) which can implement public decisions. Constraints on agents are formed by the practical deliberations of like-minded agents in relation to government policy decisions. There is a commitment to a community of practice based upon shared understandings of the public good itself. The shared understandings in the community of practice act as a guide to each individual agent's conduct. Community rules about practices, based upon the public good, might make possible fidelity by deference, and therefore, the possibility of a public official. Such community practices could then be regulated by state supervision. But this would be insufficient for acting from the public point of view. A public perspective would require that political offices be brought into this community via 'integrative practices'. These can be more or less open to a deferential conception of fidelity. For Dorfman and Harel, communities of practices, even when regulated by the state, fall outside the range required for fidelity of deference: 'This is so because the interaction of participants in a private practice with state officials is mediated through a contractual agreement whose effect is the replacement of fidelity by deference with fidelity by reason' (Dorfman and Harel, 2013, p. 85). Participants in the community of practice will involve practitioners, but also politicians and bureaucrats. It is overly simplistic to characterise politicians, bureaucrats and practitioners along an executive, legislative, administrative, practitioner axis. Politicians have a broad guiding role over bureaucrats and participants in an integrative practice. This is more than state supervision of private agents with underspecified goals. Usually, privatisation arrangements involve the state setting out desired goals and specifying contractual constraints that apply in pursuit of these goals. The state gives a degree of latitude to the private provider to meet goals within specified parameters.

> Now, the decisions and rules generated by a community of private practice striving to act within the arena of permissibility necessarily fall short of what deference to the general interest (as judged from the point of view of the relevant political officials) requires. A formally defined arena of permissibility is just an authorization for private contractors to act according to the reason conception of fidelity – that is, to pursue the general interest as filtered through their own viewpoints of what impartial concern for this interest requires.
>
> (Dorfman and Harel, 2013, p. 86)

The result of this analysis hinges on the fidelity of deference, which equates the political perspective with the public point of view. It means that:

> [I]t is in principle possible that the private employees of a private firm would be considered, for our purposes, public officials. This may be so in the (fantastic) case in which they satisfy the two conditions we have articulated: that of participation in a practice that takes an integrative form. For such a case to arise, the for-profit and not-for profit organizations must turn their backs on the private purposes that provide the grounds for their operations – to withdraw from their basic commitment to maximize profits

or vindicate certain ideals, respectively – and display fidelity of deference to the judgment of state officials in all matters pertaining to the execution of the contracted-for task.

(Dorfman and Harel, 2013, p. 88)

Now, we have gone along with Dorfman's and Harel's argument that takes as its foundation a Hobbesian model of state sovereignty. Their analysis rests on an Austinian command model of just laws handed down by a Leviathan state and does not evaluate the morality of deference. Their analysis seeks to differentiate the actions of vigilantes from the police, or bandits using force against another country from an army. What if we consider the distinction between a private, for-profit, training provider, with degree awarding powers and a university? Are these two institutions capable, in principle, of performing equivalent roles? Does the private training provider give life to the public sphere? Our answer may depend on the nature of the training and its ethical dimension in the way it goes about its work. The market, if the state is so heavily involved, is likely to fail in favour of the private providers, but if the state steps back, then the pretence involved in performance indicators means that the private providers are likely to be able to generate profit, not so much from an efficient market, but from a recent history of educational grade inflation and, therefore, a labour market situation that favours an ongoing need for credentials. The state, in part-privatising the university, in encouraging academic entrepreneurship, in encouraging managers to regard themselves as CEOs, ensures a 'rise of the social' while an economic ethic, appropriate to the private realm, is applied to the public. No longer would higher education prepare people for the public world. Arendt worried that this tendency destroys both the private and the public spheres. It is the division between these realms that concerns the likes of Dewey, Arendt and Habermas (Bernstein, 2012).

Instrumental values and privatised universities

Public officials have an obligation to determine the public interest. Dorfman's and Harel's analysis tells us that this means being guided by the state and deferring to the state. We might consider the policy regime in the English universities and point towards integrative practices involving the Privy Council's role in conferring university status on an institution of learning, or think of quality assurance systems, or consider the financial distributive system involved in the Research Excellence Framework. These combine a community of practice with the involvement of politicians in guiding bureaucrats towards adopting the public point of view. However, this construal involves a very basic assumption, viz. that the state is the public point of view. In a democratic culture the state only represents the public point of view. It manages to do so, empirically to a greater or lesser extent, because of its open structure. There are formal and informal aspects to this open structure – frequent elections, universal suffrage, separation of powers, human rights enshrined in the legislative framework, the rule of law; but there are also the more informal aspects – plural sources of information, a free press, welfare provision (including basic education), 'evidence-based' policy-making and higher education available to those who can benefit from it. So, the strong public sphere of the state reflects the public point of view because it is informed by the weak public sphere (often referred to in terms of civil society). A democratic culture informs the democratic state of the public perspective. The public point of view and the state perspective are not necessarily synonymous (under models of state authority that differ from the Hobbesian portrayal).

With a more democratic model of the state in mind, what happens to the idea of fidelity of deference? Public officials defer to the state, but the state is also responsive to public opinion. We have in Britain, to be sure, a parliamentary democracy, where decisions are ultimately made under formal conditions in Westminster rather than on the streets, but there are obligations placed upon the state as well as on public officials and private citizens in our model of governance. One obligation might be to ensure a free press and freedom of information. Another duty is academic freedom and the opportunity for people to study those things that interest them in depth. As Standish puts it:

> [I]deas of responsibility . . . extend . . . to a responsiveness an answerability to the objects of study, to the content of learning, to the subjects to which we are subject. Rather than a body of knowledge or skills to be mastered, a subject of study comes to be understood as deepening and expanding the more one pursues it: as with the vista that extends as one ascends the mountainside, one progresses towards a greater understanding of what there is still to learn. From outside one scarcely understands the problems.
> (Standish, 2005, p. 62)

The privatisation of higher education and universities is a form of censorship in liberal, democratic society. We are in danger of 'robbing the human race', as John Stuart Mill suggested, of a properly informed and critical public sphere capable of informing the democratic state. This is not just the result of epistemic problems, such as a dumbed-down, more superficial content of spoon-fed, degree-level work or scholarly shallowness – falsifying results, plagiarism. Also, in ethical terms, there is an increasing tendency to push academics to apply for grants simply for bureaucratic career imperatives rather than intellectual inquiry, whereby those who belong and have belonged to a university are disinclined to engage in the *polis*.[6] And, no doubt, therefore there is an educational deficit and consequently a democratic deficit.

The privatisation of universities is a special case because a fidelity of deference to the state is not sufficient for grasping the democratic public point of view. Rather, a higher education has a moral commitment to the public perspective, to civilisation, higher culture, call it what you will, whether a follower of

Oakeshott, Strauss, Adorno or Habermas, who all recognise this threat. So, does this mean that higher education provision can be privatised (normatively speaking) because it inherently contains the public point of view, perhaps along the lines of BPP providing professional training in law and accountancy or A. C. Grayling's New College of the Humanities? I think the answer would be that insofar as these institutions do not reflect the public perspective and then inform the state, they can be privatised, but then they cannot retain a meaningful title of university. They provide not higher education, but high-level training (in the case of BPP), or they do provide higher education but only by free-riding on a publicly orientated university (NCH in its use of the University of London's exam system).

A public community of practice, then, ought to inform the state of the public point of view. Dorfman's and Harel's analysis is reversed for public institutions like universities, whose special function is to inform, and hold to account, the democratic state. Rather than deferring to politicians, the public university's role is to inform and enable politicians, at local, regional, national and supranational levels, to guide bureaucrats. The integration of universities into the welfare state has resulted in a fundamental misunderstanding of the public role of universities, which inform the state and educate critical, reflexive citizens. The externalities involved in the exercise of these functions include the production and safe-keeping of scientific knowledge, the development of commercially valuable research, scholarly inquiry and increased skills (and sometimes higher productivity and flexibility – and therefore wage levels) in the labour market. Yet these externalities are by-products of the university's core public activity. As such, universities, because higher education ought to involve the transformation of students away from the anxious, avaricious tentacles of the self towards a deepening of intellectual interest and empathetic engagement with others, are prime candidates for the category of an inherently, inescapably public good. However, it is plausible to claim that the university is constitutive of the public sphere itself.

In chapter 11, book 3 of the *Politics*, Aristotle suggests that the people at large, rather than an elite, should hold power in the polis. People collectively are better judges than elite individuals. Jeremy Waldron refers to this as the 'doctrine of the wisdom of the multitude', and Aristotle compares such collective judgement to a 'potluck dinner' 'in the same way that a feast to which all contribute is better than one supplied at one man's expense' (Aristotle, 1981, p. 202). This doctrine of the wisdom of the multitude, however, is contingent on the people not being debased in character. The doctrine is mostly applied, in political philosophy, to legislative assemblies, but Aristotle applies it more broadly to the application of law and to making judgements where the law is silent (Waldron, 1995, p. 564). The grounds for the doctrine of the wisdom of the multitude lie in variety: 'more contributors will produce a more varied feast, and a more varied feast is better' (Waldron, 1995, p. 567), and the doctrine applies to both policy-making decisions and to ethical judgements. But the benefit of collective judgement comes not so much from a mechanical aggregation of the claims raised by participants, rather:

> [D]eliberation among the many is a way of bringing each citizen's ethical views and insights – such as they are – to bear on the views and insights of each of the others, so that they cast light on each other, providing a basis for reciprocal questioning and criticism, and enabling a position to emerge which is better than any of the inputs and much more than an aggregation or function of those inputs.
>
> (Waldron, 1995, pp. 569–570)

The polis's, or indeed the university's, job is to consider participants' views and use these to cast light on each other, illuminating those aspects in each which contribute to the truth. Much as with J.S. Mill's notion of free speech in *On Liberty*, truth emerges through the struggle of opinions in the process of deliberation. This deliberative exercise, however, misfires when the institution that is supposed to attend and protect conditions of free speech is subject to reification. For instance, there may be private benefits in the academic labour market attached to participation in the Research Excellence Framework, and these private benefits subvert normative standards in the collective exercise of scholarly inquiry. There may be private benefits for the student who copies his essays from a diligent friend studying a similar subject at another university. The right to participate in politics, or in the academic world, is a form of private property. 'But the rationale for the distribution of this right requires that each use that property, not just for his own purposes, but in a way that contributes to the excellence in judgement of the group . . . to which one belongs' (Waldron, 1995, p. 574). For Waldron, to adopt an individualistic, rather than a dialectical, attitude is a form of corruption:

> A person under the influence of money, patronage, or passion, for example, is likely to be someone who will cast his vote without listening to others (except his patron or the one who has bribed him), or who will cast it on the basis of interest or impulse irrespective of what has been said back and forth in the deliberative process. His deafness, so to speak, in deliberation is the mark of his using political property in a narrowly selfish way.
>
> (Waldron, 1995, p. 575)

So, the public university requires specific virtues to sustain itself: skill in explanation; skill in listening to others; skill in bringing the two together in a way that casts light; and skill in explaining the tentative synthesis. The skills involved relate to empathy but also to rhetoric. It is such skills in speech and writing that a higher education ought to focus upon, because they are at the heart of dialectical learning. Speech is more than reciting truths; it is a matter of articulate conversation that rests upon interdependence. We might conclude, then, in the spirit of Aristotle, that those who advocate an economistic understanding of the university do not *de jure* belong to the university.

Reification

'Reification' . . . signifies a habit of thought, a habitually ossified perspective, which, when taken up by the subject, leads not only to the loss of her capacity for empathetic engagement, but also to the world's loss of its qualitatively disclosed character (Honneth, 2012a, pp. 35–36). Honneth's conception of reification, then, involves a turn away from something akin to Buber's 'I-thou' relationship with others, something like Cavell's notion of acknowledgement or Honneth's idea of recognition. Reification is an ossifying process. Cavell hints at Heidegger's glimpse of one-track thinking when he warns us of the superficiality of abbreviations and acronyms. What, Heidegger asks, has already come to pass when people speak of 'Uni' rather than University? The designation, Heidegger claims, is 'not accidental, let alone harmless' (Cavell, 2011, p. 91).

Honneth's theory of recognition, and the struggle for recognition, is a process we can see clearly at work in the university. Without harking back to any golden era, we can see a misrecognition of scholarly work. I would add that this particularly applies to philosophy. Those involved in the philosophy of education, therefore, might be particularly sensitive to claims about the reification of education generally, and the higher education that we engage in.

A dual perspective that takes on board the normative core of the public and operates with an adequate descriptive framework that accounts for the limits of public interaction helps us to grasp the problems involved in structural transformation of public goods, such as higher education. Neither the normative political theory of, say, Arendt, nor the nuanced sociological analysis of, say, Bourdieu is sufficient to understand the diminution of the public. Joining a normative, regulative ideal to an appropriately rich descriptive sociological framework helps to throw into relief the difficulty in which the institution of the university finds itself.

For instance, the idea of the privatisation of the university is problematic not so much in terms of fidelity to reason or deference, but because the university is a pivotal institution of the public sphere. As such, the university, in lots of ways, informs and helps to guide the state, rather than holding the status of an institution *of the state*. The university, therefore, cannot be privatised because if this democratic function is central to the purpose of universities, then, regardless of where funding has come from, universities are not institutions which belong to the state.

Transparency is a key feature of the idealised market. Good quality, valid, reliable information is important for markets to operate efficiently. Key Information Sets of data, about completion rates, student satisfaction, employment statistics, proportions of graduates with 'good' degrees, etc. are assumed to lead to a more efficient market. But such transparency also brings problems. The stress laid on these targets leads institutional managers to adopt strategic attitudes: employment figures are raised by offering graduate internships, national student surveys are carefully managed in an attempt to increase 'satisfaction' ratings. The norms of strategic management, of course, are in tension with academic norms. Crass attempts to improve national student survey results essentially involve asking students to put to one side the critical attitude good scholarship demands; internships give young people work experience in the labour market but may well be regarded as exploitation. Transparency, coupled with competition, brings shallowness, duplicity, insincerity and hypocrisy. Such vices, Onora O'Neill points out, corrupt public trust and, therefore, corrode the public good of higher education (O'Neill, 2002, pp. 83–87).

The normative core of the public sphere values properly public action, not the compromise of social action that interest group competition exemplifies. As such, the degree to which the universities in the UK influence the state *qua* sectional interest groups, like the Russell Group or the Million+ Group, advocating protection for budgets related to scientific research in order to protect future economic growth or lobbying to save the budget related to widening participation, throws into relief Arendt's notion of the rise of the social, whereby supposedly public action is, in fact, institutional self-interest and economic action masquerading as political action.

Notes

1. O'Neil begins the article by pointing towards politicians' use of deliberately deceiving tactics during elections.
2. See, for instance, the *Council for the Defence of British Universities*, or the *Campaign for the Public University* in the UK.
3. See, for example, John Holmwood, 'Markets versus Publics: the new battleground of higher education' in *Harvard International Review*, Fall, 2012.
4. See Michael Barber, Katelyn Donnely and Saad Rizvi (2013), *An Avalanche is Coming: Higher education and the revolution ahead*, Institute for Public Policy Research, for an account of the threats they predict will engulf universities, including the contracting out of higher education to for-profit providers. Note that the threat of the coming avalanche is intended to encourage universities to move away from a fundamentally public purpose.
5. Empirically, of course, decisions require judgement in applying orders to changing circumstances, so this characterisation is notional rather than intended as an accurate description.
6. No doubt this isn't only a matter of the form that the university takes; it depends upon the quality of public life in general, but insofar as the university is an institution which leads and represents and protects the public sphere, we can say that the form the university takes is likely to mirror the form that the public sphere takes as a whole.

Chapter 3

The role of the university in a democracy

Universities hold a special place in a democratic society. We should think of them as essential to democracy. Of course, this does not mean there can only be universities within democratic states. Rather, it means that universities have democratising tendencies. They were places of advanced learning, where new knowledge was developed, and places of higher education. Universities produce knowledge through research and educate students who graduate with some portion of that knowledge. Academics have expertise; they are often hired as expert consultants, able to offer critical commentary on business practices or state policies.

This is a potentially dangerous claim to make, for it immediately looks like special pleading from a vested interest: an academic argument for the academy's special status. To attempt impartiality, political philosophers often make use of the idea of a 'veil of ignorance'. For example, Paul Bou-Habib relies on John Rawls' political theory in his discussion of 'Who Should Pay for Higher Education?' in an attempt to determine the fairest way to fund university study (Bou-Habib, 2010, p. 481).

Bou-Habib notes that there has been a shift across many higher education systems from taxpayer funding towards payment from the individual graduate through income-contingent loans for tuition fees and students' living expenses. These payment arrangements are often referred to as 'cost-sharing' policies. He seeks to make a normative analysis of such cost-sharing using a Rawlsian framework. However, in taking this approach, he screens out the educational content of the effect of such policies. In other words, he adopts a political normative framework which is disappointingly oblivious to its own educational consequences.

Cost-sharing in this context means 'the sharing of the higher education funding burden between taxpayers, on the one hand, and students or graduates, on the other' (Bou-Habib, 2010, p. 480). This is presented as an alternative to funding higher education through the private sphere or out of general taxation.

He runs through four arguments which crop up in discussions about higher education funding that he thinks are either implausible or indeterminate. These arguments are either intended to reject private student funding or funding from general taxation. The first points out the positive externalities produced by higher education, such as better informed voters, lower crime rates and increased economic growth. Bou-Habib suggests it is not clear why positive externalities should entail funding from general taxation. He distinguishes two views related to this: a) the fairness argument that if an activity incurs costs but produces positive externalities, then the beneficiaries owe the producer; and b) that general taxation should fund the positive externality producing activity as an incentive for those who may not have otherwise engaged in the activity. While the fairness argument is implausible, for Bou-Habib, the incentive argument is indeterminate (Bou-Habib, 2010, p. 482).

The implausibility of the fairness argument comes down to brass tacks and sustainability, according to Bou-Habib. If the free-riding beneficiaries of a good with positive externalities reap benefits without incurring costs, it is implausible to argue that tax funding is necessary to prevent an unfair distributive pattern emerging. Funding from general taxation is also unfair because it allows these free-riders (Bou-Habib, 2010, p. 483).

This, however, is misleading because Bou-Habib has shifted focus on to the issue of distributive justice in a specifically Rawlsian sense of 'who gets what and what happens to the least well-off?' Funding public goods from general taxation, however, need not be motivated by an argument from fairness in this form. The manner in which a good is funded ought to concern the meaning of the good. Bou-Habib argues that higher education would not collapse, in the way that a public television channel would, if it were funded through a market mechanism because 'there remains a benefit in higher education – improved human capital – that can sufficiently motivate its being funded by graduates themselves' (Bou-Habib, 2010, p. 483). However, as Michael Walzer and Michael Sandel, among many others, have pointed out, questions of distributive justice also relate to the way a good is provided and the resultant social understanding of that good (Walzer, 1983, Sandel, 2012). As David Marquand puts it, 'The goods of the public realm may or may not be tradable technically: the point is that, if they are traded, they will no longer be public. In Ruskin's language, they would forfeit the 'moral sign' attached to them if they could be bought and sold' (Marquand, 2015, p. 99).

Bou-Habib makes the mistake of focusing his analysis on a fixed or 'end-state' pattern of distributive justice. In examining issues of justice and higher education he locates the locus of justice in the issue of earnings. For example, fairness (and whether something should be privately or publicly funded) 'depends on whether its being publicly provided is likely to maximise the lifetime income prospects of the worst-off' (Bou-Habib, 2010, p. 491). The Rawlsian framework of analysis on offer here treats students as 'rational fools'.

Amartya Sen characterised the abstracted self-seeking individuals of rational choice theory as fools because they are only rational insofar as they are consistent in their preferences and their assumptions about welfare maximisation screen out issues important to the consumption of public goods: sympathy and commitment. Sympathy and commitment drive a wedge between personal choice and personal welfare (Sen, 1977, p. 329). As Sen puts it, 'The *purely* economic man is indeed close to being a social moron' (Sen, 1977, p. 336).

Ronald Dworkin is an egalitarian-libertarian interested in equality of opportunity and ensuring that distributive outcomes track some idea of desert (what people deserve to get). He proposes a thought experiment with echoes of Robert Nozick's 'Wilt Chamberlain example' where, in an egalitarian society, spectators at the basketball game freely donate to watch Wilt play. At the end of the season Wilt holds more money than everybody else and the egalitarian state has to (unjustly) intervene to return society back to its equal pattern. Dworkin proposes a desert island auction where shipwreck survivors bid with equal amounts of clamshells for the resources they would like on the island. If the clamshell auction begins from a situation of equality and everyone bids, then the outcome of the auction must reflect how much the bidders really value the things they are bidding for (ambition sensitive and endowment insensitive). This would mean, in relation to higher education funding, that all have the opportunity to study the course they prefer (endowment insensitive) but will pay as much as they need to realise their ambitions. However, the bidders in this auction don't know their talents so can buy insurance against bad luck (they study philosophy in a culture of greedy finance, or their university turns out to be the spurious University of Kensington).

It's not completely clear what constitutes the hypothetical insurance market and who takes out insurance when the idea is grafted on to university funding. Is it the policy-maker standing behind a veil of ignorance and choosing between different funding mechanisms or is it a student choosing a preferred method of funding? Colburn and Lazenby claim that we need only accept one component of Dworkin's view: '[W]e must think it important that someone's resource holding is sensitive to their own ambitions' (Colburn and Lazenby, 2016, p. 5) and manage to conclude that tuition fees and student loans are the most egalitarian way of funding higher education (Colburn and Lazenby, 2016, p. 14). (This emphasis fits with many claims that a gap between holdings and ambitions can be plugged with encouraging a culture of 'aspiration'.) However, this tension between individual holdings and ambitions is a narrow frame of analysis. We also need to look carefully at the social meanings that derive from different funding models.

Full funding through general taxation is crudely lumped into the high level insurance category. The model assumed in something like studying at a British university in the 1970s. Family income or lack of it does not prevent students from studying. There is an earnings premium but also a social benefit (Colburn and Lazenby, 2016, p. 7). However, Dworkin's clamshell auction also considers the opportunity costs involved and it may well be that social benefits will accrue even if university study isn't generously funded by general taxation. There may, for instance, be a much cheaper funding model that generates nearly as much social benefit. It may be that general taxation funding allows a wide, diverse group of people into higher education, but this doesn't only depend on the form of funding, but also the number of places available to students and the attitudes of institutions. The possibilities open to non-graduates are claimed to be blighted under this general taxation model of funding (Colburn and Lazenby, 2016, p. 8), but this muddies the ideal theory with the concrete situation on the ground today: 'To insure is, in effect, to take from your less financially attractive option (not attending) to subsidise your more financially attractive option (attending)' (Colburn and Lazenby, 2016, p. 8). This is the familiar claim that funding universities from general taxation robs people in traditional working class jobs (who tend not to go to university) to subsidise middle class graduates. However, good employment opportunities for people from working class backgrounds depend much more on the structure of the economy in general than the specific funding model of higher education. A 'high insurance' preference cannot be so readily equated with a general taxation funding model.

Full privatisation is taken as the no insurance at all option (Colburn and Lazenby, 2016, p. 8). Here graduates pay for themselves, and funding higher education is left entirely to the market. If average returns on graduate income are greater than the costs of attending university, then this will generate a market for student loans available for all prospective students, including those from poorer families. However, Colburn and Lazenby notice at this point that there is still a risk that some graduates will fail to find well-paid work after studying. 'In effect, it is the possibility of going to university and failing to find well-paid work afterwards that one insures against, not the possibility of going to university per se' (Colburn and Lazenby, 2016, p. 9). But given this, Colburn and Lazenby have just pointed to their own equivocation. The no insurance option is not a free market in higher education, but a willingness to adopt a risky strategy towards distributive justice that Dworkin's thin veil of ignorance is designed to screen out. It starts to become clear that Colburn and Lazenby over-determine the notion of education as insurance to safeguard individual living standards. The analysis is at once too broad brushed and then sloppily applied.

Nonetheless, they press on with their analysis. They argue a graduate tax pools risk among graduates but not among non-graduates and that the tax could kick in at an earning level that does not discourage prospective students worried about taking on unmanageable debt. However, they claim that this could disincentivise people to study subjects that appear to offer high income returns. This system is not therefore ambition sensitive and may well reduce total income levels and tax revenues. The insurance here is, in other words, costly. The standard objection to a graduate tax scheme is that it is difficult to enforce on geographically mobile graduates. Outside of the British tax system, British graduate earnings are difficult to tax. But the objection based on disincentives is odd. A graduate tax would surely function as a general disincentive to study any subject, if the incentive is primarily financial. Given that some large employers are no longer insisting on university degrees as a prerequisite for employment, this practical concern may be misplaced. If large accountants and similar employers no longer require degrees for new accountants and a graduate tax provides disincentives to study, then the risk would not be to overall income levels but to university funding itself. The insurance market itself here looks in danger of collapse.

Finally, Colburn and Lazenby turn to their final, preferred, model: an income contingent state-backed loan. A good system, they argue, will not subsidise university at the expense of people who don't go, and is ambition sensitive in terms of reflecting the costs or benefits of people's choices. The state-backed loan smoothes the risk of going to university by basing repayments on sufficient income, but does not take funds from people who don't attend university. The state-backed loan, Colburn and Lazenby insist, doesn't involve disincentives to study financially rewarding degrees (Colburn and Lazenby, 2016, p. 11). They are not entirely clear why this is so. They claim that 'Under the state-backed loan, you know that when you have completed your repayments there will be no more additional financial burden to bear. You know that you will not have to subsidise the choices of others who choose less financially rewarding subjects'. The first point to make is that fee levels may well be set at a point which already cross-subsidises between different subjects, therefore the loan repayments may well subsidise others. Given the high anticipated default rate (in England the RAB rate stood at an embarrassingly high level of 45% until it was dropped to 20–25% in January 2016) anticipated under the existing English state-backed loan system, it is clear that almost half of the money lent out is ambition insensitive under this scheme. The £21,000 repayment threshold is likely to be held down in order to generate returns from fiscal drag over time, the student loan book is likely to be sold off at some point which will put upward pressure on the interest rates charged and there is a heavy upward pressure on university fee charges, especially from institutions with a keen eye on international students. The second point to make, then, is that the state-backed loan scheme is not ambition sensitive because the ambitions of the insurance scheme itself have been removed from the analysis. Universities with a strong international brand are able to benefit from such a scheme. This is a central problem with Dworkin's analysis. He assumes that markets and insurance markets are themselves morally neutral. However, in choosing between different policy options we should attend to the internal effects of the good on offer. Colburn and Lazenby's analysis runs up against the difficulties involved in applying the idea of risk-smoothing through hypothetical insurance where they address the issue of personal income level where repayment should begin. They suggest that repayments should only start when personal income is above average income to smooth risk:

> [W]e believe you would choose to structure your debt so that repayments only began after you earned an income that was higher than average. This is to smooth the risk of university. By placing repayments at this level,

prospective students can be confident that university will not leave them very badly off with unmanageable debts.

(Colburn and Lazenby, 2016, p. 12)

This recommendation, however, is financially naïve because the higher the repayment level, the less money can be recovered from the loans. This naïveté is also demonstrated in their thinking on loan defaulters. Colburn and Lazenby argue that degree subjects with higher rates of default should be subsidised more: 'This will ensure that students undertaking particular subjects share the risk together, with those successful in the job market picking up the costs of those who default' (Colburn and Lazenby, 2016, p. 13). However, we need to move beyond such monocausal, static thinking. Earning power, and propensity to repay the loan, will not only track degree subject choice (and particular subjects will be more and less desirable to employers through time) but also institutional status, a graduate's prior education, family connections, personality type, self-confidence, articulacy and a host of other factors, including gender and ethnicity in relation to prevailing social attitudes. In other words, the thin veil of ignorance in the hypothetical insurance scheme is quickly swept away in the debt-laden graduate's reality. To assume that, say, physics graduates can subsidise philosophy graduates ignores too many other dimensions that will bear on future graduate earnings. Moreover, a subject-sensitive subsidy would suffer from the same disincentive problem that led Colburn and Lazenby to dismiss a graduate tax funding policy. Ambition sensitivity in the idea of higher learning as insurance runs up against the problem of information asymmetry in the insurance market.

We should also think more carefully about what universities insure against. Rather than thinking of a degree in terms of personal income insurance, consider the possibility that studying, really studying, makes a person more interesting, develops her opinions, makes her into somebody with something worth saying, yet prepared to listen to others.

Christopher Martin points out that those studying higher education funding should be wary of any reductive income maximizing assumptions involved in preference satisfaction:

> [T]he particular preference being satisfied differs depending on the individual. For some, accessing higher education is about charting a path to a scholarly life, for others it's a gateway to a lucrative profession. Still others choose it in order to broaden one's own horizons. No singular human need is being served by the provision of higher education.
>
> (Martin, 2016, p. 3)

This is certainly true. There is a pluralism in terms of preferences within the system. This pluralism of preferences is internal within the individual too. It's simply not the case that I study for higher income and you study in pursuit of a scholarly vocation. There is always a bundle of preferences, but it is important to recognise that the preferences at stake here, the hopes of the students for their future, are forms of commitment and it is commitments that are screened out by the egoistic assumptions underlying an economistic or catallactic funding system.

Within universities knowledge emerges out of 'communicative' rationality: it's the process that produces, not this grouping or that grouping. The groups are always reified anyway. Do all teachers teach? Do all students study? Don't students teach and teachers study? If we impose a market framework upon the distribution of a good there can be a danger of assuming that the nature of that good is held constant, but market norms change meanings: just look at how the social meanings of football change when money enters the game, or how a home becomes property with yield potential once values begin to inflate. The process of educating produces but it's always ongoing. The process requires particular norms which are sustained by institutions. In the end, it's the attitudes attached to these norms which hold value. David Estlund in *Democratic Authority* uses the metaphor of a jury deliberating to explain this. He is thinking about legitimate law backed by expertise, but I think the same holds for education. The formal strictures of a trial – testimony under oath, balanced arguments by prosecution and defence are all important to the jury's deliberations (Estlund, 2008). Similarly, there are educational procedures that help sustain ethical attitudes that are more likely to generate attitudes conducive towards communicative reason and yield knowledge, truth and new technology.

Many universities are ancient, indeed older than nation states. They have their origins in the authority of the Roman Catholic Church, established by papal authority and granted the autonomy to educate the clergy. From here, there remains the tradition of professional education in medicine, in law, architecture, education itself and branching into state services of policing and nursing. But this old model is changing fast. The ancient ideal with vague aspirations to truth, goodness and beauty can be readily exploited for gain. There is an interesting situation currently in process in Malta where an institution called the American University of Malta is proposed to be built in Zonqor Point, in a national park and outside of Malta's usual development zones. The controversial project is supported by foreign investment arguments for economic growth, though the 'university' seems to be classed as a higher education institution rather than a university, neither is it American, it is backed by a Jordanian hotel business. The case seems to typify the way in which higher education is regarded by policy-makers as an instrumental economic good which generates jobs, brings in foreign investment and has economic multiplier effects on the local economy. Many local people in Malta protested against the decision to build the American University of Malta at Zonqor.

The expansion of higher education has been justified on different grounds, but these grounds usually demonstrate a *catallactic bias* (see Heath, 2006). In other words, the justifications for universities usually foreground economic gain. For instance, higher education brings increased productivity and this contributes to higher growth rates. In a globalised economy, post-industrial nations, it is argued, can only compete with low cost economies by developing high-skilled production. Highly skilled jobs require highly educated graduates to fill them. Second, and related to high-skill production, universities can produce commercially exploitable new technologies. Third, higher education attracts overseas capital. The reputation of British universities and the draw of developing fluency in speaking English attract students from overseas. Fourth, higher education helps to support the economy at local and regional levels as well as the national level. The development of higher education institutions in areas suffering from post-industrial decline provides employment and leads to a multiplier effect on the local economy. Fifth, university degrees bring a greater likelihood of increased income over the course of a lifetime. In England (and other countries like the USA and Australia) this point has been made repeatedly in order to justify large increases in tuition fees. Sixth, universities educate the state bureaucracy and politicians. Seventh, university medical schools train the clinical staff in hospitals. Eighth, business schools provide qualifications for senior business administrators. Ninth, university research provides the material for the curriculum of the school system. Tenth, teachers are usually trained in university education faculties.

Now, all of these functions share an instrumental attitude. The university's role is a strategic one where the end is met by the institution of higher learning or research. However, these contingent functions contradict an underlying democratic purpose held by universities and higher education. The economic functions of universities are not 'pre-political' but contingent upon political concerns. This chapter sets out the general argument that the good of universities should be considered first in democratic terms. This stands at odds with the argument set out by Stefan Collini in *What Are Universities For?* (2012), where Collini asks us to consider what good science and technology is for.

After the Great Depression of the 1930s Karl Polanyi developed the idea of a 'double transformation'. He argued that the commodification of goods which ought not to be treated as objects for sale destabilised human society. The shift towards marketisation had to be met with a reactionary opposition in order to bring society back into line. Yet, as Nancy Fraser points out, in the wake of capitalism's problems in the early twenty-first century, there has been no double movement, equivalent to the establishment of the welfare state or the New Deal (Fraser, 2013, p. 127). For Fraser the problem seems at first glance to stem from the financialisation of production and globalisation that renders the nation state relatively weak to implement a Keynesian response in and among depressed economies. Post-industrial societies, where capitalism is dominated by finance, seem to hold no identifiable social force capable of acting as a 'counter-hegemony' to capital (Fraser, 2013, p. 124). Yet these explanations are insufficient. Fraser argues that it would be beneficial to spread the net of analysis wider: alongside the Bretton Woods institutions of the mid-twentieth century and the establishment of welfare states in response to the crisis of capitalism, there were also a range of emancipatory movements that spread through democratic societies in the 1960s and afterwards. Protest movements often focused on issues of recognition rather than redistribution, and they were deeply critical of the exclusions and hierarchies involved in institutionalised welfare and social protections. Emancipatory protest movements do not easily fit with Polanyi's double movement, however. Accordingly, Fraser argues that we ought to think in terms of a triple movement to analyse the grammar of social, political and economic change. Market, state and political movements pushing for emancipation are all relevant poles in this political dance: 'the conflict between marketization and social protection cannot be understood in isolation from emancipation' (Fraser, 2013, p. 129).

Fraser's analysis is relevant for the transformation of the meaning of the university as well as the politics of crisis. The debate surrounding the marketisation of universities too often presents the issue of issues as a choice between bureaucratic state and market, between regarding higher education as a branch of the welfare state or as a commodity to be delivered and consumed. Neither position leaves room for the notion of emancipation, which is decidedly odd given that education is often intuitively allied with greater freedom. Fraser contends that a political focus on emancipation concerns an impulse to overcome domination, but this does not automatically bring positive effects since emancipation may strain existing solidary bonds or 'transform the ethical substance undergirding protection' (Fraser, 2013, p. 130). Fraser thinks that markets and states throw up injustices that lead to responses from emancipatory movements, but that emancipatory movements also result in responses from markets and states. Emancipatory movements in the postwar twentieth century were, of course, associated with the universities in the USA and Europe. However, in the decades since the late 1960s, universities have entered a new world where they are encouraged to compete for status. As state funding for universities has declined and graduate numbers have risen, pressure has increased on appearances. The status and reputation of universities has become their primary focus. Universities have shifted away from an ideal concerned with emancipation through the development and dissemination of knowledge and understanding towards a competition for status and recognition that has resulted in a zero-sum game of league table competition in individual countries and internationally. Here, the generation of knowledge and understanding, of a commitment to truth or the public good, becomes secondary to concerns about institutional status and branding.

While Fraser describes struggles between market, state and emancipatory forces, it is worth digging a little deeper into the ideas of competition and cooperation. Joseph Heath outlines five different mechanisms of cooperative benefit.

Heath argues that catallactic, market fetishizing thinking results in a tendency to misconstrue the welfare state as residual. In other words, the market provides goods where possible, but the state steps in where necessary. The welfare state becomes regarded as essentially redistributive and egalitarian. Heath argues this is a misclassification. The state often takes a lead role in promoting certain forms of cooperative benefit, and delineating the different mechanisms of cooperation enables a clearer view of the normative foundations of the welfare state. I strongly suggest that this form of thinking also misconstrues higher education as essentially concerned with social mobility, increased growth levels and efficiency. After all, it is such rhetoric that justified increased state spending on education, including higher education, in the UK from 2001 under the New Labour Government. To understand why universities are much more than functional institutions promoting growth, or their own reputation, we should turn to a close analysis of cooperation.

Begin with a state of nature, a situation without cooperation. Why might anyone choose to interact? Heath argues there are two types of reason. One is where individuals agree to engage in actions that bring positive externalities. Another is where they agree not to engage in activity that leads to negative externalities. Heath wants to ignore the second type because agreement between people to leave each other alone is a minimal form of cooperation. It seems plausible, however, to argue that universities have transformed from institutions concerned with promoting emancipation into organisations with a tacit agreement to leave each other alone as they pursue increased brand value. In other words, there is a collective resistance to admit to a transformation in purposes since that would devalue the collective brand of 'universities'.

He proposes there are five types of cooperation that can arise: i. economies of scale; ii. gains from trade; iii. risk pooling; iv. self-binding; and v. information transmission mechanisms. The idea behind Heath's argument is that if the primary purpose of public institutions is to secure cooperation, then these can be analysed in terms of these five types of cooperation and the extent to which they limit free-rider strategies (Heath, 2006, p. 330).

Universities are institutions that enable advanced specialisation, and in theory, collaboration. Academics and students are organised into departments, faculties and research centres. Economists will tend to approach a question from a different perspective from political theorists; psychologists will take a different tack from philosophers. If there is self-interest for each to answer the question satisfactorily, then there is an incentive for reciprocal cooperation. The reciprocity involved in such joint ventures enables trust to develop between participants.

Economies of scale also relate to the second mechanism through specialisation. Gains from trade mean that the farmer will cooperate with the blacksmith because of their different needs, preferences and abilities. Cooperation between different people allows for gains in trade in consumption and in production. Industry and academia are encouraged to cooperate through, for example, knowledge transfer partnerships or through requirements to demonstrate research impact or research engagement. Universities and business might have specialist resources that enable gains from trade through cooperation. There is a difficulty that is brought into focus here though. If the university is concerned with the production and dissemination of knowledge and the business is concerned with profit levels, then cooperation between the different institutions may well be strained.

Cooperation helps to reduce uncertainty. Risk-pooling refers to the idea that individuals and organisations are risk-averse. Cooperatives spring up among producers as a form of insurance, for instance. Universities, state bureaucracies and private firms might share risk through secondment schemes for staff with particular expertise.

Self-binding cooperative mechanisms are those which employ cooperation to constrain future choices. If I lack self-control I might hand you my car keys before the party so I cannot drive home. Over time, preferences can be inconsistent. For example, a business might want to hire staff as soon as possible rather than wait for better-trained employees. Collaboration with a suitable degree programme could be a form of cooperation that enables a more efficient long-term outcome. Cooperative agreement among academics in a department for high entry grade requirements for students should help maintain good academic standards.

Cooperative interactions also allow agents to save on learning costs. The preservation, development and dissemination of knowledge require a system of trust. Heath points out here that:

> The norm of truth-telling is the most apparent example. As the story of 'the boy who cried wolf' reminds us, individuals whose behavior is determined by their own self-interest, rather than by the norms governing the relevant language game, undermine the integrity of the system.
>
> (Heath, 2006, p. 328)

The depth of learning involved in higher education goes beyond mere imitation, though admittedly this will be involved too, so learning is itself highly susceptible to free-rider problems. Researchers have been caught falsifying their own work and articles have been retracted. Frameworks intended to help preserve the ethical integrity of research have become common at universities and at national levels. For instance, there is the *Singapore Statement on Research Integrity* (2010), the *European Code of Conduct for Research Integrity* (2011) and in the UK the *Concordat to Support Research Integrity* (2012). There are also widespread concerns about students 'cheating' in their studies through plagiarism or falsifying results.

However, at what point does collaboration between private industry and public university become exploitative? To what extent might the private firm be buying kudos from the university's involvement, or intervening in research publication for reasons of self-interest? Or, as Christopher Newfield argues, does commercially oriented university research merely provide private firms with high-quality research at lower costs than they would incur if conducting the research themselves (Newfield, 2008, pp. 208–214)? Kneller et al focus on collaborations between universities and industry in Canada, Japan, the UK and USA, but their focus is on ways to prevent censorship of publications and 'lock up' of new inventions through intellectual property management. For instance, in the UK they make much of the Lambert Agreement for collaboration that ensures private firms can only control intellectual property and publication in exchange for covering the full economic costs of research. Kneller et al point towards this as a way forward for Japanese and North American collaborations (Kneller et al, 2014). It is worth noting, however, that these collaborative arrangements between industry and universities are non-cooperative except in the context of a policy environment that encourages universities to work with private industry. Universities are encouraged towards greater collaboration under the assumption that gains from trade will tend to follow. However, corporate funding of university research is likely to produce findings that benefit the funder. On the surface, there appears to be gains from this trade: university researchers are paid from a private source and the sponsor receives the research findings, but the gains here are purely financial. The research looks more like a marketing exercise rather than scholarship or science. Of course, the sponsor has bought the veneer of objective research.

Heath points out that each of these cooperative mechanisms has been put forward at one point or another as the key reason for social order. So, Hume argued that self-binding explained the basis of civil association, Locke thought that gains from trade led to the need for property rights, Hobbes saw the basis of the state as an insurance scheme that protects us from fear and Rousseau saw cooperation as an ongoing matter that allows us to deliberate and learn from one another in a process of general will formation. The point of this analysis of cooperation is to turn attention towards re-examining the type of collective action problems that social institutions attempt to solve. For instance, to take a concrete example, there is a great deal of focus within higher education on employment (or underemployment) of graduates after they finish their studies. One increasingly common feature of undergraduate degrees in the UK is more focus on group projects. A general intention is, among other things, to prepare students for working in teams within the context of employment. One of the central problems of cooperation that Heath notes is moral hazard in group action, or shirking. To overcome shirking, one strategy frequently adopted is to form small groups where strong relations of trust are encouraged to form in order that the group polices itself. A team like this, however, will police itself according to norms internal to the group. The self-binding mechanism can be seen to be relevant where a constitution limits the legislature. Like an uncodified constitution, the academic norms of commitment to truth and knowledge can also lead to cooperation even in a competitive context. So, for instance, academic roles like acting as an external examiner for another institution, or working on peer review, aid information transmission through a self-binding mechanism (Heath, 2006, p. 336).

It becomes relevant that Heath excludes the idea of social status from his analysis:

> Although it might be argued that healthy self-esteem is one of the positive benefits of social interaction, I am inclined to analyse it in terms of its

opposite, and regard low self-esteem as a potential negative consequence of social interaction. Social interaction, according to this view, elicits dominance behaviour, which in turn generates status hierarchy. Self-esteem is generated by the perception of one's own position in this status hierarchy. Refraining from dominance behaviour is therefore a form of cooperation. Self-esteem, from this perspective, is not a social good, but merely the absence of a bad.

(Heath, 2006, p. 330)

It is unfortunate that Heath does not take this analysis further, focused as he is on the positive aspects of cooperation. An orientation towards self-esteem, a concern about our appearances in the eyes of others, a concern with branding, with 'likes' and 'favourites' on social media in a virtual world has a significant impact on higher education and the university itself. This turn towards self-esteem coincides with a financialisation of society to contribute to a process of de-democratisation in democratic societies.

Since Habermas analysed the transformation of the public sphere (Habermas, 1992b, 1996) and even since Calhoun (2006) noted a mirroring tendency in universities, the public sphere has undergone another significant transformation. Dutch-disease is the term often used to designate unbalanced economies, after oil discoveries caused the Netherlands to concentrate too much on oil and gas production at the expense of other sectors in the economy. There is a similar unbalancing caused by focus on financial services. Just as Wall Street and the City of London have come to generate huge economic growth in the USA and Britain since the 1980s, there has also been a financialisation of higher education. The very liquidity of finance that allows such great gains also makes possible large losses in purely financial terms, but also democratically. The nation state, or the EU at the supranational level, can no longer contain production as it did in the industrial age. The loss of political control over production dampened the economic efficacy of the post-industrial state and alongside this came the transfer of risk away from the state and on to the backs of individuals.

The public sphere became too expensive to maintain and competition through rankings and league tables replaced more substantive notions of hierarchy. League tables reflect but also generate inequalities in status. One trouble with such competitive inter-institutional arrangements is that incentives are based on envy and shame. In a battle between universities for relative league table position, there is no distinction between getting better, in terms of the performance indicators, and rivals performing worse. This leads to a situation where the performance in the league table counts for much more than the substantive activity that is supposedly being indicated. If a rival institution cuts costs by hiring fewer academics, but maintains its league position, then the institution has made an efficiency gain regardless of what happens below the surface of maintaining rank position. Its competitors are forced to do likewise. Of course, dropping down the league is a source of institutional shame and this provides incentive to the institution. But shame also takes another form here, for in pursuing systemic performance targets the academic is forced to be someone inauthentic. In Bernard Williams' words:

> The root of shame lies in exposure in a more general sense, in being at a disadvantage: in what I shall call, in a very general phrase, a loss of power. The sense of shame is a reaction of the subject to the consciousness of this loss . . . it is 'the emotion of self-protection'.
>
> (Williams, 1994, p. 220)

This is interesting in its relation to civic engagement and capacity for action because Arendt points out that shame and embarrassment form a barrier to action in the public realm since, for her, being forced to act is a contradiction. The academic world, insofar as it is a public sphere, must be a realm of free action. Instead, the modern scholarly ethic exhibits signs of inflamed *amour-propre*.

Chapter 4

Academic authority, trust and reliance[1]

As far back as the 1950s Hannah Arendt warned that the concept of authority had almost lost its meaning under attack both from the left, where it was confused with tyranny, and from the right, where it was confused with unfreedom (Arendt, 1993b). Against these positions, Arendt argued that authority enables citizens to act in a public capacity. This is a fundamentally important aspect of education. In this chapter I explore authority in English higher education, where market asymmetries and 'producer power' have been seen as impediments to a contestable market. Policies designed to enable a market mechanism to function more effectively are likely to damage relations of trust between academic teachers and students. This is because authority loses its moral aspect when recognised only in functional terms.

Authority is grounded in the notion of moral tradition (Arendt, 1993) rather than orderliness, or some vague promise about improved employment prospects for those who do as they are told. Arendt, in fact, connects her conception of authority as *auctoritas* – making the world, creating the possibility of action – with a sharp critique of so-called child-centred education in 'The Crisis of Education' (Arendt, 1993). In higher education contexts where students are encouraged to consider themselves consumers of positional goods, we tend to get the same abdication of educational responsibility for the world that she saw in a child-centred, responsibility-abdicating, school education in the 1950s. This chapter looks towards the context of education, and specifically examines higher education in England, to draw out the relationship between authority, trust and reliance.

Authority demands obedience, so it is not surprising that the concept is confused with lack of freedom, or with power or violence. But authority is not concerned with external means of coercion; rather it is recognised. As Arendt says, 'where force is used, authority itself has failed' (Arendt, 1993, p. 93). But neither is authority concerned with persuasion because persuasion 'presupposes equality and works through a process of argumentation' (Arendt, 1993, p. 93). So, authority involves obedience but neither force nor persuasion. Why would I obey somebody who held no power over me, or who had made no attempt, or tried but failed, to persuade me? Obedience might come from trust, rather than power or persuasion. When we trust somebody else, or some institution, we recognise some moral commitment held. I try to switch between thinking about authority and trust in educational and political terms through the argument. My claim is that education is primarily a political (rather than an economic) good.

There are various ways in which political philosophers have attempted to ground the concept of state authority: through security (Hobbes); by consent (Locke); through participation in democratic will formation (Rousseau); by appeals to fairness alongside freedom (Rawls). These are only some well-known varieties of how political authority is grounded in the question of political obligation. For some, such as Robert Paul Wolff, authority cannot be grounded at all, since it always and everywhere limits autonomy (Wolff, 1998, p. 18). Indeed, Wolff says elsewhere, 'Claims to authority, the exercise of authority, and the submission to authority have no place whatsoever in any of the characteristic educational relationships of a university' (Wolff, 1969, p. 100).

It is tempting to agree, when we think in terms of education, perhaps a higher education most of all, to think in terms of the development of autonomy, rather than in terms of authority. This becomes all the more obvious when Wolff tells us that 'Authority is the right to command, and correlatively, the right to be obeyed' (Wolff, 1998, p. 4). Of course, when we construe authority in Wolff's deontic terms of issuing commands or imperatives in return for obedience, it appears to us as an entirely inappropriate concept with which to view pedagogic relationships, especially (perhaps) in an environment where students are highly indebted through tuition fees which they incur in return for the possibility of higher earnings after graduation. Wolff defines authority in terms of command, which he can dismiss as immoral if it is never legitimate for an autonomous person to command another. Wolff is quick to draw a common distinction between *de facto* and *de jure* authority, and proposes that the fundamental task of political philosophy is to give a deduction of the concept of legitimate authority:

> To complete this deduction, it is not enough to show that there are circumstances in which men have an obligation to do what the *de facto* authorities command. Even under the most unjust of governments there are frequently good reasons for obedience rather than defiance. . . . [A] man may be right to comply with the commands of the government under whose *de facto* authority he finds himself. But none of this settles the matter of legitimate authority. That is a matter of the *right* to command, and of the correlative obligation *to obey the person who issues the command*. . . . Obedience is not a matter of doing what someone tells you to do. It is a matter of doing what he tells you to do *because he tells you to do it*. Legitimate, or *de jure*, authority thus concerns the grounds and sources of moral obligation.
>
> (Wolff, 1998, p. 9)

Wolff's defence of philosophical anarchism, and his dismissal of the exercise of authority in the educational relationships in a university, are only as good as the terms in which he seeks to define authority. Wolff's command theory of authority falls into a tradition: the command theory of law, which includes Hobbes, Austin and Kelsen, but the idea that authority concerns only commands and obedience misleads us. As Goldstone and Tunnell explain:

> It is wrong to define 'authority' as 'the right to command A to (not) do x,' because commanding is only one type of activity that authorities engage in, and not the essence of authority. Not only do authorities decide that A will do x, they decide or rule or judge that something is the case. An umpire in a baseball game, for example, may issue commands, but he also decides or rules that a pitch is a ball, or that a base runner is out. If he *says* that a base runner is out, then the base runner *is* out; the umpire's decision *makes* it so. When a spelling-bee judge declares a word to be spelled (in)correctly, then his decision is binding, even though he is mistaken. (His decision might be appealed, of course.) When a judge renders a verdict, which is clearly an exercise of authority, he is not giving commands, rather he is announcing his decision. When a judge pronounces sentence, he is doing just that, not commanding anyone to do anything. But when the judge tells the bailiff, 'Take him away,' then he is commanding. Although both announcing decisions and commanding may initiate action, nonetheless announcing decisions must be distinguished from commanding A to (not) do x. The definition of 'authority' as 'the right to command' assimilates diverse modes of authority to one – namely, commanding.
> (Goldstone and Tunnell, 1975, p. 134)

Wolff's *de jure* concept of authority allows him to express his argument in terms of command and obedience, which are unlikely to appeal to teachers interested in cultivating attitudes and persons who would want to pursue a higher education. The authoritative tutor is not someone who commands obedient students in the seminar. Rather, the authoritative academic cultivates an authoritative relationship of trust with students. Just as an umpire or judge has authority to make decisions (and sometimes might issue commands), an academic or teacher has authority to organise a course of study, holds a right to award grades and a right to establish and apply a system of standards (Silk, 1976, p. 273). But the academic does not hold this authority in her person, it is not the experience she has, her personal qualities or her academic qualifications which bring this authority. The authority of the academic ought not to be considered in the causal terms which the command theory invites: your command causes my obedience. Rather, as Peter Winch pointed out, 'Authority is not a sort of influence . . . but an *internal* relation. The very notion of a human will, capable of deliberating and making decisions, presupposes the notion of authority' (Peters and Winch, 1967, p. 98). This is an interesting turn of phrase, because Winch is pointing out that participating 'in rule-governed activities *is*, in a certain way, to accept authority' (Peters and Winch, 1967, p. 99). The academic belongs to a particular culture. Or, as Michael Oakeshott puts it, the academic belongs to a certain manner of thinking and employs a particular language. Oakeshott draws a distinction between a text and a language in education, and these fit with a vocational and a university education, respectively. It is Oakeshott's view that a vocational education concerns not how to use a particular language, but 'how to use those products of . . . thought which contribute to our current manner of living' (Oakeshott, 1991, p. 192). Consider how far removed Oakeshott's understanding of a university is from the perspective of an undergraduate student keen to acquire a university qualification which will maximize future income. Oakeshott says that a university:

> [I]s an association of persons, locally situated, engaged in caring for and attending to the whole intellectual capital which composes a civilization. It is concerned not merely to keep an intellectual inheritance intact, but to be continuously recovering what has been lost, restoring what has been neglected, collecting together what has been dissipated, repairing what has been corrupted, reconsidering, reshaping, reorganizing, making more intelligible, reissuing and reinvesting. In principle, it works undistracted by practical concerns; its current directions of interest are not determined by any but academic considerations; the interest it earns is all reinvested.
>
> (Oakeshott, 1991, p. 194)

The hypothetical student here has little interest in *attending to* the intellectual capital that makes a civilization, and little care for any interest it earns in being reinvested. The academic authority of the educator rests on what Max Weber termed the traditional authority of the 'cultivated man', rather than the rational-legal credentials of the expert:

> Behind all the present discussions of the foundations of the educational system, the struggle of the 'specialist type of man' against the older type of 'cultivated man' is hidden at some decisive point. This fight is determined by the irresistibly expanding bureaucratization of all public and private relations of authority and by the ever-increasing importance of expert and specialized knowledge.
>
> (Weber, 1991, p. 243)

The academic educator holds a sense of deriving authority from the intellectual discipline, the manner of thinking she seeks to introduce to her students. Her students, on the other hand, seek the expertise that brings increased employability in the labour market, while senior administrators and policy-makers involved in the development of the concept of student partnership hold to a command conception of authority. The teacher and the student hold different understandings of commitment to one another within the context of a privatised, marketised English higher education. The student believes in a functionally relevant higher education experience (providing opportunities to develop skills and understanding) yet cannot rely on academic authority to fulfil commitment to the student given the low status of teaching, the weight of student numbers and, most importantly, the student's private understanding of the self in everyday *life*. The relevance of the world is lost on universities and students thinking in careerist terms.

Roger Brown, a British higher education policy analyst who is highly critical of marketisation, describes higher education not as a 'search good' where value can be determined prior to consumption, nor as an 'experience good' where value is determined as the good is consumed, but as a 'post-experience good':

> [H]igher education is actually a '*post*-experience good', the effects of which may not appear for many years and may not even be traceable to a particular educational experience. . . . Because higher education is an intangible product, and because it involves a judgement-based, customized solution, as in any professional service, it is not always clear to either the teacher or the student what the outcome will be.
>
> (Brown, 2011, p. 24)

Brown points out that this characteristic feature of the good of higher education renders problematic quality indicators in the marketplace, designed to act as proxies for price signals. Individual students cannot value education as they 'consume' it because of epistemic asymmetry between even good students and good teachers. I hope to show that the real difficulty with valuing the good of higher education goes well beyond the claim that we can only grasp its true worth at the very end of our lives. The analytical path down which discussion of the economics of information leads encourages us to conceive of higher education in a particularly shallow manner. There seem to be two problems with this. First, higher education's value is regarded primarily in private, individualistic terms. Second, higher education's value is construed in epistemic terms. A good higher education provides practical and propositional knowledge to the individual. This knowledge yields increased productivity. Spending on higher education (by the state or by individuals) is rationalised in instrumental terms. This apparently simple argument is deeply flawed and we can begin to see why through an exploration of university education as a post-experience good. A version of this apparently simple argument which sees higher education in terms of 'human capital' or a source of endogenous growth is playing out in the UK (but especially England), Australia and the USA, but the idea has become hegemonic that higher education carries instrumental value. State policies are intended to release or encourage that instrumental value as economies 'upskill'. Such a policy stance towards higher education involves a fundamental category mistake that pertains to the transformative purposes, coinciding with an instrumentalised conception of higher education. In short, when we regard education as 'adding value' to persons through education, we miss a fundamentally important moral role that education takes on. Teachers, colleges and universities play a vital role in identifying students with talent and potential. The students' grades are a reflection of educators' judgements about the students. Students, their families, their future employers are put in a position of trust towards the educators' judgements – the authority of teachers' judgements is at stake, but this authority does not have the status of a command. Or, to take a different approach, consider the possibility that higher education is about supporting the public sphere. Universities' first duty is to the public and developing competent persons capable of acting in the public sphere (Smith, 2010). The democratic state in this context should trust universities to carry out this role. However, moral concepts like trust are disappearing from the education system. We will do well to remember that a higher education is more than the development and transfer of knowledge and skills from one generation to another. It is, more fundamentally, the development and transfer of authority between generations. This is an authority to act in the world. To be sure, higher education is neither necessary nor sufficient for this, it is merely one way in which a public institution has, historically at least, fostered the capacity for action among citizens.

In the UK, the Higher Education Academy (abbreviated to HEA – a body formed to promote teaching and learning in higher education by the umbrella group Universities UK that represents British universities) has advocated a policy of 'student partnership'. The founding Chief Executive of the HEA, Paul Ramsden, submitted a report to the then Minister for Universities, Bill Rammell, on 'The Future of Higher Education Teaching and the Student Experience' in 2008. This was intended as a reference point for policy decisions related to teaching and the student experience over the subsequent ten to fifteen years. In the report, Ramsden acknowledges global competition as a key threat, and proposes a vision to establish UK higher education as 'an engaged partnership between students and providers'. By way of elaboration, he claims that students should be 'collaborators' in institutional structures and processes relating to teaching and assessment and 'central contributors to the business of enhancing the student experience'. He envisages students as part of a community of learners working with academics and 'sharing responsibility' to enhance teaching, assure quality and maintain standards.

Ramsden's rationale for this partnership model is primarily market-driven. On the one hand, he argues, student partnership will help entrench future UK competitiveness by consolidating a special feature of the UK 'brand' that is encapsulated in the phrase 'intimacy of pedagogical relationships'. On the other hand, partnership counters any notion of students as passive consumers of their education, which Ramsden recognises as one of the most negative potentials of marketisation.

Regardless of the merits or otherwise of Ramsden's claims, the conception of students as partners, proposed as the medicine for improving the student experience and as antidote to a passive consumerist approach to education, has been adopted and keenly promoted by UK higher education bodies, including the Quality Assurance Agency (QAA), which oversees qualification standards in UK universities, the Higher Education Academy (HEA), which is intended to improve teaching and learning throughout UK universities, and the Students' Union (NUS), and consequently by many individuals within universities with a stake in advancing learning and teaching.

Universities have made extra efforts to step up student representation in matters of governance and quality assurance, and the HEA in particular has promoted student partnership in curriculum design and delivery. In case there is any doubt about what is meant by student partnership here, let us give just one example. A recent large funding project run by the HEA was entitled 'Students as Partners in the Curriculum', and the bidding criteria clearly specified that students should be treated as equal rather than subordinate partners. Project teams were required to comprise representatives from both student and staff communities in almost equal number, and listed principles of working with students as partners included developing 'shared purpose, values and principles' and 'joint decision making and accountability arrangements'. The logic of student partnership can also be seen in a recent Business, Innovation and Skills report on *Improving the Student Learning Experience – a national assessment* (BIS, 2014). The report attempts to track student satisfaction over the previous two years and pays particular attention to the mechanisms used to gauge student satisfaction with institutions' attempts at 'student engagement' in terms of representation in matters of governance, feedback from students, their ability to shape their academic experience and to what extent students can see the impact of their feedback (BIS, 2014).

The implication here is clear: that when it comes to making and evaluating changes to curricula, students and teachers should have equal status and equal say. Other projects and literature proceeding from the students as partners movement echo or even exceed this principle of equality by elevating students to leadership roles, such that students are identified as 'co-designers of courses', 'pedagogical consultants' and 'strategy developers'.

An understanding of expert authority of the teacher is negated. It is not that students should not be involved in educational matters or have a voice. Rather, the claim here is that undermining the authority of the teacher to limit the impact of a consumer model of higher education is detrimental to both student and teacher when it comes to the main task of a higher education – learning and specialising in a subject discipline of choice.

Advocates of the market often point towards a particular form of market failure caused by asymmetrical information. Akerlof (1970) sets out the problem related to markets where the quality of the good on offer is subject to uncertainty on the part of potential consumers. Akerlof explains that there are many sorts of market where buyers use some sort of market statistic to judge the quality of prospective purchases. This generates 'incentive for sellers to market poor quality merchandise since the returns for good quality accrue mainly to the entire group whose statistic is affected rather than to the individual seller.

As a result there tends to be a reduction in the average quality of goods and also in the size of the market' (Akerlof, 1970, p. 488). Epistemic asymmetry of information in the market, between buyers and sellers (but also what we might consider a moral asymmetry between well-intentioned and malicious buyers and sellers) causes the market to degrade and eventually shrink as bad quality merchandise crowds out good quality offerings. Immediately, we should notice that this market relation between purchasers and providers has a reifying effect. If we consider a particular university degree as the product, then the degree is not synonymous with a higher education. Two friends on the same degree course may have been taught by different people, held different discussions in tutorials, read different books, taken different modules and options within the same degree course. Both may graduate from the same university course with the same degree class, but we should not pretend that their education was the same. Roger Brown's wish to identify higher education as a post-experience good is in part a recognition that education, as a relational good, is highly differentiated between different individuals undergoing different experiences with different effects at different points over the course of a lifetime.

In the economics of information, post-experience goods are also sometimes referred to as 'credence goods' (Darby and Karni, 1973). Dulleck, Kerschbamer and Sutter explain that:

> Repair services, medical treatments, the provision of software programs, or a taxi ride in an unknown city are prime examples of what is known as a credence good in the economics literature. Generally speaking, credence goods have the characteristic that though consumers can observe the utility they derive from the good ex post, they cannot judge whether the type or quality of the good they have received is the ex ante needed one. Moreover, consumers may even ex post be unable to observe which type or quality they actually received. An expert seller, however, is able to identify the type or quality that fits a consumer's needs by performing a diagnosis. He can then provide the right quality and charge for it, or he can exploit the information asymmetry by defrauding the consumer.
> (Dulleck, Kerschbamer and Sutter, 2011, p. 526)

The notion of a credence good adds another dimension to the concept of the post-experience good. If the consumer of a higher education can roughly estimate the utility of that higher education, she may still struggle to grasp whether that higher education was what she needed before she began to study. Moreover, she may well be unsure of the quality of her higher education even at the end of life. A decision to consume a credence good, whether it's related to expert health care, car repairs, a taxi journey in an unfamiliar city or a higher education, involves trust or some sort of reliance. The university student and the motorist with a car that will not start both place themselves in a position where they must trust or rely upon a potentially fraudulent provider. The moral component involved in trusting a credence good is relatively unexamined largely because literature on credence goods remains within the field of (supposedly) value-free economics, while literature on the concept of trust remains within the field of moral philosophy. I wish to point out that there are different sorts of credence goods. Sometimes credibility relates mainly to the functional aspects of a good and involves the recipient of the good relying on it to function appropriately. At other times, however, credibility relates mainly to trust and a moral commitment between the consumer and producer. To be sure, at the empirical level, credence goods involve both moral trust and reliability. However, keeping these analytically distinct throws into relief the altered grounds of authority and power in relations between academics and students.

Fair trade coffee or organic pork products carry a 'kite mark'. The kite mark represents a set of standards involved in the production of the good through a vertical supply chain. The consumer of the credence good trusts in the meaning of the kite mark, and the observation of standards set by the authority of the institution represented by the kite mark. Advanced division of labour renders the consumer relatively powerless to determine production standards of the various inputs at each stage of production, so the consumer places trust in the authority of the kite mark and the institution this represents. The university might be considered in a similar way. The authority of the university is delegated by some higher authority such as the Pope, historically, or the state, for instance via the Privy Council in Britain.

Zdenko Kodelja argues that authority involves trust. This is implicit in Arendt's conception of authority – an idea that we have almost lost sight of. Authority, on a standard analysis, takes two forms: epistemic and deontic authority, also sometimes expressed as 'an authority' and 'in authority'. R.S. Peters argued that epistemic authority, being an authority, grounds deontic authority, being in an authoritative position to issue imperatives:

> Usually we think that what makes professors epistemic authorities is their de facto knowledge. But this knowledge itself is not sufficient for being an epistemic authority or, more precisely, for being a de facto epistemic authority as De George interprets it. In his opinion, 'we make someone a de facto authority by believing what [the person] says.' Therefore, a university professor is for students a de facto epistemic authority if, and only if, they believe – at least to some extent – 'what [the professor] says when [he or she] teaches. If there is no such' student, 'then no matter how' knowledgeable the professor is, he or she 'is not a de facto epistemic authority.' Thus, what makes the professor a de facto epistemic authority is not his or her knowledge, but rather the students' belief. However, they would not believe if they knew that the professor did not have the knowledge they supposed.
> (Kodelja, 2013, p. 323)

In other words, the university teacher's authority over students rests upon recognition of that authority by those students. The teacher holds authority, in other words, to the extent that she is trusted by the student. The relationship between authority and trust is familiar to readers of Locke's liberal social contract theory. According to Locke, in society the overarching good is the common good, but the uncertainty involved in political life can sometimes mean that political authority fails to sustain the common good. Locke turns to the notion of fiduciary trust as a model for ruling. Here citizens should remain vigilant towards those they trust in authority. Emily Nacol says, of Locke's liberal idea of trust, that:

> The trust model is appropriately open and flexible, but this elasticity contains the potential both for profitable political relations and for profound betrayal. That is, a trust can be either a means of security and benefit or a source of insecurity and loss; it always holds the seeds of both, as risks do.
> (Nacol, 2011, p. 581)

It is tempting to portray Locke's liberal theory of trust in shallow, transactional terms, whereby the citizens accept the authority of the state so long as the government acts for the common good. However, the citizens take on a role whereby they are required to exercise judgement over whether their trust is being honoured by the trustee state. At the heart of Locke's social contract lies the risk: agents in the state of nature enter into an agreement to give up their natural rights in exchange for civil rights on the understanding that the government will support the common good. The source of the authority of the state is therefore the will of trusting, consenting citizens, but their trust and consent are always and everywhere provisional.

Trust and authority have generally declined as risk management has been incorporated into a bureaucratic ethic associated with the modern office. It should come as no surprise that talk of obedience problems and discipline in primary school classrooms has risen as the authority of teachers, lecturers and academics has become transformed into a bureaucratic system. Gradually, education is losing its moral dimension.

Trust, Katherine Hawley argues, following Annette Baier (1986), is a moral quality, more than mere reliance. Trust involves commitments and promises (though commitments can also arise out of conventions and social norms), when trust fails betrayal is involved. Moreover, Hawley finds it analytically helpful to examine the concept of trust in opposition to distrust and non-reliance. An increasingly transactional relation between students, teachers and universities could be argued to have altered relations in terms of trust and authority. In effect, new arrangements for higher education finance (such as £9,000 annual tuition fees in England and the highest levels of educational indebtedness in the world) generate a situation where trust becomes distrust, and academic authority becomes a service provider. The imposition of high-level fees radically alters academic relations. The credence good is no longer imbued with credibility, trust in the good begins to evaporate. This is because the social rules and conventions involved in the interpretation of what it means to study at a university are altered. Universities generate, for instance, expectations that students (as consumers) should expect to rely upon. The shift from trust to reliance undermines legitimate authority, or possibly, for some (students and academics), brings a sense of betrayal. A predominant policy response to this situation is to encourage universities to engage in practices which increase 'student partnership'. However, this partnership takes place at a formal policy level rather than being organically embedded into the meaning of belonging to the university as a student. Hawley argues that distrust 'is nonreliance plus a tendency to resentment, a tendency to judge the distrustee negatively, or tendency to think that an apology is warranted: distrust is something like disappointed trust, though perhaps not preceded by an episode of trust' (Hawley, 2014, p. 9). For Hawley, it is 'appropriate to trust or distrust someone to do something only if that person has an explicit or implicit commitment to doing it' (Hawley, 2014, p. 9). This means that trust involves reliance and some extra sense of commitment. Often, this extra sense of commitment is thought to be some positive view of the motives of the trusted. If I trust you to teach me Locke's theory of just property acquisition I might assume you have the right sort of motive for teaching me Locke. This might be your intellectual interest in Lockean political philosophy. Russell Hardin, for instance, suggests that when we trust someone, we expect the trustee to take on our interests within his own. The student expects and trusts his teacher to look out for the student's interest, while the same student might rely on his laptop to store essays and readings. There is no expectation that the laptop has intentions which take into account the student's interests. Karen Jones, on the other hand, has argued that trust requires an attitude of optimism or hope, an affective attitude rather than a belief, that the trusted will be positively moved by the thought she is being trusted (Hawley, 2014, p. 5). But Hawley is keen to demonstrate that such a motive-based idea of trust cannot explain distrust.

Hawley argues that the appropriateness of relations of trust or distrust hinges on an explicit or implicit commitment from the trusted towards the trustee.

> To trust someone to do something is to believe that she has a commitment to doing it, and to rely on her to meet that commitment. To distrust someone to do something is to believe that she has a commitment to doing it, and yet not rely upon her to meet that commitment.
> (Hawley, 2014, p. 10)

The problem of the university teacher's authority turns on the teacher's commitment and purposes. It is likely that the university teacher understands her commitment in epistemic terms or in terms of attitude towards developing a sense of intellectual curiosity. The student, however, is encouraged by higher education policies and practices to understand the university teacher's commitment on a different horizon of skill development in preparation for paid employment. The bureaucratic manager is keen to understand the academic's commitment in terms of targets, various league table positions and research evaluation scores.

In a focus on relations between teachers and students we should notice that the student who distrusts his teacher might distrust a particular attitude in his teacher: 'Perhaps', Hawley writes, 'expecting the distrustee to have an interest in frustrating our interests' (2014, p. 6). But, Hawley points out, such negative expectations are not necessary for distrust: we would distrust a liar or a cheat even if he held no interest in frustrating our interests. Hawley's point is that motive-based accounts of trust in general cannot cope with the concept of distrust. But, it's worth pausing to reflect on her analysis. The idea of students as consumers, armed with information about previous students' satisfaction levels, and the powers to influence course content and the form assessments should take, places the student and the academic teacher in opposition. The market model of consumers and producers encourages the student to adopt a distrustful stance towards the teacher and to regard the academic's interest as distinct from the student's interest. In other words, a non-moral, thin, functional conception of higher education precludes trust, and therefore precludes the recognition of authority, which in turn renders impossible an acquisition of authority by students through education. Less skeptical student-consumers might rely on their tutors and lecturers to hand over the learning materials required to pass the qualification, but such reliance actually turns a potentially authoritative educational relationship into a power relationship.

Credence goods, like organic meat, fair trade coffee or windscreen glass, are substantively different from a credence good such as higher education. While kite-marked windscreen glass involves reliance that the glass will shatter relatively safely in an accident, a university education ought to involve a trusting commitment between students, academics and the university itself. However, the lifeworldly horizon of the university appears differently to policy-makers, senior managers, future employers, students and academics. Different relationships of trust, authority and obedience obtain in the interactions in the different relationships. For instance, the students and staff might rely on or trust the university administrators to organise facilities for teaching students, while the administrators might rely on students and staff to fulfil their roles. The instrumentalised climate of high-fees, highly indebted higher education helps to generate an attitude from many students, administrators and academic teachers that students are, indeed, justified in regarding themselves as consumers, or lecturers are justified in delivering a body of knowledge. Student partnership recommends policy initiatives such as involving students in choosing and designing assessment methods, deciding upon curriculum content, involvement in faculty and university committee work. From a consumer perspective this can be understood in terms of an increase in student power and student voice.

The practices and policies involved in a marketised higher education system are indeed transformative, but not in educational terms. Educational authority becomes power in the labour market, trust becomes distrust or reliance, commitment to diligent study evaporates and reliance on support from the *alma mater* turns into a functional reliance on the academic teacher to provide knowledge.

The policy of student partnership does not generate mutual relations of trust between the students and their academic teachers. The moral relations of trust and authority are all too easily transformed in an overly instrumentalised higher education into strategic relations of power and distrust. Recall for Hawley that distrust was a reliance from the trustee towards the relied upon, coupled with a lack of commitment from the trusted. Formalised student voice and engagement to help design curriculum or determine modes of assessment, or 'inclusive' representation (without providing appropriate support and training) imposes student engagement from outside the teacher-student relationship. The outside imposition, unless done in a way that takes pains to protect the authority of the academic teacher, undermines relations of authority and trust between students and their teachers at university. Educational (intellectual) commitments (a tacit background contract between teacher and student) between students and teachers reduce, damaging the legitimacy of the teacher's authority. Authority, without recognition (from the student) becomes pure power, and the purpose (or output) of the process of higher education is no longer the gradual development of authority (in the student becoming a graduate) from the university via academic teachers, but the acquisition of power to be held in the labour market. Relations of trust and authority degrade in a culture of instrumentalism, and this degradation can be seen as a fundamental inefficiency and a misdirected waste of time and effort. Onora O'Neill makes much the same point about trust in conditions of transparency. Where outcomes and targets are tracked, the incentive to game the outcomes increases, trust reduces and authority diminishes (O'Neill, 2002). The policy of student partnership, therefore, unless very carefully introduced in ways which protect academic teachers' authority, only helps to further hollow out higher learning.

Conclusions

Discussion of the concept of authority too often involves a confusion between epistemic and deontic varieties of authority, and between power and authority. The example of *de jure* authority in higher education systems illustrates this confusion and shows us how authoritative relationships can be eroded and transformed into relations involving distrust. Moreover, authoritative teachers making judgements about their students and taking responsibility for preparing students to act in the world show us that there is meaningful instrumental value attached to authoritative teachers. Attempts to marketise higher education erode this value, which we can associate with liberalism via Locke.

Higher education ought not to be regarded as a search good, experience good, nor as a 'post-experience good'. We should instead consider higher education as a credence good, however, a credence good which involves trust (and therefore authority) rather than mere reliance. The trust and authority involved in such a credence good render policies oriented towards student partnership problematic insofar as these undermine the academic teacher's authority and, therefore, the purpose of higher education to pass on a sense of authority from one generation to the next. Higher education must be understood in more than functional terms. Its purposes reach beyond professional training, income generating research and the development of scientific knowledge towards Oakeshott's language of a university education.

The state in democratic society ought to preserve the legitimate authority of institutions which help to sustain a democratic public sphere. Ultimately, it is a pluralist system involving different sources of authority in society that underwrite an attitude of critical trust towards the state itself. Advocates of marketisation of university education should understand the full costs of their preferred policy, in both educational and political terms.

Note

1 This chapter is derived in part from an article published in *Educational Philosophy and Theory* on 7th June 2016, available online: http://www.tandfonline.com/10.1080/00131857.2016.1153451

Chapter 5
Higher education and citizenship[1]

Liberal and republican varieties of citizenship

There are two broad conceptions of citizenship which we can look towards. On the one hand we have the ancient, republican tradition of citizenship, and on the other, the modern, liberal understanding of the citizen (Touraine, 1997, pp. 77–89). Michael Ignatieff sketches the distinction:

> The one defends a political, the other an economic definition of man, the one an active – participatory – conception of freedom, the other a passive – acquisitive – definition of freedom; the one speaks of society as a *polis*; the other of society as a market-based association of competitive individuals.
> (Ignatieff, 1995, p. 54)

Contemporary higher education, where students pay high tuition fees to acquire degrees which will provide skills for the 'real world' of work and academics produce research which sustains 'evidence-based' policy or 'impacts' upon 'end-users', exhibits developments which all speak to the liberal conception of the citizen, rooted in 'life' rather than 'worldliness'. The participative, political citizen is subsumed within the economic, instrumentally rationalist individual. Here, the capacity for *action* is diminished and replaced by steering mechanisms whereby individuals respond instrumentally and strategically to their environment. The tensions between the private and the public, between economics and politics, between life and world, between state, market and *polis* can be seen throughout the twentieth century. However, these tensions are particularly clear in education, and clearer still in higher education. Moreover, the financial-economic crisis experienced from 2008, and the 'austere' governmental response to it, is pulling these tensions to breaking point. Civic relations between persons pursuing a common good are replaced by market relationships alleged to result in efficient outcomes. However, these seemingly efficient outcomes occlude the public value of civic virtue.

The liberal language of contract has entwined these values of citizenship and value for money. The citizen is replaced with the taxpayer, who has been reified, turned into someone concrete who demands his or her money's worth from the public sector. The social contract is reduced to a transaction between consumers and producers. The liberal perspective on the university looks to issues of 'fairness' and seeks that institutions widen participation, but this neglects the broader and, perhaps, deeper issue of the degradation of the good of the university (Sandel, 2012, p. 108.)

Authority, accountability and value for money

The managerialism that we see in our education system and in our universities is intended to result in efficiency, and, therefore produce value for money. Focus is set on learning outcomes, teachers should be paid, in part, according to the results of their teaching and research quality is graded according to where it is published. In the USA private higher education providers argue that university accreditation should depend on 'student outcomes' rather than 'input measures' such as the number of staff with PhDs. Performance indicators, in short, form a representation of real work being done, and performance indicators have to be gauged accurately. This, in turn, means that the intangible qualities, especially those internal to processes at hand, rather than 'outcomes', will be dismissed as too ephemeral, or perhaps, too costly to play a part in the exact business of determining performance. All too often, moreover, the most straightforwardly measurable factors are those which can be counted in cash terms. Accountability measures tend to focus on inputs and outputs but neglect the ethical matter of how something is done. It is, then, the academic ethic which is corrupted by both a bureaucratic state and a market-oriented environment.

The idea of accountability, however, comes not from management theory but from representative democracy. To be accountable can involve financial liability, but it can also mean liable to be called on to provide an explanation. As citizens we hold our representatives accountable through various channels: through surgeries, meetings, public debate and elections. As citizens we hold neither lecturers nor teachers, nor any other public sector worker, to account. Rather, as citizens we entrust the state with the role of policing public professions. And this is why those elements of the state bureaucracy charged with monitoring quasi-public goods are so visible. Accountability, as we experience it, is about the state being seen to act appropriately, rather than acting appropriately per se. Accountability has a dramaturgical significance. This explains the crude character of accountability mechanisms: league tables, key information statistics. The issue of holding academics accountable is, in fact, not a matter of accountability, but of authority. In the name of accountability the *legitimate* authority of the academic is usurped. This, however, is not to make the argument that academics should not be publicly accountable. Rather, it is to say that accountability measures should preserve those realms which are open to abuse by office holders, rather than determine those offices. This tendency, however, actually serves to detract from the accountability of the state and governing parties, for one way in which governments are held accountable is through their policies and the behaviour of ministers being left open to scrutiny by the citizenry. One channel of criticism has traditionally come from academe because academics have expert knowledge which can challenge the wisdom of state policy. But, since control of what people within universities teach and research comes increasingly under the auspices of state regulation, the accountability of government is reduced, thereby diminishing the legitimacy of government, since it is no longer so open to criticism, and the legitimacy of the university, as a democratic voice which can mobilise challenges to a scientised politics, is also undermined. Amy Gutmann makes this very point in relation to schooling, but it holds equally for university education:

> The legitimacy (as distinguished from the justice) of liberal democracies is generally based upon a theory of the consent of citizens to democratic rule. Yet most citizens of liberal democracies have no real choice but to obey the government of the society in which they were born, raised and educated. Although they have no real option to leave, they might at least not be required to accept their state uncritically. That option is a real one only if they are intellectually exposed to alternative political systems and ways of life more common within other political systems. Schools [and universities more so] are uniquely equipped to supply children [and adults] with the knowledge and intellectual skills necessary to appreciate alternative political philosophies and ways of life.
> (Gutmann, 1996, p. 276)

Citizenship and education

Modern political thought displays a tendency to draw a distinction between citizens and state (with an intermediary stage of 'civil society'). But, if we recall Aristotle, we know that citizens are those who are fit to obey and to govern. Citizenship, therefore, implies active participation, not through a civil society which sits below the state, but more directly: through office holding, as well as, more or less tacitly, through obeying the laws made by all citizens in common. Ignatieff reminds us that:

> Civic-virtue, the cultural disposition apposite to citizenship was thus twofold: a willingness to step forward and assume the burdens of public office; and second, a willingness to subordinate private interest to the requirement of public obedience. What Aristotle called the 'right temper' of a citizen was thus a disposition to put public good ahead of private interest.
> (Ignatieff, 1995, p. 56)

Largely because of the overwhelming influence of the universalistic, liberal idea of the citizen, the importance of civic virtue and its development is under-emphasised.

But, in terms of a political aspect to education, it is this idea of developing virtue, of some kind, which has most often connected political and educational theories. Prominent examples include John Dewey's pragmatism, J.S. Mill's liberalism or Jean-Jacques Rousseau's participatory democracy. Less frequently cited examples might include Oakeshott's conservatism, Hegel's focus on *Bildung* in relation to education (Jessop, 2012, p. 299) or Habermas' critical theory.

The Aristotelian idea of citizenship, which combines, at once, ruling and being ruled, is not, however, the only model on offer. The Platonic version of citizenship, for instance, draws a sharp distinction between rulers and ruled, or the *aristoi* and the *pseudo-aristoi*. This idea, and similar variants, led to a conception of civic education which lays stress on the need to inculcate, on the one hand, an ability within the citizenry to choose leaders effectively, and on the other, to foster political loyalty. Eamonn Callan writes that:

> The efficacy of representative institutions in elevating the *aristoi* to political office and keeping out the *pseudo-aristoi* depends on what ordinary citizens do in that sphere of political participation, modest though it might be, that representation entails. The supposed superiority of democratic aristocracy over plain old aristocracy requires that citizens have the ability 'to discern the talent and character of candidates vying for office, and to evaluate the performance of individuals who have attained office'.
> (Callan, 1997, p. 110)

Now, for Callan, the development of such an ability comes through what Michael Walzer describes as 'vicarious decision-making' or sense of 'democratic play'. Callan explains that:

> This is the making of vicarious anticipative and retrospective judgements, sometimes in deliberative solitude but more often in dialogue with others, about the proper conduct of public officials. . . . In a representative democracy, vicarious anticipations and retrospections regarding the decisions of office holders are a profoundly serious endeavour. That is largely because the skill and insight we develop in playing the game are what we rely on to evaluate the performance of office-holders and to measure the talent and character of candidates for office. The talent and character of candidates has to do with the quality of the decisions they are likely to make, just as the merit of current office holders depends on the quality of decisions they have made. So citizens who are inept participants in Walzer's democratic play will be in no position to tell the difference between the *aristoi* and the *pseudo-aristoi*.
> (Callan, 1997, pp. 110–111)

But Callan here forgets himself. He now wants to deny that such democratic play is, in itself, an educative process. The ability to play this game of citizenship proficiently comes from practice as well as from some antecedent teaching in the rules of the game. If citizens inhabit an open political culture which encourages democratic play, most will, eventually, learn to play the game well. Moreover, inept participants here are not those who fail to distinguish correctly the *aristoi* from their pseudo counterparts. No one can be entirely sure of this. But those who refuse to take part in the game are more likely to be poor democratic citizens.

Callan misconstrues Walzer's idea. The point of anticipative and retrospective deliberation is not to draw the Platonic distinction between those who are and those who are not capable of rule. Rather, it seeks to collapse this dualism. As Walzer clearly puts it:

> Vicarious decision-making precedes and follows actual decision-making. In our minds, if not in fact, we imitate the Aristotelian ideal: We rule and are ruled in turn. We decide and we (usually, but not always) abide by the decisions of others. It's not the case, then, as elitist writers have argued, that citizens merely reaffirm or reject their leaders at periodic intervals. . . . The study of politics should have this purpose: It should help ordinary citizens reflect upon the most important matters of state. It should prepare leaders, would-be leaders, and vicarious leaders – which is to say, it should prepare all of us – for the democratic business of taking stands and shaping policies.
> (Walzer, 1980, pp. 159–160)

Through a dialogic process of this democratic play, citizens learn to be better citizens. They learn to make up their minds on salient political issues of the day and to make decisions. This democratic play, however, does not teach citizens to discriminate between rulers and ruled. Rather, vicarious decision-making is an act of citizenship in itself. It implies what Hannah Arendt called isonomy, or formal political equality in terms of a capacity for action. Now, in an increasingly de-politicised culture it is precisely these sorts of 'skills', or rather dispositions, that universities (and schools) should encourage in their teaching, and not simply focus on those skills deemed appropriate by careers officers and employers for the time being. If society is to describe certain abilities as 'key skills', surely the most relevant are those which allow us to engage as citizens. This would mean, in practical terms, an understanding of, and an ability to use, rhetoric, logic, grammar (the Trivium as it was once known in the mediaeval university) and critical capacities. But formal skills alone are not enough, for some sense of the duties of citizens towards others is also required, as is an understanding of the world that individuals live within. Michael G. Gottsegen sums this up succinctly:

> By one account the paramount need is to equip the youth of today with the practical skills that will be necessary in the world of tomorrow. Especially in a world that is changing as fast as ours, it is argued, there is little point in conveying knowledge which quickly becomes obsolete. . . . [H]owever, a skill-oriented pedagogy which does not undertake at the same time to bind

men to their past, and thus to their world, constitutes a danger to that very world of which the proponents of 'relevant' skills believe themselves to be so mindful. More important . . . than the imparting of skills is the imparting of an ethos of worldliness and world-concern which the teaching of skills alone will not serve to inculcate.

(Gottsegen, 1994, p. 112)

The republican, in addition to an understanding of the world, requires an artillery of skills to engage in the agonal realm of politics; the liberal citizen can call upon a set of formal political and civil rights and duties bestowed by the state. The latter citizen appears politically passive; the former appears active.

However, the republican citizen is active in the public sphere only to the extent that he is already free. Ignatieff writes that:

> Since Aristotle assumed that political discussion was an exercise in rational choice of the public good, he also assumed that the only persons fit for such an exercise were those capable of rational choice. And the only ones capable of rational choice were those who were free. Dependent creatures could not be citizens: slaves, those who worked for wages, women and children who were both subject to the authority of the domestic *oeconomia* were excluded from citizenship. Adult male property owners were the only persons vested with civic personality.
>
> (Ignatieff, 1995, p. 56)

Citizenship has always been an exclusionary category: exercising political choice and decision-making require an independent mind, and this in turn requires material and social independence. Property holding guaranteed independence and rationality free from material concerns. So, while there is a clear contradiction between a republican, property-based mode of citizenship and its liberal, rights-based counterpart, we can also see such property restrictions in the ideas of liberals like Locke who saw rights based in property relations. However, the republican view is more than a defence of property or gendered privilege. Citizenship required certain intellectual, social and economic prerequisites for good judgement in the realm of politics. Moreover, as Ignatieff points out, the property required for citizenship was landed, rather than held in moveable assets. As such, property holding citizens also held a patriotic interest in the state. The point, however, is that political freedom did not stand independent of cognitive capacities, status and material wealth.

In the civic republican tradition, juridified bureaucracy was anachronistic. Offices were rotated among citizens; the establishment of a permanent bureaucracy was resisted because this might invite a separation of specialist bureaucratic interests in opposition to the public interest. This explains why the republican tradition is wary of the concept of civil society, informed, but also dominated, by the state. For republicans, citizenship is self-rule, taken in turns by members of a coherent community.

But, of course, this rule of self-rule is indeed a myth. The profits of office mean that office holders want to hold on to their positions. The civic concept of citizenship has to be supplemented by a discourse on corruption (just as the civic university requires a discourse on the degradation of its purposes). Ignatieff writes that republican 'Citizenship implied a tragic and often nostalgic sense of lost human possibility. Civic life was a ceaseless struggle to preserve the human good – the *polis* – from the forces within human nature bent on its deformation into tyranny' (Ignatieff, 1995, pp. 58–59).

Civil, political and social rights

Certain material conditions have to be met to help ensure the virtue of citizens. Just as private civil and political rights balance civic community, these in turn have to be balanced with social rights. The problem is that reconciling these requires that we accept their contradictions. Formal legal equality is rather empty without the social and economic equality necessary for the exercise of legal equality. Indeed, the formal legal rights of citizenship were concretised in the founding of the modern welfare state. This welfare state should be seen as an expression of those social rights which underpin purely abstract, formal civil and political rights. The state once saw its role as the guardian of equal citizenship balancing the undermining forces of the market economy. It is because of such social rights that citizens could count on protection against illness, old age, illiteracy and unemployment. It was a welfare state founded upon universal benefits which strengthened the civic ties between individual citizens and between their private and the public interest: 'Taxation was thus explicitly conceived as the instrument for building civic solidarity among strangers' (Ignatieff, 1995, p. 67).

Presently, however, the welfare state has a rather different image. In place of acting as a kind of civic cement, the welfare state is painted as an institution which provides disincentives to work, supports the feckless, removes individual responsibility, is an unnecessary drain on national income and is overly bureaucratic. Far from building solidarity among strangers, the taxation paid to fund the welfare state, *once value for money is demanded from welfare services*, actually serves to undermine civic ties. For the norm which underlies the purpose of the welfare state is diluted. Either welfare provision brings people closer together in the spirit of solidarity, creating civic bonds, or public services are delivered in a way which aims at efficiency which will break down civic ties between people.

Citizenship and university education

The erosion of civic ties is demonstrated in the case of a higher education system which takes the efficient training for future employment of students as its main aim. Students no longer receive a rounded, civilising education:

> [O]nly 2.6 per cent of American students major in English. Almost as many major in catering, domestic science, and hotel management. The British

figures are heading in the same direction. It may or may not be a good thing to teach young persons the art of portion control, or to give them diplomas in the wiles of advertising, but such students are not being turned against western civilization. They are being so unblinkingly trained to take their place in the modern consumer society that to encounter a decent scepticism about western civilization would do them good. . . . [P]rofessional training is not enough for the whole of life. It is not exactly news that the holders of MBAs have been known to commit fraud, to throw their workers on to the street needlessly, to sacrifice production to financial manipulation, and to behave as badly as Thorstein Veblen complained that financiers behaved a hundred years ago. If they behave badly because they have been badly trained, what they lack is not a training in analytical techniques but a sense of the duties of the powerful and the clever to the less powerful and the less clever.

(Ryan, 1999, pp. 154–155)

Veblen's complaint about financiers is prescient, but a 'vocational' education is usually nothing of the sort. How many of the students and graduates of these courses really have a calling for hotel management? Vocational courses are merely those which point towards a training for a future career. Ironically, of course, such career-based courses have flourished at precisely the same time as the idea of a career, in the sense of engagement in uninterrupted professional employment, is disappearing (Williams, 1988, pp. 52–53).[2] While it is still possible to conceive of, and look forward to, a legal career or the vocation of the priesthood with reasonable confidence, for instance, we cannot look forward to a career in politics, or in television or even hotel management with the same degree of confidence. It only really makes sense to speak of a political career in retrospect. A formal university training is a strict requirement for lawyers, it is not for television producers, journalists or politicians. Formal training may help in some ways, but this only means that we can call such training 'vocational' in the very loosest sense. Intuitively, then, it seems to make more sense to think of a career in hindsight. If the notion of a career as uninterrupted progress can no longer be generally relied upon, then it does seem odd that education, and higher education most markedly, has become much more career oriented. It could be argued that education, and university education with it, has gradually become integrated into the wider framework of the bureaucratised welfare state. After all, the welfare state provides for citizens in need of some assistance, but the need for this should vanish if we educate and train citizens to be able to provide for themselves, usually through employment. In this sense, a university education geared towards future employment would allow the state to step back from its responsibilities to provide wider social rights. Putative students are being misled. The instrumental university has become a tool to provide more efficient labour markets, where vocational education generates a supposedly level playing field that will allow the state to withdraw from other forms of welfare provision, such as unemployment benefit, allows employers to withdraw from work-related training and proposes that the individual student shoulders the brunt of the costs. This credentialist promise, however, of a ticket to a career, is a trade borne of desperation. The degree appears attractive because employment is becoming more precarious.

The transition to a more instrumental idea of the university was begun at the end of the nineteenth century when science became a means of capital accumulation through the application of discoveries in the fields of physics and chemistry to commodity production. This was the result of advances in science itself but also because of a greater willingness on the part of capitalists to invest in research and development, a spirit which was fostered by increased industrial competition and a sufficient level of surplus capital. This industrial development created a demand for scientific-technical education which was complemented by the rationalisation of state administration which compounded the demand for technocrats. Tony Smith explains:

> No longer was the goal of a university education the formation of character. Rather than being oriented towards the ideal of *Bildung* [self-formation], the university now had the goal of producing persons capable of discovering and applying technically employable knowledge. No longer was the ideal the well-rounded humanist of the *Universitas litterarum*. Instead the ideal became the specialist, one who concentrated on a particular area and was able to produce causal knowledge of the regularities of that object realm.
>
> (Smith, 1991, p. 196)

But, although the ideal related to the specialist, this was combined with a notion that we can all be specialists because the logic at work here was to *produce* a band of trained researchers capable of making further efficiency savings or finding or creating new markets for goods and services.

Higher education now cannot be claimed to remain the preserve of an elite. Instead, it has become one agency among others charged with increasing the opportunities of individuals. And opportunity, because it is conceived in a strictly materialist fashion, is synonymous with production and consumption: job opportunities, career prospects and earnings potential. This is most evident in the new subject areas: leisure and tourism studies; media studies; fashion design; business administration (but we might also include things like education studies too). Ronald Barnett points out that these:

> [N]ewer forms of study are not merely operational but are instrumental in character. That is, they are designed to bring about technical effects on a taken-for-granted world (or slice of it). They are built around a technical interest in the world in which the world is objectified and externalized, and it is understood to be a suitable vehicle for instrumental operations to be

wrought upon it. The action that they encourage can be said to be critical, but its critical component is arrested at the instrumental level. It is a critical action that accepts the world largely as given and seeks to produce more effective operations within it. Transformations are entirely acceptable *providing* that they produce greater profitability, power and security.

(Barnett, 1997a, p. 79)

It could, however, be suggested that this is nothing new. Universities, in their mediaeval form, were, after all, about training for the elite professions of law, medicine and public administration. But Barnett argues that the link between the university and work was entirely different in the mediaeval period. He refers to Basil Bernstein on this point:

The mediaeval curriculum might, in the professional schools, have contained an operational character, but it was not instrumental. . . . Not only were the studies framed in the larger curriculum of the Trivium (grammar, logic and rhetoric) and the Quadrivium (arithmetic, astronomy, geometry and music), but the Trivium, 'as exploration of the word' took precedence over the Quadrivium, 'as the exploration of the world'. 'The construction of the inner was the guarantee for the construction of the outer. In this we can find the origin of the professions'. But we have been seeing the abandonment of the inner world, except that the inner world is now finding its way back in the form of an instrumental control of the self by the self (in other words, *self-control*). As a result, 'knowledge, after nearly a thousand years, is divorced from inwardness and literally dehumanised'.

(Barnett, 1997a, p. 79)

Knowledge, however, is also divorced from a public form of outwardness. Once knowledge acquires a private instrumental value, a value without a public value, it is also dehumanised because it forecloses the possibility of action. The outer, it should be noted, develops the inner; the Quadrivium builds our understanding of the Trivium. Private, instrumental values attached to knowledge curb the *vita activa*; outward, public oriented values enable it to flourish.

It is here that citizenship, earning income and education come together. We are regarded as citizens to the extent that we can partake in social life, and social life has come to mean, for many, little more than production and consumption. And so good citizenship loses its ties to traditional ideas of virtue and worldliness. Instead, virtue is demonstrated by secular signifiers: what we can consume, and those things we consume are primarily determined by what we earn, and how we earn it, since leisure time is also required to consume. What we earn has, in the past, been largely determined by educational background (or rather what we earned was determined by class background and this correlated with educational background), and so, it follows, some kind of flow between the roles of citizenship, employment and education can be expected.

Of course, this is all entirely contingent. The idea that those with more material goods live fuller lives is precisely the inequality that democracy attempts to iron out. What we have is a democratic state which reinforces this message which celebrates consumption and encourages fairness through encouraging what it calls a 'meritocracy'. However, the merit rewarded in this system is that which corresponds with the *status quo ante*. This takes away the critical voice of dissent, and leaves us as narrower, more limited, citizens. As citizens we can take part in the life of society but we cannot mount a political challenge to the world we inhabit and the corruption of the goods we value. In short, and in Arendtian terms, the idea of citizenship has shifted from a political to a social meaning.

In our rather impoverished understanding of higher education, learning is either productive, in that it is regarded as an investment which will pay dividends in terms of future earnings, or it is consumptive, in that it is like a leisurely activity, a kind of high-minded frivolity. But this is to mistake education for training or entertainment. While education, Arendt maintains, belongs to the realm of the world, training and entertainment relate to life. Education introduces learners to the world, it teaches them to question it in a process of becoming, and education ensures the continuance of the world. Training and entertainment, on the other hand, are consumer goods, destined to be used up:

> *Panis et circenses* truly belong together; both are necessary for life, for its preservation and recuperation, and both vanish in the course of the life process – that is, both must constantly be produced anew and offered anew, lest this process cease entirely. The standards by which both should be judged are freshness and novelty, and the extent to which we use these standards today to judge cultural and artistic objects as well, things which are supposed to remain in the world after we have left it, indicates clearly the extent to which the need for entertainment has begun to threaten the cultural world.
> (Arendt, 1993, p. 286)

Arendt here compares the worldly realms of culture and art with the business of earning and entertainment. But the point pertains equally to education. In a rush to provide equality of opportunity, to broaden the range of groups participating in higher education, and in connecting efficiency indicators to teaching and research, we have forgotten the purposes of education generally, and higher education specifically. As higher education comes under the fiscal pressures of austerity, the need to recall those purposes is urgent.

Higher education should not be necessary for developing basic democratic virtues, such as toleration, truth-telling and a predisposition to respect others. What universities can do, however, is encourage the kind of vicarious decision-making advocated by Walzer. As Gutmann puts it:

> [L]earning how to think carefully and critically about political problems, to articulate one's views and defend them before people with whom one

disagrees is a form of moral education to which young adults are more receptive [than young children] and for which universities are well-suited.

(Gutmann, 1999, p. 173)

Democratic citizenship and academic autonomy

But what is taught is not the only directly relevant factor. For the idea of democratic citizenship not only offers a platform from which to criticise the vocational nature of much of what is taught in universities, it also offers a defence of institutional, scholarly autonomy. Academics can (sometimes) be regarded as an especially important category of citizen:

> Control of the creation of ideas – whether by a majority or a minority – subverts the ideal of *conscious* social reproduction at the heart of democratic education and democratic politics. As institutional sanctuaries for free scholarly inquiry, universities can help prevent such subversion. They can provide a realm where new and unorthodox ideas are judged on their intellectual merits; where the men and women who defend such ideas, provided they defend them well, are not strangers but valuable members of a community. Universities thereby serve democracy as sanctuaries of nonrepression.
>
> (Gutmann, 1999, pp. 174–175)

Democratic states can support democratic legitimacy by respecting academic freedom and the freedom of the academy. The academic freedom of scholars is neither a right of citizenship nor a contractual right of university employees, though it is most obviously expressed through permanent academic tenure (Shils, 1997, pp. 80–82). It is the democratic purpose of the university, and not contracts held between employers and employees, which grounds the freedom of academic scholars.

> The core of academic freedom is the freedom of scholars to assess existing theories, established institutions, and widely held beliefs according to the canons of truth adopted by their academic disciplines, without fear of sanction by anyone if they arrive at unpopular conclusions. Academic freedom allows scholars to follow their autonomous judgment wherever it leads them, provided that they remain within the bounds of scholarly standards of inquiry.
>
> (Gutmann, 1999, p. 175)

In return for this freedom scholars have a duty to observe scholarly standards of inquiry. To neglect this would make the freedom of the scholar indistinct from more general freedoms of speech that all citizens hold. To be sure, it is precisely a blurring of these categories which occurs when an academic scholar takes on the role of a consultant. One way, then, that we might assess the decline in academic freedom would be through the increasing *expectation* that academics behave like consultants, and, connectedly, the increasing prevalence of short-term temporary employment contracts for academics. Of course, the notion that academics can also act as consultants reinforces the pressure to keep levels of pay down and to offer temporary employment. The myth we are encouraged to believe in is that good teachers and good researchers will also be able to function as successful consultants in the real world of business. Seldom do we come across the point that education, from a normative point of view, takes as its task the preservation of the world, which entails a cultivation of civilization, while the 'real world' of private business and industry, in fact, belongs to a life process and sometimes does considerable harm to the world in concrete terms.

Now, one form which academic freedom takes is the ability for academics to be able to control the educational environment within which teaching and research takes place. The institutional administration of universities, however, varies between cultures in important ways.

> Whereas German universities were generally self-governing bodies of scholars who made administrative decisions either collegially or through democratically elected administrators, American universities (with few exceptions) are administered by lay governing boards and administrators chosen by those boards. Therefore, while the scholar's right of academic freedom in the German context could readily be extended to a right collectively to control the academic environment of the university, the academic freedom of faculty in the American context had to be used as a defense *against* the universities' legally constituted (lay) administrative authority. Recurrent threats by universities' trustees and administrators to the academic freedom of faculty members made it easy for faculty to overlook their stake in defending their universities against state regulation of education policies.
> (Gutmann, 1999, p. 176)

When we look to the administration of British higher education we see a marked shift from a more or less Germanic model of governance to an American system of management (Salter and Tapper, 2000). The crucial difference, however, is that in British higher education institutions, professional administrators, teaching and research staff with administrative responsibilities and lay members of universities' governing bodies are all guided by the norms laid down by state determined performance indicators which attempt to reproduce a market, or at least a competitive, environment. The public good of the university is polluted, degraded and colonised by both state and market.

The managerial argument against the kinds of points I sketched out above claims that academic freedom is the slogan which academics appeal to whenever their authority is undermined. Academic freedom, so the argument goes, is a concept which applies to the freedom of students just as much as academic staff. Therefore, academic freedom entails duties towards teaching students well.

The managerialism of today's university culture is no more than enshrining this duty in the procedures of faculty against the vested interests of academic staff. In response to this it can be said that there is obviously a duty to teach students well, to operate a fair admissions policy, as far as possible, to assess students' work fairly and accurately, to allow students to have control over what they study even. Academic freedom is not a freedom to provide poor teaching or poor research. It is, in fact, a freedom to do good research and good teaching, whatever form this takes – and that is a judgement for the academic community. The problem with the managerialist approach is that its procedures have never been discursively redeemed in argument. Rather, performance indicators and working practices have been handed down by the state to the administrators of our universities based on business norms (Kedourie, 1989, pp. 27–34) which (generally) regard students and their families as consumers demanding higher education. Of course, this denies the legitimate authority of academic staff over their students, which is not to say that students have no claim to academic freedom, but, rather, that academic freedom could best be served through procedures settled on – though they remain fallible – by participants: the academic community (and not only its managers), the state and the wider public.

With regard to citizenship, however, universities not only help to create citizens through teaching students, they also, through the academic freedom of faculty staff, help to lead political debate in new, or old and forgotten, directions. The autonomy of the modern university is rooted, like the idea of the active citizen, in the protection of democracy against the threat of domination. The academic freedoms of scholars and universities guard against political repression for all citizens, not only scholars. This is so precisely because the rational pursuit of truth lies at the heart of the intellectual exercise.

But the freedom of faculty scholars does not have to be directly impinged upon to infringe the academic freedom of universities. Central to understanding this is the idea that an academic community of scholars creates its own scholarly standards. Democratic societies can 'foster the general freedom of conscious social reproduction within politics by fostering the particular freedom of defending unpopular ideas within universities' (Gutmann, 1999, p. 177). This marks the difference between populism and democracy. We can, and should, defend unpopular ideas if these ideas meet other standards of legitimacy. In this case, this means meeting standards of scholarly merit. To undermine academic freedom means to undermine an important distinction between democracy and populism. So, academic freedom (from accountability mechanisms and to cultivate civic engagement) is important to democratic citizenship because it serves as a block to a rather insidious form of tyranny. The scholarly university, that is, the true university, provides a space for action in which students and scholars share a public, civic-minded ethic and supports students and academics in their democratic forays into the public realm. The league-table obsessed, branded, performative empirical reality of universities in the twenty-first century may speak of widening participation, but the hierarchical system they represent only reinforces the inequality of citizens (Delbanco, 2012, p. 135). At the normative level, however, the university, insofar as it supports and encourages an active, worldly, republican conception of citizenship, in both teaching and research ought to be regarded as a public good, only guided by market norms at the margins, only steered by state bureaucracy peripherally. The resuscitation of the authority of the university depends upon such scholarly integrity.

Notes

1 This chapter appears in *Journal of Philosophy of Education*, (2013) vol. 47, no. 1, pp. 112–127.
2 Williams writes that 'Career is still used in the abstract spectacular sense of politicians and entertainers, but more generally it is applied, with some conscious and unconscious class distinction, to *work* or a *job* which contains some implicit promise of progress. It has been most widely used for jobs with explicit internal development – "a career in the Civil Service" – but it has since been extended to any favourable or desired or flattered occupation – "a career in coalmining". Career now usually implies continuity if not necessarily promotion or advancement, yet the distinction between a career and a *job* only partly depends on this and is often associated also with class distinctions between different kinds of work'.

Chapter 6

The ivory tower and public life

British society, like many others around the world, has witnessed a significant shift in the boundaries between the public and private spheres since the 1980s. Whilst some of the political rhetoric has altered – Thatcherism unashamedly promoted the suitability of the market for allocating resources, Blair has spoken loosely of some 'third way' between market capitalism and state socialism – the privatisation of the public realm has continued. In a bid to make state institutions more efficient and present value for money to taxpayers, state services have either been privatised (in the everyday sense of that term, they have become privately owned – often by massive corporations) or pushed into a pseudo-competitive environment.

Privatisation and the rise of the social

According to John Clarke and Janet Newman, the privatisation of the public sphere can be categorised into three different types:

> First, there is privatisation as the direct sale of public assets to the private/commercial sector, as in the case of public utilities like gas, water and electricity. . . . The second form of 'privatisation' can be found in the processes of undermining the boundaries between public and private sectors by means of sponsored competition and restructuring. . . . This second sense of privatisation involves a degree of *de-differentiation* – a reduction, though not necessarily a removal, of some of the distinctions between the state and the market (or the public and private sectors) through the requirement that public organisations come to behave 'as if' they were commercial corporate entities. The third, and rather different, sense of privatisation is the shift of responsibilities from public to private understood as the familial domain. . . . This meaning of privatisation is also part of the wider agenda about the transfer of resources (via taxation policies), choices (empowering the welfare consumer) and duties (enforcing parental responsibilities) away from the state to the private realm of the family.
> (Clarke and Newman, 1997, pp. 27–28)

However, this absence of state provision has been replaced by an increased level of state surveillance, regulation and intervention. What we are witnessing here is not only a shift away from the public to the private sphere but also a greater degree of monitoring of the private realm by the state. In a sense, we are beginning to see a collapse of this public-private distinction.

Now certainly universities, and university departments, are faced with a compulsion to behave *as if* they were businesses. But Clarke's and Newman's other senses of privatisation are relevant to higher education too. For example, it has become commonplace for universities to contract out support services, such as catering and cleaning. One wonders when teaching and research might come to be seen as supporting services. Clarke's and Newman's third understanding of privatisation concerns a shift of responsibility from the public or state sector to the familial domain. This too is evident in higher education systems all over the world, as expansion of university education, along with the idea that the fiscal benefits of a university education accrue to the individual, has led to students and their families contributing financially towards tuition fees and meeting living costs. In this sense a degree of responsibility for funding university education has moved from the responsibility of the state towards a partial responsibility of the individual student and his or her family. Moreover, in an attempt to ensure 'value for money' from the university system, the state has introduced a raft of monitoring agencies such as the research councils, the Quality Assurance Agency and the Institute for Learning and Teaching which then transformed into the Higher Education Academy which academics are encouraged to join.

In the current funding climate many academics regard the privatisation of university education along the lines followed in the USA as a path which leads away from the heavy handed state intervention of the past years in the UK. This, however, is a mistake. The attempt to achieve greater levels of efficiency through competitive structures in a quasi-market context results perversely in increasing state interference. In the British higher education system, state and market are not diametrically opposed to one another. Rather, each reinforces the other.

The point so far, which is hardly contentious, is that the UK higher education system, despite being largely state funded and becoming increasingly state controlled, is clearly moving in the direction of privatisation. But I want to say more than this. What Clarke's and Newman's typology misses is the increasingly goal-oriented, instrumental, marketised, individualised nature of the mass higher education system. The privatisation of the university is particularly insidious precisely because the academy is marked out as a sphere of freedom. Moreover, the privatisation of an educative institution results in individuals who pass through that institution internalising its norms and values. In short, the contemporary UK university system represents a rise, to invoke Arendt, not simply of *homo faber*: an elevation of the realm of work over all other aspects of the world, but, to be sure, a victory of *animal laborans*: the focus falls on labour. What I mean by this is that higher education has come to be seen as an extension of schooling. It concerns itself not so much with education or self-development of the individual, but with instruction and training for specific, career-oriented ends. A university 'education' now has become a means to an end rather than an end in itself. The vocationalism which imbues the current debate on higher education in Britain serves to undermine education itself. Further, to regard higher education as simply a means to a career, or as a gate-keeping device for holders of office (Gutmann, 1999, pp. 181–185), raises deep problems for any society that claims to be democratic. The public sphere, it seems, is withering away in the face of civic privatism. One symptom of this is the instrumentalisation of education. Even the meaning of higher education is shifting towards a notion of training and away from a focus on the development of an individual's critical capacities. Increasingly, the scope for participants to act within the academy is being curtailed. As Alain Touraine put it: 'Technical [or instrumental] reason is rarely discussed, because it is clear to most people that it leaves them no choice as to the end of their actions' (Touraine, 1995, p. 101).

Universities are no longer run by administrators, academics and students. Rather, bureaucratically determined performance indicators steer university governors. There is, because of a concentration upon instrumental rationality, little possibility for action. Management has replaced action. Administration has replaced political discourse within the life of educational organisations. In this respect, instrumental reason leaves no choice, no scope for deliberation. If, for instance, a university is to maximise its income according to certain funding formulae, then its strategy is to an extent predetermined. The organisation's functions, then, are always already steered by the imperatives of subsystems. This, perhaps, goes some way towards explaining why we find it difficult to refer to an *idea* of the university, or even to speak of the purposes of universities. The notion that we can decide for ourselves what the idea of the university is or ought to be has been taken away. The business of education nowadays requires that organisations concerned with teaching, learning, and research function efficiently. They are administered like the *oikos*. Only secondly are they educational institutions. It is in this respect that the legitimacy of public institutions has been replaced with a private notion of accountability.

The public sector must be seen to deserve its funding. This focus on appearances is particularly worrying: what is important is that public services look productive. In the context of universities this is manifestly obvious. Consider the emphasis on the volume of research produced by academics, or the kudos attached to the number of graduates who find employment soon after matriculation, or the number of first class degrees awarded by an institution. Each of these, and there are many other criteria employed in an attempt to rank institutions, make an attempt to show how useful universities are, and this is attempted via various measurements. What is happening here though is an attempt to replace judgement with a form of instrumental rationalism. This is the nub of my argument. A rationalised, juridified educational system is too rigid to deal with the creativity and complexity involved in education. A university education still looks like education, but is, in fact, something else. Degrees are still awarded, but the meaning of a degree has changed. Research is still carried out, but research grants are based on a contractual model. So, philosophers are asked to explain how their research will be of value to research users, for instance.

The drift from democratic education

What I would like to explore is a deeper conception of privatisation than that offered in Clarke's and Newman's typology. The modern academy stands in danger of losing its democratic role. I want to show that academia is now bound up in wider social processes identified by theorists of modernity. To paint in broad strokes: the contemporary university is a bleak place. Here we see in concrete terms Arendt's 'rise of the social' – a culturally impoverished realm, colonised by instrumental reason.

In 'The Crisis in Education' Arendt portrays education as essentially conservative in the sense of conserving the world against the new while enabling us to remake the world through action:

> Basically we are always educating for a world that is or is becoming out of joint, for this is the basic human situation, in which the world is created by mortal hands to serve mortals for a limited time as home.... To preserve the world against the mortality of its creators and inhabitants it must be constantly set right anew. The problem is simply to educate in such a way that a setting-right remains actually possible, even though it can, of course, never be assured.
>
> (Arendt, 1993, p. 192)

Now, it seems that it is just such a setting-right that the current climate in university education does not allow. Because so much emphasis is placed upon acquiring skills for employment, in today's universities the connection between past and future is broken. This problem is only exacerbated by new technologies which seem to be updated ever more rapidly. For example, in a bid to keep markets in computer hardware and software buoyant, operating systems and word processing packages and processor chips quickly become out-dated as new, supposedly more effective replacements come on to the market. These new systems demand new skills and expertise to make use of them. Whilst large companies are able to keep up with the investment costs of such technologies, it is more difficult for publicly funded schools and universities to keep pace. Hence we are left in a paradoxical situation whereby the institutions which, according to the rhetoric of lifelong learning and the knowledge economy, are supposed to train individuals are prohibited from doing so because of the costs involved in acquiring the relevant equipment and expertise. These institutions of learning, or training, have difficulties in acquiring up to date technologies because of their prohibitive cost, or personnel skilled in the use of such tools because these people's skills can reap higher rewards in the private sector. The point to take from this, however, is that universities can no longer attempt to link past and future when they take as their task simply keeping pace with the present, and even this eludes them by and large.

The crisis in education, for Arendt, reflects the loss of the world. We can see that her argument is borne out in various ways when we look at our present situation within British academia. Consider for instance the quality assurance mechanisms proposed in the UK's Teaching Excellence Framework. This 'framework' is intended to oversee a 'kite-marking' scheme which will validate teaching quality in higher education, the results of which will allow successful institutions to raise tuition fees. But it is precisely this attitude that we can consider teaching as a technique which Arendt laments. She points out that the reduction of teaching to a skill means that the teacher leaves the students to their own devices and robs the students of the most legitimate source of authority: the teacher's own person, who knows more and can do more. As such, the non-authoritarian teacher, who abstains from threats of punishment and compulsion because he relies on his own authority, becomes an impossibility (Arendt, 1993, p. 182).

Now, this science of pedagogy, and I include in this all the talk of core or transferable skills which seem so attractive to employers, has been made possible by a basic pragmatic assumption about learning. Learning was replaced with doing:

> The reason that no importance was attached to the teacher's mastering his own subject was the wish to compel him to the exercise of the continuous activity of learning so that he would not, as they said, pass on 'dead knowledge' but, instead, would constantly demonstrate how it is produced. The conscious intention was not to teach knowledge but to inculcate a skill, and the result was a kind of transformation of institutes for learning into vocational institutions which have been successful in teaching how to drive a car or how to use a typewriter or, even more important for the 'art' of living, how to get along with other people and to be popular.
> (Arendt, 1993, pp. 182–183)

As education has become imbued with a technical rationality, as it has come increasingly to refer to instruction and training, it removes itself from reality. Despite successive Secretary of States' injunctions to make universities relevant to the real world, in fact training in 'competences' and 'core skills' relates not to understanding the world, but instead offers individuals a method for dealing with life. Education has switched from being a caretaker of the world, a realm in which the social fabric of the lifeworld is reproduced and understanding developed, into a tool for the individual's material survival.

This Arendtian distinction between the world and life and between work and labour is particularly useful when comparing education as it is and as it ought to be. P. Herbst has argued that education must always be conceived as work, but presently it corresponds more closely to alienating labour. The category of work belongs to artisan craftsmanship, whilst the idea of labour is more at home on the Fordist production line. The point of work, for Herbst, is more than its product:

> The opus . . . is the point of the workman's work; if the opus is well done, he has not worked in vain. I shall argue that in order to work well, a workman needs to love or value that at which he works and if so, he aims at good workmanship. The excellence of an opus will be sharply distinguished from its instrumental goodness, and in particular, from its propensity to procure satisfaction for consumers.
> (Herbst, 1973, p. 59)

Herbst argues that consumer satisfaction cannot be a sufficient measure of excellence of a product since advertising and marketing take as their purpose to encourage consumers to re-order their preferences. Moreover, the consumer may hold irrational preferences. It may be, for instance, that many valuable goods are not consumed but preserved and cherished: it sounds odd, for example, to claim that the value of justice lies in its consumption. Presently, knowledge in all its forms seems to be valued, in the main, in instrumental terms. Academics no longer simply belong to the academy, but instead contract their expertise out to private business or the state. The academic in this way acquires the status of consultant. However, in certain fundamental aspects, the academic and the consultant differ. Whilst the academic is allowed the freedom of the academy, he or she has a definite independence. The academic is free from convention. The consultant, on the other hand, is bound by the status quo because he or she lacks the critical potential of the academic. In the end the consultant's role is to acquiesce to her or his employer's preconceptions. Perhaps it is in this sense that we are witnessing the proletarianisation of the academic. As Michael Oakeshott puts it:

> [I]n a society (such as ours) which has a high standard of practical relevance, universities have often to be defended. And the usual defence is either to show that they also contribute (at least obliquely) to the prosecution of current undertakings, or to claim for them the status of an 'amenity' – that is, a piece of costly nonsense protected by our sentimental attachment from designed and immediate destruction but not so well protected against the imposition upon them of alien directions of activity.
> (Oakeshott, 1991, pp. 194–195)

But such a defence is much too weak. Universities have a variety of functions. Of course, different institutions may have a different emphasis. So, for instance, some colleges may take as their role the education of the local community, whilst other universities see themselves as part of a research elite. But, to say that different organisations have different priorities does not mean that we should do away with an *idea* of a university.

Herbst's argument is that it does not make sense to value education in relation to an end product. The practical worth of understanding can only be judged, and not prejudged. This means that education and scholarship must always belong to the category of work rather than labour. While labour is contingently related to its product, work is not. Labourers in a production process may not even know what their labour produces since in labour the product and productive process are conceptually separate:

> Work is non-contingently related to its product. The description of the process and the description of the product may be described in terms of workmanship, the productive work as aiming at these excellences. Education is a case in hand. To be educated, is to bear the marks of having been through the educational process. Thus finished product and productive processes are correlatively understood.
> (Herbst, 1973, p. 60)

This is not the rather vapid point that an educated individual has had an education, but that:

> The adequacy of work and the excellence of its product are *judged* together. If the unified conceptual scheme is abandoned, this advantage is lost and the point of the work is no longer clear. It is then, poor thing, fed into the machine of means and ends and justified by the calculus of his satisfactions.
> (Herbst, 1973, pp. 60–61)

When worker becomes labourer the authority to remake the world is replaced with alienation. So good research, or good teaching, or good learning, or good scholarship cannot be determined by the outcomes of these activities alone. The activities themselves have to be conducted in a certain way or, more accurately, in a certain spirit. This is far from a methodological prescriptivism. Scholarly activities should be undertaken in circumstances which allow the scholar to be free to value the particular activity at which he or she is engaged on its own terms. Hence, the scholar who is working studies in order to understand and not simply to achieve some (perhaps connected) end. Education is thus a thing in itself. It is not a set of skills which can command a particular salary. To regard education as a means to an end is to undermine education in the first place. As Herbst argues, in terms of research:

> Research labourers do research katatelically, though not necessarily without results, if 'results' are a kind of pay-off to society or to some interest represented in it. (Discoveries of genuine interest to intellectuals are not excluded). A research labourer works in the spirit of labour. He puts his highly-trained labour force at the disposal of society or its agencies. He

works in its interests, and conceives that to be its point. The beneficiaries generally reward him, but not from love of the intellectual enterprise. The beneficiaries use him, even as he will presently use his students, or prepare them for social use after they have obtained their 'qualification'.

(Herbst, 1973, p. 70)

Beneficiaries of research labour pick and choose the most useful results with no regard for intellectually reputable work. It seems, in some senses unfortunately, that British academe is no longer some kind of ivory tower. Rather, our universities, insofar as they have come to be held accountable to the state, and responsive to research 'users', have become the habitus of the educational labourer.

I think that at least two main reasons can be identified as responsible for this colonisation of the university lifeworld. Firstly, the arrival of a mass higher educational system. And secondly, a changing idea of what constitutes knowledge. I will address the second point first.

For all the talk of postmodern play, in terms of the education system, we seem to live in a world where we are forced to recognise the uncertainty of our futures, which constantly remain in flux. However, the material that is taught in schools, colleges and universities is increasingly presented as skills for life. It is as though acquiring certain skills will shield the individual from life in a world which will otherwise be nasty, brutish and short. In this way life and the world are disassociated from one another. Education no longer refers to a process of allowing individuals to belong to the world. Instead, we have a regime of training and instruction which students consume. But surely this is nonsense. Knowledge cannot be consumed. Understanding cannot be taken in and used up by individuals. The idea of education and learning presupposes a worldliness which exists prior to individuals. But, this worldliness is intersubjectively constituted. Individuals, through their understanding, add to and change knowledge. The world, for Arendt, is made up, not of people, but of the spaces between people. It is, in other words, a public space. However, the mass higher education system is privatised. The notions of transferable skills, individual learning accounts, tuition fees, that the rewards of higher education accrue to the individual, and that the purpose of education is to produce higher rates of economic growth all belong to the *oikos*. Now, one of the central problems with this is that the private sphere, the realm of instrumental reason, lacks creativity and even, perhaps, humanity. A world composed of individuals who act instrumentally will be an alienating, disenchanting imprisonment. Of course, whilst education helps to create citizens who compose the world, the world also produces its own education system.

Technical skills and lifelong learning

We currently have a more accessible higher education system than ever before. Those who problematise our university education system and policies directed at it as populist are themselves criticised as elitist. The tensions involved in a mass university system are clear: higher education is intended to provide higher learning to an ever-widening constituency of students on a historically low-cost basis. But the ivory tower has become the Tower of Babel. A mass higher education system is being portrayed as a kind of short cut to the heaven of increased economic growth in a knowledge driven economy. However, as it stands, the style of learning and scholarship which contemporary universities in Britain offer is inappropriate to the task in hand. The university nowadays has no clear purpose beyond providing a general training for employment, or more generally, producing technically exploitable knowledge.

Michael Oakeshott distinguishes between technical and practical knowledge. To be sure, it is practical knowledge which is elevated in university education today, insofar as learning, or lifelong learning, is oriented towards a career and as far as doing has been substituted for learning, as Arendt puts it. The problem, however, arises in the manner that doing is taught. For Oakeshott, practical knowledge cannot be taught via distance learning packages or through a textbook. It is only experience which teaches us this practical knowledge. But, when universities, for instance, attempt to teach such practical knowledge in the context of a mass higher education system, they are bound to fail:

> Technical knowledge . . . is susceptible of formulation in rules, principles, directions, maxims – comprehensively, in propositions. It is possible to write down technical knowledge in a book. Consequently, it does not surprise us when an artist writes about his art, he writes only about the technique of his art. This is so, not because he is ignorant of what may be called aesthetic element, or thinks it unimportant, but because what he has to say about *that* he has said already (if he is a painter) in his pictures, and he knows no other way of saying it. And the same is true when a religious man writes about his religion or a cook about cookery.
>
> (Oakeshott, 1991, p. 14)

Technical knowledge is, then, according to Oakeshott, an impoverished and incomplete form of knowledge. As he puts it:

> Technical knowledge can be learned from a book; it can be learned in a correspondence course. Moreover, much of it can be learned by heart, repeated by rote, and applied mechanically: the logic of the syllogism is a technique of this kind. Technical knowledge, in short, can be both taught and learned in the simplest meanings of these words. On the other hand, practical knowledge can be neither taught nor learned, but only imparted and acquired. It exists only in practice, and the only way to acquire it is by apprenticeship to a master – not because the master can teach it (he cannot), but because it can be acquired only by continuous contact with one who is perpetually practising it.
>
> (Oakeshott, 1991, p. 15)

Michael Polanyi makes a very similar point on skills. He takes it to be a

> well-known fact *that the aim of a skilful performance is achieved by the observance of a set of rules which are not known as such to the person following them.* For example, the decisive factor by which the swimmer keeps himself afloat is the manner by which he regulates his respiration; he keeps his buoyancy at an increased level by refraining from emptying his lungs when breathing out and by inflating them more than usual when breathing in: yet this is not generally known to swimmers. . . . [T]he principle by which the cyclist keeps his balance is not generally known. The rule observed by the cyclist is this. When he starts falling to the right he turns the handlebars to the right, so that the course of the bicycle is deflected along a curve towards the right. This results in a centrifugal force pushing the cyclist to the left and offsets the gravitational force dragging him down to the right. This manoeuvre presently throws the cyclist out of balance to the left, which he counteracts by turning the handlebars to the left; and so he continues to keep himself in balance by winding along a series of curvatures. A simple analysis shows that for a given angle of unbalance the curvature of each winding is inversely proportional to the square of the speed at which the cyclist is proceeding. But does this tell us exactly how to ride a bicycle? No. You obviously cannot adjust the curvature of your bicycle's path in proportion to the ratio of your unbalance over the square of your speed; and if you could you would fall off the machine, for there are a number of other factors to be taken into account in practice which are left out of the formulation of this rule. Rules of art can be useful, but they do not determine the practice of an art; they are maxims, which can serve as a guide to an art only if they can be integrated into the practical knowledge of the art. They cannot replace this knowledge.
> (Polanyi, 1998, pp. 49–50)

The argument here is that the logic of mass, vocationally oriented universities, such as we have in the UK presently, points towards an emphasis upon a form of technical knowledge, an instrumental notion of understanding. Whilst Arendt argued that the crisis in education stemmed from a replacement of learning with doing, Oakeshott and Polanyi are critical of the one-dimensional nature of learning in the twentieth century. All of them, however, agree that the problem is derived from a crisis in tradition. In the same vein we can say that the training in skills which employers and governments demand asks too much of our universities because the idea of a skill is intimately connected with practice in a particular context. To speak of skills as transferable across a variety of settings is to make a category mistake. Skills are specific, and cannot transfer their appropriate context. There may, however, be more than one context in which a skill is appropriate. This though is a separate matter.

Much of the force behind the arguments for a 'learning society' or 'knowledge economy' rests on the need for people to be adaptable enough to cope with uncertainty and a rapidly changing, risky environment. The paradox here lies in the fact that individuals are being asked to equip themselves with technical knowledge to manage a riskier future. However, as Oakeshott notes, technical knowledge is susceptible to precise formulation and this gives it the appearance of certainty. Surely, though, such rigidity is out of place if the world is becoming so much less certain. What must be remembered is that education ought not to serve only to maintain present social, political and economic arrangements. Our current mass higher education system lacks a critical logic.

Let me turn now to explore the idea of the university, and to consider why there is so little talk of the purposes of higher education. This will be discussed in the context of the mass higher education system which has developed in the UK alongside the production of knowledge in a culture of application. Peter Scott argues that knowledge outputs are expected to be useful and that knowledge is the outcome of a negotiation between 'practitioners' (producers, brokers and users). He claims basic research methodologies and commercially profitable knowledge forms are all produced via these negotiations. This social knowledge, Scott claims, follows a new pattern of production in a knowledge economy where economic production tends to be organised around various forms of knowledge. This makes the production of knowledge a central economic and social activity that erodes the professional monopoly of academic researchers and erodes any claim to autonomous academic work because the production of knowledge becomes so intertwined with other forms of economic production and social reproduction (Scott, 1995, p. 148).

However, there is a problem in this account. It is erroneous to suggest that a knowledge driven society is somehow new. Scott also implies a balance between the various spheres of society in their impact upon knowledge. We do not have *fairly* socially distributed knowledge precisely because the main agents in the process of knowledge production are large commercial firms and a state which seeks to emulate these firms insofar as it regards itself as a broker between the universities which it partly funds and research 'users'.

There is, I think, much confusion over what higher education and universities do. Even academics are wary of speaking about the purposes of a university. But to talk of purposes is not necessarily to regard universities as instrumental institutions. Neither does it imply some kind of foundationalist stance. The purposes of the university are connected to universal values such as science, scholarship and truth. Surely, it is the case that, rather, the current developments in higher education are foundationalist. They are seemingly grounded in bringing education closer to the 'world of work' or the 'real world'.

Perhaps this confusion arises out of the meaning of the university itself. The idea of the university invokes a certain romanticism. It is bound up in grand ideas of truth, freedom and solidarity. But, in Britain, universities are, on the whole, rather recent institutions, though, I would argue, founded on an older idea. As Scott puts it, universities are modern institutions:

> Two hundred years ago there were only six in Britain. . . . Together they enrolled fewer than 5,000 students. In no sense did they form a 'system'. Not

until the mid-nineteenth century were there any public policy interventions to shape, or reform, what today would be regarded as higher education. Even a century ago the number of universities had barely doubled, to 14, although the number of students had risen fourfold, to 20,000. There was still no national system, despite the chartering of new universities in the North and Midlands and the first tentative state subsidies for technical education. When the Robbins report was published in 1963 there were still only 24 universities, with a further six, the first wave of 'new' universities in the process of formation. But a national system had begun to emerge as a result of the activities of the University Grants Committee. . . . [This] demonstrates that the ancient pedigree of the universities is largely a myth. The universities themselves are recent foundations. Although it can be argued that the survival of the 'university' as an institutional ideal suggests that present universities, however young, are heirs to a deeply rooted tradition, it is just as plausible to argue that the persistence of the label proves how adaptable an institution the university has been over the centuries. The university has survived so long because it has changed so much.
(Scott, 1995, pp. 14–15)

Scott, here, is somewhat misleading. Of course universities have changed over the years, but this does not preclude the fact that they appeal to some idea of truth, justice and a free academic community. The fact that knowledge is fallible, or that what we regard as right sometimes becomes problematic, or that the academic community has never been completely free, does not detract from these ideas. After all, they are ideals. As Jaspers argues:

The university fulfils its task – research, instruction, training, communication – within an institutional framework. . . . The university exists only to the extent that it is institutionalized. The idea becomes concrete in the institution. The extent to which it does this determines the quality of the university. Stripped of its ideal the university loses all value. Yet 'institution' necessarily implies compromises. The idea is never perfectly realized. Because of this a permanent tension exists at the university between the idea and the shortcomings of the institution and corporate reality.
(Jaspers, 1960, p. 83)

To be sure, the threat to the university from functionalism or instrumental reason is not a uniquely contemporary problem. Jaspers wrote in 1961 that:

Either we will succeed in preserving the German university through a rebirth of its idea in the decision to create a new organizational form, or the university will end up in the functionalism of giant institutions for the training and development of specialized scientific and technical expertise. This is why it is crucial to envision . . . the possibility of a renewal of the university on the basis of its idea.
(Habermas, 1989, pp. 100–101)

Any claim that the university is becoming an extension of schooling, that university students no longer 'read' for a degree in the same way that perhaps they once did or that an instrumental attitude to knowledge held by society has impoverished arts based disciplines is not new. What does seem new, however, is the state's role in the organisation of universities. Student consumers, ranked status and inequality, precarious and alienated labouring academics, tuition fees and lack of maintenance support for undergraduates, a state sponsored imperative to publish a certain quantity of work regardless of its quality, the University for Industry, the emphasis on 'transferable' skills (if, indeed, skills can be transferable in any meaningful sense) all point towards an instrumental model of the university. Let me be clear, though. I do not wish to assert that the university, or knowledge generally, has no instrumental role at all. Habermas explains that:

> Universities must transmit technically exploitable knowledge. That is, they must meet an industrial society's need for qualified new generations and at the same time be concerned with the expanded reproduction of education itself. In addition, universities must not only transmit technically exploitable knowledge, but also produce it. This includes both information flowing from research into the channels of industrial utilization, armament, and social welfare, and advisory knowledge that enters into strategies of administration, government, and other decision-making powers, such as private enterprises. Thus, through instruction and research the university is immediately connected with functions of the economic process.
> (Habermas, 1987, pp. 1–2)

However, the production and transmission of technically exploitable knowledge, or the education of officeholders, as Amy Gutmann puts it, is not the only task of the university. Universities should ensure that its graduates are

> equipped, no matter how indirectly, with the minimum of qualifications in the area of extrafunctional abilities. In this connection extrafunctional refers to all those attributes and attitudes relevant to the pursuit of a professional career that are not contained per se in professional knowledge and skills.
> (Habermas, 1987, p. 2)

Habermas is here thinking of leadership characteristics, professional judgement, self-discipline and all of the other 'skills' that are demanded by employers nowadays. However, he writes, 'the university certainly does not produce the virtues of these unwritten professional standards, but the pattern of its socialization processes must at least be in harmony with them' (Habermas, 1987, p. 2). In other words, such qualities are not skills to be taught but virtues that can be developed less formally through the culture of an organisation and its institutions.

The university should also 'transmit, interpret, and develop the cultural tradition of the society' (Habermas, 1987, p. 2). Lastly, a university should provide a form of political education; its task is to help to form the political consciousness of its members. A university, or even a higher education system in what was once called the 'learning age', cannot restrict itself to economically necessary functions like a utilitarian knowledge factory. As Habermas argues:

> In every conceivable case, the enterprise of knowledge at the university level influences the action-orienting self-understanding of students and the public. It cannot define itself with regard to society exclusively in relation to technology, that is, to systems of purposive-rational action. It inevitably relates also to practice, that is, it influences communicative action. Nevertheless it is conceivable that a university rationalized as a factory would exert an influence on cultural self-understanding and on the norms of social actors indirectly and without being conscious of its own role in doing so.
> (Habermas, 1987, p. 4)

In other words, Habermas is calling for a more self-reflexive university. The notion that a university education which does not directly address its cultural hermeneutic role or admit that its own institutional culture will impact upon its students, graduates and staff is simply naïve.

Chapter 7

The corruption of democracy and education

The idea of social and public service provision through competitive markets imposed by the state marks a pivotal moment in the history of the welfare state. A contestable market would inject dynamism at minimal cost. One policy feature of recent political administrations in Britain has been marketisation of public services, begun under Margaret Thatcher and continued under John Major and then Tony Blair.

Subsequent administrations in the UK and in Australia and New Zealand, by and large, followed suit and then accelerated the process further. In this chapter I want to explore the trend towards the imposition of market norms in areas of life governed previously by social norms or ethical considerations. The problem is that the imposition of market mechanisms on universities in Britain is destroying the fabric of institutions which were once widely regarded as holding a comparative advantage over their international equivalents. An education from a British university once carried a special cachet. Desmond Ryan points out that certain factors marked out the British university experience as special, involving:

> An unusual degree of formative contact with critical and creative minds at work, its most outstanding graduates, socialized to expect fulfilling work, often compete to work in sectors allowing the most liberated exercise of the mind. Higher education became the live germ of a post-manufacturing production system with a competitive edge in imaginative ideas.
> (Ryan, 1998, p. 4)

Insofar as a marketised higher education environment no longer seems capable of providing such an experience, this is one example of what Habermas refers to as a colonisation of the lifeworld. He argues that this is bound up in the complementary process of cultural impoverishment. Somewhat abstractly, the spheres of science, morality and aesthetics come to differentiate themselves from one another. This rationalisation process leads to a loss of meaning – via disenchantment; and a loss of freedom – as actors in the social lifeworld lose autonomy and find themselves trapped in an iron cage.

Justification of the market

These processes, I think, can be seen in the current UK higher education system. Although, of course, they are in no way limited to the UK with issues surrounding the role of the market in higher education pressing concerns in the USA, Australia, New Zealand, Canada, South Africa and parts of South America. The international tendency over the past twenty years has increasingly given a greater role to the market in higher education, as universities compete for students and funding increasingly comes from students through loans. The higher education policies of successive governments in Britain have pointed towards a commodity-oriented form that manifests itself in a dual process of reification and juridification. In other words, higher education becomes increasingly commodified and tied up in regulations in order to enable this. These domestic processes are compounded by the development of the global market in higher education. Under the rules of the global market, Tokyo University competes with Harvard, the commercial University of Phoenix competes with the University of Wolverhampton. The ideal of open competition to which this view appeals, however, betrays a certain naïveté of universities. These institutions, despite carrying the title of university, serve very different constituencies and hold differing purposes. Accordingly, whilst these institutions all offer degrees and employ academics, they do not all compete within one homogeneous market. Rather, the market place in which universities compete is highly differentiated. However, the argument here is not so much about the complexity of a globalising higher education market but the justification and appropriateness of the market for universities.

Those who advocate the distribution of goods via market mechanisms usually do so on grounds of the epistemic justifications of the market. This, however, depends on the market being placed in an oppositional relation to the state. At its simplest the epistemic justification for the market is expressed in L. von Mises' 'calculation insight', which John Gray summarizes:

> The Misesian insight is that in any modern economy there will be billions of market exchanges and therefore billions of prices. In the production of any consumer good, for example, producers will need the guidance provided by the prices of many capital goods and these prices will typically be subject to constant change. Mises's argument is that, without market pricing of assets, their relative scarcities are unknowable, since simulating market pricing is a calculational impossibility in an economy where billions of market transactions take place and pricing is in a state of dynamic flux.
> (Gray, 1992, p. 6)

So, given that there are 'limitations to the knowledge that any particular individual or subset of individuals in society can possess[, h]ence, there are limitations to the knowledge at the disposal of any central planning board in a planned economy' (O'Neill, 1998, p. 129). However, the epistemic justification of the market is based upon more than a problem of calculation. According to John Gray, Hayekian advocates of the market argue that the market itself is an epistemic device, 'a discovery procedure for transmitting and indeed generating information that is dispersed throughout society' (Gray, 1992, p. 7). Rather than the market resolving a calculational difficulty, the market serves to transmit local knowledge of fleeting economic conditions, what we often refer to as entrepreneurial insight. It is such entrepreneurial knowledge that, by its nature, cannot be collected by any central planning board:

> The epistemic role of the market, accordingly, is to generate and to make available for general use information (transmitted via price signals) that is irretrievably scattered and cannot be subject to centralisation. The information embodied in market pricing, since it is not the property of any one market participant, is a sort of holistic knowledge of the whole society, a public patrimony that it is the state of central planning to fritter away. It is this depletion of the stock of knowledge embodied in markets that explains the universal impoverishment of socialist systems.
>
> (Gray, 1992, p. 7)

We might similarly question the human impoverishment of capitalist systems. The implication of Gray's claim that market systems do not impoverish the goods they distribute is weak. Indeed, it is just this kind of claim that I call into question. To distribute a good via a market can, in some cases, alter the meaning of that good. This poses problems if this good was previously distributed according to its publicly held meaning. Take the good of health care, for instance. Health care, we might say, is most effectively distributed according to criteria of illness, disease and trauma rather than ability to pay. If we distribute the health services according to ability to pay, then the meanings attached to the good of health care alter. So, for example, in private practice, plastic surgeons in Hollywood get rich on breast implant operations that are undergone in the hope of higher career earnings as a 'perfectly' formed movie actress. The surgeon here is employing surgical skills on members of the public, but it would be difficult for this surgeon to maintain that he is engaging in public health care. The example is extreme but it does illustrate how the meanings we attach to shared goods, such as a health care or education system, or a university or system of universities, become distorted when they are no longer allocated according to their meaning. In the plastic surgery example, where it seems reasonable to ask, is that public patrimony which is guaranteed by the market? Of course, it could simply be that even the market is never perfect, but it might still remain the 'most efficient communicative device we could have to enable production and consumption to grow and contract in the appropriate places' (O'Neill, 1998, p. 129).

In addition to entrepreneurial, local, particular knowledge, Hayek's argument rests on the idea that not all knowledge is propositional in its form. In other words, knowledge can also be practical too. It can be embodied in skills and know-how, knowledge which, it is argued, could not be passed on to a centralised planning body because it can only be vocalised or articulated in practice. In short, the defenders of the market argue that a division of knowledge in society renders central planning ineffective but epistemic problems can be overcome by pricing. As O'Neill explains it:

> The price mechanism is presented . . . as a solution to this problem of the division of knowledge in society. By serving as a numerical index of changes in the relation between the supply and demand for goods, it communicates between independent actors the information that is relevant to the coordination of their economic activities. And . . . information of such changes is all that is relevant to actors for them to be able to adjust their activities appropriately.
>
> (O'Neill, p. 133)

The claim made by Hayek, and those who espouse the benefits of the market, is that the price mechanism communicates all information required to coordinate action and that the coordination of actions can be ensured via the communication of information. If this is so then the entire project of deliberative democracy can be written off, or at least, the public sphere can be reduced to the market.

Firstly, the price mechanism fails to communicate sufficient information to coordinate action in a competitive market system. Consider competing producers in a market context. It is in the interests of both producers to withhold information from the other in order to establish and maintain a competitive advantage. These producers will keep their plans secret from one another and, therefore, the coordination of the producers' actions will be inhibited. When demand for a good rises against supply, the price signal pushes producers to raise production levels and consumer demand dampens. However, over time this leads to surplus production causing demand to slump and falling prices, leading to a subsequent rise in demand and another boom.

What we have here is the usual explanation, invoked by both Marx and Hayek, for the business cycle. But what it adds up to is that the market, we can see, communicates not information, but misinformation over time, and it does this because economic agents are instrumental and purposive in their self-interested outlook.

But, information alone is insufficient to coordinate action. For instance, knowledge that supply of a good will outstrip demand is of little use to a producer who seeks to coordinate action, unless, of course, she is the sole producer. Even with mutual knowledge of projected discoordination, O'Neill explains, 'no adjustment by any particular actor of his or her own actions will necessarily lead to coordination. There must be some mechanism whereby producers can mutually adjust plans in order that activities be coordinated' (O'Neill, p. 137). Competitive markets under normal conditions, just as they block the transfer of information and lead to the promotion of misinformation, also lack any mechanism for mutual adjustment. These problems pertain to the market because agents within it are self-interested, but this self-interestedness is required for the price mechanism to operate effectively.

It is claimed that the market, however, manages to transmit information which other distributive mechanisms cannot cope with. On the one hand, it is argued that local, entrepreneurial knowledge can be transmitted via the market; on the other hand, it is argued that practical, uncodifiable knowledge can be carried through the price mechanism. Local and practical knowledge, the argument goes, is wasted on the state. Now, we might have some sympathy with this claim. Look, for instance, at the kind of state planning that was involved in UK Higher Education's Quality Assurance Agency, which attempted to ensure good quality teaching. The Teaching Quality Assessments, however, made little space for practical or local knowledge. It is small surprise then that teaching quality is now proposed to be ensured through a Teaching Excellence Framework to mirror a Research Excellence Framework. But the argument at stake here is not between state and market, but between state, market and public institution. We can think of universities as public institutions, once upon a time at least, located within civil society and pursuing their own goals. The academic community, by and large, operated in a communicative manner, academics sought truth through their research and passed on understanding to their students and wider publics via publication. When we look at the ways in which markets operate in practice, they hardly seem to protect local or practical knowledge. The spread of the market tends to dissolve the understandings of the less powerful. As O'Neill puts it:

> The growth of global markets is associated with the disappearance of knowledge that is local and practical, and the growth of abstract codifiable information. . . . The claim that the market allows the full use of particular knowledge is not empirically confirmed. Some of the reasons for this . . . have to do with features of market economies that tend to be missed in the abstract models of catallaxy that Hayek presents. There is the significance of the power of different actors in the market. The knowledge of weak and marginal actors in markets, such as peasants and indigenous populations, tends to be lost to those who hold market power. The epistemic value of knowledge claims bears no direct relation to their market value.
> (O'Neill, p. 139)

It might be argued that while markets fail to coordinate plans and generate misinformation in theory, and extinguish local and practical knowledge in practice, they are still the most efficient devices for distributing goods. So, it is to issues of efficiency that I turn. It might, however, be worth bearing in mind that self-governed universities, when they worked well, could manage to coordinate plans, transfer information and preserve local and practical knowledge. It could be that the academy of scholars and scientists forms an effective distributive mechanism. It would be supremely ironic if the scholarly and scientific norms of academe were to be torn apart by the complementary colonising forces of state and market.

Efficiency and optimality

Government policy, over recent years, has focused on the inefficiency which is argued to be inherent to the public sector. Oliver Fulton outlines some of the then recent changes in the UK education system:

> At the policy level, recent changes in primary and secondary education include the introduction of a national curriculum, the virtual abolition of the long established structures of local democratic control and independent national inspection, and the quasi-privatization of schools; while in higher education the number of autonomous universities has been nearly doubled, the established mechanisms of academic planning and control have been downgraded or replaced, and student demand has become one of the main vehicles for differential funding of institutions. At the same time, the education system's outputs are changing dramatically: both qualification levels (as proportions of the relevant population cohorts) and the demand for non-compulsory education are rising at rates that, as recently as five years ago, were regarded by policy-makers and analysts as possibly desirable but certainly unattainable.
>
> (Fulton, 1994, p. 223)

Efficiency, so the argument goes, can be injected into the public sector via the imposition of market norms. Market mechanisms will serve to do away with inefficiency and bureaucracy. Public services, such as the state education system, or the National Health Service, will therefore be rendered less costly to the tax paying public. The price of this, however, is the obliteration of public space.

Allen Buchanan outlines two efficiency arguments (that I will address here) for markets based on Paretian optimality – where there is no feasible alternative state of the system in which at least one person is better off and no one is worse off, and diachronic efficiency, that is, efficiency that approximates the idealising conditions of the market over time. The concept of Paretian efficiency is problematic when making comparisons between different systems since what it means to be better off will vary between systems. Buchanan writes that claims for market efficiency rest on two grounds:

> (1) a theoretical statement that exchanges in the ideal market reach an equilibrium state that is Pareto Optimal [an equilibrium state where no one can be made better off without someone being made worse off] . . . and (2) the assumption that actual (nonideal) markets, or feasible modifications of actual markets, sufficiently approximate the efficiency of the ideal

> market to make them preferable to nonmarket arrangements. . . . Since the immensely strong conditions that define the ideal market are never met in actual markets, the case for the market on grounds of efficiency depends on the extent to which actual markets do approximate, or can be modified to approximate, the ideal market.
>
> (Buchanan, 1985, pp. 14–15)

Here I will ignore some of the detailed technicalities of welfare economic theory surrounding Paretian optimality. Indeed, the concept of Pareto Optimality pertains to a 'zero sum game' which, in itself, I wish to argue, is not suited to an analysis of education with its emphasis on development and learning. Consider, for instance, the idea of Paretian efficiency applied to the distribution of higher education. Working out the Pareto-efficient distribution of the good would involve determining the ideal levels of stock held in libraries, the ideal staff to student ratios and, importantly, the ideal attitudes to be held by staff and students since all of these factors contribute to the system of higher education. These factors cannot be regarded as simple inputs to the higher education system which have some kind of optimal level. All talk of levels in this context is somewhat empty when what is at stake is not only a quantitative issue but also a matter of obtaining appropriate books for the library, appointing suitably qualified and competent staff to engage in teaching and research and ensuring that academics hold appropriately scholarly attitudes to their work. In other words, the notion of efficiency fails us when it has to be balanced against matters of human judgement. Moreover, as Buchanan points out, the Paretian concepts of optimality and superiority are worthless when attempts are made to put them to use in comparing the efficiency of different economic systems. Whilst the theory of Pareto Optimality is concerned with efficiency within a given system – the Paretian Optimal point being where no one can be made better off without making somebody else worse off – in terms of intersystemic comparisons this makes no sense because each system to be compared would have to comprise individuals with comparable interests. Of course, any two systems comprised of individuals with comparable interests would also be comparable systems once it is conceded that our interests are contingent upon our environment. This brings in a circularity to the idea of intersystemic comparison which renders the notion of comparing the efficiencies of systems meaningless. Buchanan writes:

> It is not simply that there are practical difficulties (lack of information, for example) which hinder intersystemic efficiency comparisons. Rather, there is not even a *theory* of intersystemic efficiency comparisons in the same sense in which there is a theory of intrasystemic efficiency comparisons. All arguments concerning the relative efficiency of rival systems of social organization would appear to have an irreducibly intuitive element.
>
> (Buchanan, 1985, p. 44)

The rather vaguely articulated concept of diachronic efficiency fares badly in this respect too. The idea behind diachronic efficiency is based upon the notion that, over time, non-ideal markets will approximate the conditions of the ideal market through competition. It is as if the all too visible hand irons out structural deformations in non-ideal market conditions. But this argument is rather weak. Structural imbalances within a market can be perpetuated by any market-oriented policy that assumes an already existing competitive element. Just as negative liberty cannot ensure freedom among unequal actors, a market framework cannot automatically deliver efficiency if the system concerned already suffers from structural deformations.

My line of argument will, therefore, focus instead on the impoverished analysis which market-based libertarian thought provides and on a discussion of how the scope of the market should be limited. Of course, there are problems associated with an abstracted argument which pertains to markets. However, here I want to concentrate on the arguments which have lain behind the privatisation and marketisation of social goods in a quest for efficiency which has been the legacy of a welfare state that has come to be seen as a fiscal millstone in an age when the state sees itself as accountable to some reified notion of 'the taxpayer' rather than to its citizens.

Diachronic efficiencies of the market, as I pointed out, are those efficiencies which accrue from competition over time. These efficiencies will, it is argued, arise whether or not a market is ideal or nonideal. Buchanan explains:

> Competition among producers reduces costs of production, since producers who fail to develop and utilize less-costly methods of production are replaced by those who do. Competition among entrepreneurs reduces transaction costs, because the entrepreneur who can match buyers with sellers with the least expenditure of his own resources can charge less for his services and capture a larger share of the market. Finally, the need for information on the part of the producers, consumers, and entrepreneurs creates a market for information. In each of these respects, competition in nonideal markets generates incentives for behavior that tends towards the more perfect satisfaction of the conditions of the ideal market, in particular, zero transaction costs, full information, and zero information costs.
>
> (Buchanan, 1985, pp. 15–16)

Crucially, and as celebrants of the market have themselves emphasised, markets deal with and utilise information efficiently. Markets contain large quantities of complex information which allow prices to move over time, although no individual or group requires all or even part of this information for the system to tend towards an efficient outcome. The market, in other words, enables participants to save on information (Buchanan, 1985, p. 16). It is this tendency towards efficiency which appeals to policy-makers who have had to deal with the repercussions of Nozickian arguments about the minimal state alongside a welfare state that is becoming increasingly expensive to maintain.

Markets in an educational context

In the realm of education policy one suggested avenue for more efficient provision of education, which the Major Government briefly put in place for nursery funding, is the voucher system. Similar ideas, however, lay behind the confusing package of plans for 'individual learning accounts', which the Blair Government briefly established in 2000 under the banner of lifelong learning. The individual learning accounts were weakly regulated and fraud was widespread, as 'training providers' cashed in credits without providing education. Advocates of a voucher system for education accept the need for compulsory education and the need for parents to be provided with the means to educate their children. Under such a system the administrative and managerial roles, once undertaken by democratically accountable bodies such as the Local Education Authorities, would be replaced with educational or training institutions run on a commercial basis. Indeed, this is the policy route that the UK's Conservative governments followed in the late 1980s and early 1990s. Particularly obvious examples of this come with the 1988 Education Reform Act and the 1992 Further and Higher Education Act. The former Act introduced Local Management of Schools, which was

> designed to give schools greater autonomy in managing their resources and to increase the proportion of LEA [Local Education Authority] funding allocated on the basis of pupil numbers. Since its introduction, the extent of the [budget] delegation has been increased and the pupil-led funding principle strengthened. LEAs retain control of capital funds, central government grants and certain other items. They are, however, then required to pass on at least 85 per cent of their remaining funds to the schools and colleges, retaining only sufficient to discharge their statutory duties and to provide other essential LEA services.
>
> (Macfarlane, 1993, pp. 115–116)

In the case of the post-16 education sector, the imposition of a market or business framework was even more blatant:

> The 1992 Further and Higher Education Act significantly changed the status of post-16 colleges by making them corporate bodies – freestanding, autonomous institutions responsible for their own affairs. As business organisations they have their own legal identity with the power to manage their assets and resources, employ staff, contract to provide services, engage in consultancies and join in cooperative enterprises with other companies. . . . With incorporation, college governors acquire the status of company directors and become subject to various Companies Acts that increase

their responsibility and accountability. They are given ultimate authority over colleges' general strategy, the curriculum, personnel management, student services and external relations. They can be held legally responsible if a college goes into insolvent liquidation and forced to make a personal financial contribution if it can be proved that they have failed to monitor their college's affairs properly.

(Macfarlane, 1993, p. 108)

Currently then, the British education system operates along lines that have been designed to approximate a market model. This is shown in an information fetishism (without regard for the quality of that information). Witness testing in primary and secondary schools at certain 'key stages' (indeed, many educationalists have argued that the effect of testing children has been detrimental to the teaching and learning of pupils because the tests have such a narrow focus). Published national results of such testing exist to facilitate a consumer choice to be made by parents between institutions; and school inspectors judge the quality of education on offer in institutions. However, 'quality' here seems to be determined independently of resources available to schools.

The further education sector has become imbued with this market rationale too. Institutions are forced to compete with one another for students, and this has resulted in colleges merging together or closing down entirely.

Universities, of course, do not escape this invisible hand either. When once the Higher Education Funding Councils collated together a variety of performance indicators which then influenced funding levels, now the performance indicators serve as a price signal for student-consumers. League tables rank institutions in very general terms, and sharp distinctions are drawn between 'research' and 'teaching' universities generating increasing inequality between different universities. Behind the market mentality which has shaped education policy lies an instrumental rationality where students are seen to consume education and training and institutional reputation becomes more important than substance. Here individuals achieve competences which will allow them to buy into the labour market; institutions compete for research contracts from industry; and the 'post-industrial society' supposedly benefits from an expanded skills base. However, the problem with this is that it offers a one-dimensional framework which is oriented towards short-term economic growth. The emphasis in this lies on developing rather low-level skills which students, and their families, pay for themselves. Desmond Ryan worries that:

Quite how the graduates of the massifying system will do in the labour market remains to be seen. What we have already seen is that they have been paying a higher price for a lower quality good than earlier student generations. What makes this behaviour [instrumentally] rational is the general knowledge that the price will go on rising for a quality which can only fall.

(Ryan, 1998, p. 32)

Drawing the boundaries of the market

Theorists such as Jürgen Habermas, Michael Walzer, Russell Keat, Michael Sandel and Elizabeth Anderson have argued that the question of whether we should organise our lives around the notions of market or state is no longer pertinent. Instead, the salient point for them is that both individuals and the community depend upon one another: community stagnates without the individual, but the impulse of the individual fades without the sympathy of the community. Similarly, it is no longer plausible to argue that either the state or the market ought to organise our lives. The problem, instead, is where should the boundaries of the market be set?

This is not the same as an exclusive focus on the question of which goods ought to be amenable to the market; that is, what goods can be bought and sold? Russell Keat in 'The Moral Boundaries of the Market' argues that this fails to capture all that is at issue, and could be misleading:

> For example, any worries that one might have about the extension of the market to include higher education are unlikely to be confined to the possibility of qualifications such as university degrees becoming straightforwardly purchasable. They will additionally, and perhaps more significantly, be directed at the possible effects of market forces on the character of educational institutions themselves, on the kinds of commitments and attitudes that may be encouraged in their participants, and so on.
> (Keat, 1993, pp. 13–14)

So, it is not enough, in dealing with the problem of where to set boundaries to the market, to list commodities that should not be bought and sold. Rather, what is required is an investigation into the reasons why certain goods are not amenable to market arrangements. In short, it is the attitudes and culture which sit alongside competitive market structures that are the problem and not simply the market mechanism in itself.

Norman Fairclough has argued that public discourse has undergone a process of 'conversationalization' which accompanies the commodification of public discourse (Fairclough, 1994). Fairclough examines the connection between the conversationalization of public discourse and a shift in authority in favour of 'the public', epitomised by a shift in authority from 'producers' to 'consumers'. He seeks to problematise the *prima facie* 'democratic' consequences of this process. He suggests that the 'cultural value and significance of conversationalization is more ambivalent, and that the evidence of conversationalization indicates caution about such [democratic] claims' (Fairclough, 1994, p. 253). Fairclough suggests that we can think of this process of commodification and conversationalization

> in terms of the weakening of boundaries between 'orders of discourse' . . . between on the one hand the discursive practices of the market in the more traditional sense, and on the other hand the discursive practices of politics,

public services like health and education, government and other forms of public information, and even the arts. In part, this is a matter of the colonization of these domains by market *discourses*.

(Fairclough, 1994, p. 253)

Such market discourses are exemplified in educational courses which are 'sold' as 'products' which are 'designed' and 'implemented' to meet the 'needs' of 'customers' and 'clients'. For Fairclough, such a language of sales is deeply problematic:

> The increasing salience and generality of promotion as a communicative function consequent upon commodification is having pervasive and I believe profound effects upon public orders of discourse. . . . [I]t is becoming increasingly difficult to differentiate 'informative' discourse from 'persuasive' discourse . . . since information is so widely covert promotion. From the point of view of text users and consumers, there is I think a generalization of distrust: we don't read documents like university prospectuses as we used to, we are too 'knowing' about their promotional designs upon us.
>
> (Fairclough, 1994, pp. 257–258)

So, according to Fairclough, the promotion of commodities leads to problems of sincerity and authenticity. The market here cannot allow us to make any properly informed choice. Moreover:

> [T]he impact of promotion is not only upon those discursive practices which overtly sell organizations like universities to the 'public' [or mass]. The elevation of promotion in the hierarchy of institutional practices tends to mean that *all* the practices of an organization (even for instance the 'internal' discursive practices of teaching and so forth in universities) come to be constructed with a view to their *promotability*.
>
> (Fairclough, 1994, p. 258)

Money and complex equality – Appropriate distributive justice

However, I wish to question the suitability of such market norms within the sphere of education. Is education, to use Michael Walzer's phrase, a sphere where we can block exchange? Or, does 'the market' have a legitimate role to play in the provision of education and training in order to ensure that such provision is as efficiently allocated as possible? I will begin with a general discussion of money and markets and attempt to link together those arguments which call for the scope of the market to be limited.

Marx on money is, unsurprisingly, damning:

> What I have thanks to money, what I pay for, i.e. what money can buy, that is what I, the possessor of money, am myself. My power is as great as

the power of money. The properties of money are my — (its owner's) — properties and faculties. Thus what I am and what I am capable of is by no means determined by my individuality. I am ugly, but I can buy myself the most beautiful women. Consequently I am not ugly, for the effect of ugliness, its power of repulsion, is annulled by money. As an individual, I am lame, but money can create twenty-four feet for me; so I am not lame; I am a wicked, dishonest man without conscience or intellect, but money is honoured and so is its possessor. Money is the highest good and so its possessor is good. Money relieves me of the trouble of being dishonest; so I am presumed to be honest. I may have no intellect, but money is the true mind of all things and so how should its possessor have no intellect? Moreover, he can buy himself intellectuals and is not the man who has power over intellectuals not more intellectual than they? I who can get with money everything that the human heart longs for, do I not possess all human capacities? Does my money thus change all my incapacities into their opposite?

(Marx, 1977, p. 109)

Marx, like Walzer in his *Spheres of Justice*, is concerned to show how money is the 'galvano-chemical power of society' (Marx, 1977, p. 110); money, Marx argues, is the universal whore, the universal pander. Walzer's concern over money relates to this function of money as the universal pander because it is in this capacity as a solvent that money breaks down the barriers between spheres of life that Walzer would like to see kept in place. Otherwise, Walzer argues, goods lose their inherent value. For instance, a work of art will not be valued for its inherent beauty, or any statement it makes, when it has been purchased as a piece of investment which will increase in financial value. Indeed, an important painting may as well be locked in a vault if its only function is to accrue in financial worth over time.

In *Spheres of Justice* Michael Walzer seeks to defend a particular view of distributive justice which he calls 'complex equality'. He argues that distributive justice concerns being and doing, just as much as holdings. It relates to how we produce as well as how we consume, and concerns issues such as status as well as land, capital and possessions. Different political arrangements and ideological perspectives determine different distributions of goods, whether power, honour, status, membership, love, knowledge, wealth, security, offices and work or more material goods like food, housing, health care and education. Walzer's argument, which Michael Sandel made slightly more recently (Sandel, 2012), is that there is no truly universal medium of exchange: money cannot buy everything and this is true both empirically and normatively (Walzer, 1983, pp. 3–4). Moreover, Walzer says, there is not (and neither has there been) a single criterion for all distributions. 'Desert, qualification, birth and blood, friendship, need, free exchange, political loyalty, democratic decision: each has had its place, along with many others, uneasily coexisting, invoked by competing groups, confused with one another' (Walzer, 1983, p. 4).

Now, in modern societies, Walzer argues, there exists a high degree of differentiation between various 'spheres' of life. Within each sphere particular social activities take place and particular forms of social relationships are appropriate. Each sphere involves its own special rules. For instance, actions which might be permissible within the sphere of the economy – say, taking profit – ought to be considered impermissible within the sphere of religion. Social goods then, ought to be distributed according to their own specific social meaning:

> All distributions are just or unjust relative to the social meanings of the goods at stake. . . . When medieval Christians, for example, condemned the sin of simony, they were claiming that the meaning of a particular social good, ecclesiastical office, excluded its sale and purchase. Given the Christian understanding of office, it followed – I am inclined to say, it necessarily followed – that office holders should be chosen for their knowledge and piety and not for their wealth.
>
> (Walzer, 1983, p. 9)

Similarly, Van Gogh's *Sunflowers* should be valued for its aesthetic worth and not for its million-dollar price tag.

What Walzer wishes to prevent is the 'dominance' of certain social goods. He hopes that this can, in part, be done via a defence of the 'plurality' of social goods:

> Walzer maintains that it is precisely the specificity – or, as he terms it, the 'plurality' – of these social goods (which themselves also vary between different societies at different times) that makes it impossible to defend principles of distributive justice of the kind standardly proposed by political philosophers, whether these are egalitarian, desert-based, Rawlsian, Nozickian or otherwise. For these typically involve either mistakenly assuming that all such goods are somehow commensurable with one another (e.g. that they are different ways of achieving the single good of utility, or even measurable in monetary terms), or attempting to apply to every social good a principle that is in fact appropriate only to some.
>
> (Keat, 1993, p. 9)

So, for Walzer, social goods should be distributed according to criteria appropriate to those goods, according to those goods' own social meanings. Further, each sphere should be prevented from dominating other spheres. As Keat explains: '[P]eople's success in one sphere must be prevented from enabling them to achieve corresponding success in another, despite their lacking the attributes that would justify such success according to the criteria regarded as appropriate in that other sphere' (Keat, 1993, pp. 9–10). A plurality of social goods, Walzer argues, must be maintained in order to prevent the dominance of one good, or one set of goods, which in turn can determine the value of goods in other spheres of distribution. Alongside this dominance comes monopoly too.

A dominant good's value can be upheld by the strength and cohesion (derived from the possession of the dominant good) of its owners:

> I call a good dominant if the individuals who have it, because they have it, can command a wide range of other goods. It is monopolized whenever a single man or woman, a monarch in the world of value – or a group of men and women, oligarchs – successfully hold it against all rivals. Dominance describes a way of using social goods that isn't limited by their intrinsic meanings or that shapes those meanings in its own image. Monopoly describes a way of owning or controlling social goods in order to exploit their dominance. When goods are scarce and widely needed, like water in the desert, monopoly itself will make them dominant. Mostly, however, dominance is a more elaborate social creation, the work of many hands, mixing reality and symbol. Physical strength, familial reputation, religious or political office, landed wealth, capital, technical knowledge: each of these, in different historical periods, has been dominant; and each of them has been monopolized by some group of men or women. And then all good things come to those who have the one best thing. Possess that one and the others come in train.
>
> (Walzer, 1983, pp. 10–11)

It is probable that some notion of technical knowledge as a dominant good lies behind the current rhetoric of lifelong learning, whereby education and training are coming to be viewed in terms of their potential for economic growth. Further, the status of technical knowledge as dominant good might go some way towards explaining the marketisation of further and higher education: students may well be more willing to invest and finance their own education because they suspect that a high degree of technical knowledge brings with it the possibility of a whole host of other goods. However, notice that even in this brief *ad hoc* example another good to be considered has sneaked in: the universal pander, money, or the 'sphere of money and commodities', as Walzer is wont to call it. This sphere, for Walzer, poses the greatest threat to pluralism. As he puts it:

> One can conceive the market as a sphere without boundaries, an unzoned city – for money is insidious, and market relations are expansive. A radically *laissez-faire* economy would be like a totalitarian state, invading every other sphere, dominating every other distributive process. It would transform every social good into a commodity.
>
> (Walzer, 1983, pp. 119–120)

Here, it seems, there are echoes of Georg Simmel's description of the anonymous nature of money: in market exchange between buyer and seller no questions need be asked and no answers given.

Money . . . makes possible the secrecy, invisibility and silence of exchange. By compressing money into a piece of paper, by letting it glide into a person's hand, one can make him a wealthy person. Money's formlessness and abstractness makes it possible to invest it in the most varied and most remote values and thereby to remove it completely from the gaze of neighbours. Its anonymity and colourlessness does not reveal the source from which it came to the present owner: it does not have a certificate of origin in the way in which, more or less disguised, many concrete objects of possession do.

(Simmel, 1990, p. 385)

Simmel describes money in this way in the context of bribery and, for Walzer, this is illuminating because it shows up the boundary between the legitimate sphere of money and those places where it does sometimes operate but should not: 'Dishonesty is always a useful guide to the existence of moral standards. When people sneak across the boundary of the sphere of money, they advertise the existence of the boundary. It's there, roughly at the point where they begin to hide and dissemble' (Walzer, 1983, p. 98). The sphere of money and commodities then is all the more difficult to bound because of its depersonalised nature. As Walzer says, 'Money is innocent until proven guilty' (Walzer, 1983, p. 98).

However, no matter how difficult it may be to enforce a boundary around the sphere of money, Walzer maintains that such a boundary does exist: there are things which stand, or ought to stand, outside the cash nexus. To limit the dominance of wealth, Walzer proposes a list of 'blocked exchanges', a list of things that cannot be had for money (Walzer, 1983, pp. 100–103). Briefly, according to Walzer, the following should not be bought and sold:

1. Human beings – Slavery is ruled out. Whilst labour power and the things people make can be sold, people and their liberty cannot. 2. Political power and influence – votes can't be bought nor officials bribed. 3. Criminal justice cannot be bought, otherwise it ceases to be justice. 4. Freedom of speech, press, religion and assembly. 5. Marriage and procreation rights. 6. The right to leave the political community. 7. Exemptions from communally imposed work, e.g. military service or jury service. 8. Political offices. 9. Basic welfare services such as those provided by the police or primary and secondary education. 10. Desperate exchanges, what Walzer refers to as 'trades of last resort'. 11. Prizes and honours, if an honour is bought then it loses its meaning as a reward for achievement. 12. Divine grace. 13. Love and friendship. Of course, as Walzer realises, money can buy things that make one a more likely candidate for lovers and friends, but any direct purchase is blocked. 14. Criminal sales. Illegal goods and services such as heroin, blackmail and stolen goods are prohibited from sale. Consider how these blocked exchanges relate so readily to the activities of a public institution like a university where academic work, ideally, is based on freedom, honour, truth, honesty, sincerity and authenticity.

The meanings of goods

There are, however, problems with Walzer's thesis. As Keat points out:

> [T]he question of what we regard as legitimately bought and sold is by no means the same as what we regard as legitimately produced and distributed specifically through the mechanisms of a market economy. (Indeed, in light of the . . . experience with the European exchange rate mechanism, some might like to protect money itself from the market!)
>
> (Keat, 1993, p. 13)

The problem, rather, is the effect which market forces might have on the character of certain goods. Walzer wishes to rely on some notion of the social meaning of goods in order to decide whether or not goods can be regarded as candidates for blocked exchange. However, he neglects the possibility that the impact of market forces upon goods might transform the way that people think about those goods. The important point perhaps is not, as Walzer suggests, whether goods can be bought or sold, but how they are regarded. Elizabeth Anderson argues that we can grasp the nature of goods by considering the ways we value and use them (Anderson, 1993, p. 144). And for Keat too it is necessary to focus on social meanings rather than legality (Keat, 1993, p. 14). So, if the crucial point relates to the 'public imagination', then 'a system of blocked exchanges, however successful, may still prove seriously inadequate in preventing the colonizing tendencies of the sphere of commodities' (Keat, 1993, p. 14). Given this, then the market is not only the sphere of commodities, that is what can be purchased, but also what is socially meant by this term. If this is so, Keat argues, then 'the dominance of the market domain might itself take the form of an illegitimate extension of its social meanings and norms to other institutions and activities, without these being straightforwardly (re-) located within the market' (Keat, 1993, p. 15).

The question at issue here is much broader than which goods can and cannot be sold. Rather, what needs to be clarified, as Charles Taylor writes:

> [I]s the family of conceptions of the good life, the notions of what it is to be human, which have grown up with modern society and have framed the identity of contemporary people. . . . [I]t is only by articulating these conceptions that we can identify the conditions of a legitimation crisis of contemporary society. For these will define the terms in which institutions, practices, disciplines, and structures will be recognized as legitimate or marked out as illegitimate.
>
> (Taylor, 1981, p. 111)

Taylor singles out several important features of the modern identity (which also shed some light on Walzer's list of blocked exchanges, insofar as these blocks seem to shield vulnerable aspects of the modern identity). These features, for

The corruption of democracy and education 109

Taylor, have 'played a vital part in developing and sustaining our sense of ourselves as free agents' (Taylor, 1981, p. 114). The first of these is equality. So, the modern identity is incompatible with slavery, for instance. Hierarchy is anathema to modern society. Another, connected feature, is that one must be the subject of rights. Certain freedoms in modern society are guaranteed: 'One must be able to choose and act within limits free from the arbitrary interference of others. The modern subject is an equal rights-bearer. One's having this status is part of what sustains one's identity' (Taylor, 1981, p. 114). Alongside the sense of ourselves as equal rights-bearers, the modern identity also requires a conception of what Taylor refers to as 'efficacy'. This is the ability to effect our own purposes:

> Subjects without efficacy, unable to alter the world around them to their own ends, would be incapable of sustaining a modern identity or else would be deeply humiliated in their identity. . . . The very fact that we command so much private space is very important for our sense of efficacy as, for example, the ability to move around on our own which the car gives us.
> (Taylor, 1981, p. 115)

The modern identity, for Taylor, is defined in part by an instrumental attitude towards nature: '[I]t is an affirmation of our autonomy . . . that our purposes are not imposed on us by the supposed order of things. The instrumental stance towards nature is meant to be a spiritual declaration of independence from it' (Taylor, 1981, p. 116).

Certainly, the modern identity fits well with the consumer society.

> [T]he consumer society comes to us dressed up in a form that meshes with . . . the aspirations of the modern subject. Thus we are invited as consumers to acquire and furnish a private space as the condition of an autonomous, self-contained, unmediated existence. . . . Much advertising plays on this aspiration to the private sphere: the ads always show happy families filling those interiors, driving away in those cars, surrounding those barbecues, etc. Of course what is not justified is the continued increase: why should the mobile private space we travel in become ever more rapid and high-powered? Why must labor-saving mechanization continue without stop, even up to electric tooth-brushes and similar absurdities? This could never be justified intellectually, but somehow the implication is that more and more powerful accoutrements mean more of the fulfillment that they are meant to make possible.
> (Taylor, 1981, p. 119)

The modern identity supports the consumer society. It also helps us to understand the processes at work which are leading towards the instrumentalisation of education. Learning is coming to be seen more and more in terms of competences and the economic benefits such competences might deliver. The 'consumer' of a university degree, for instance, is not so much attempting to understand a certain body of knowledge, rather, he or she is bolstering his or her curriculum vitae: higher education is recalibrated as *Success as a Knowledge Economy* (BIS, 2016). The understanding involved in intellectual work has become subordinate to the qualification conferred upon the graduate. And thus the meaning of education has started to shift from developing a public understanding of knowledge, open to criticism, to a private meaning where the skills picked up during a course of study, and embodied in a certificate, can be traded in for a job.

Ronald Barnett has written about the changing meaning of the university. 'What, if anything', he asks, 'does the title "university" mean in the modern world?' (Barnett, 1997b). He suggests that the university comprises a multitude of meanings and that this is a problem:

> [I]n a mass system, it can mean all kinds of things. Institutions that we call 'universities' can have a variety of functions and forms. Large or small, research-based or not, campus-based or distributed, focused on full-time or on part-time courses, with face-to-face or distance learning, and with courses having an explicit orientation towards the world of work or built around disciplines: we can happily call all of these universities and feel no unease.
>
> (Barnett, 1997a)

But, if this is the case, then this means that there is no particular sense of what the university stands for. Participants in university life no longer decide the meaning of the university through discourse; instead the market decides and the meaning of the university dissolves and loses its essential qualities. Moreover, as an instrumental rationality takes over, those features that were once central to the idea of the university have begun to fall away: the university was built on a project of knowledge, but knowledge is becoming prized for its effectiveness rather than its truth. Finally, educational institutions and universities have become:

> [O]rganisations characterised by missions, plans and decision-making according to financial and numerical performance indicators. This move inserts instrumental reason and power structures into what has traditionally been the site of communicative reason between equals. The university as an 'academic community' was largely a myth; but now, even the myth is hardly sustainable. The university, as an organisation, takes on the economic and instrumental rationality of the wider society.
>
> (Barnett, 1997a)

Desmond Ryan makes a connected point, which relates the internal organisation of the university to the idea it appeals to:

> In being organizationally reconfigured to take on a politically decreed role in the economy, they [the universities] have lost the right to collectively

self-manage their own work, the vital ingredient in the discipline of originality. Losing that self-management has turned their occupants into employees, to be deployed as utility dictates. Losing the discipline of creativity under criticism has brought the consequential loss of their cultural role in British society. From *producers of cultural norms* which animated a dynamic sector of society they have become the *consumers of procedural dogmas* emanating largely from the moribund sector of society which had never had much regard for their products and which the universities were bidding to displace: manufacturing industry. From being to a large degree ends in themselves, they are now means to the ends of the politicians in office, as in Italy or Indonesia. From cultural capital for society they have become political capital for governments. University 'chief executives' no longer claim that their institution is based on an Idea, but emphasize its functionality, its 'fitness for purpose', its accountability.

(Ryan, 1998, p. 5)

Much of the confusion over the idea of the Idea of the University stems from a misunderstanding that the Idea pertains to one single purpose that universities appeal to. As I argued in the previous chapter, it is perfectly acceptable to hold on to an Idea of the University which contains a bundling of functions, all of which, however, can be pursued within an academic ethic.

Market norms and the good of higher education

Anderson argues that the norms structuring market relations typically display five features: 'they are impersonal, egoistic, exclusive, want-regarding, and oriented to "exit" rather than "voice." Norms with these features, though not governing all market transactions, are characteristic of the market' (Anderson, 1993, p. 145). I will try to explain these five features of market norms.

Norms governing market relations are impersonal. As Anderson puts it, they are:

> [S]uitable for regulating the interactions of strangers. Each party to a market transaction views his relation to the other as merely a means to the satisfaction of ends defined independent of the relationship and of the other party's ends. . . . The impersonality of market relations thus defines a sphere of freedom from personal ties and obligations.
>
> (Anderson, 1993, p. 145)

Although, she notes, the market's impersonality has been evolving for centuries, it still manages to discriminate on the grounds of race, ethnicity, gender and sexual orientation.

The market domain is egoistic. The market leaves those parties within it free to pursue individual interests without considering others' interests. In the market we have to look after ourselves, and each of us defines and satisfies our interests independently of others. But, Anderson points out that this private use of reason only operates in relation to private goods that are exclusive and rivalrous in consumption. Exclusive goods are those whose benefits are limited to the purchaser. If I cannot exclude people from enjoying the flowers in my garden, it becomes impractical to charge a market price for the good. Goods are rivalrous in consumption if the amount consumed reduces the amount left available to others. Anderson points out that the use-value of commodities is rivalrous, while socially shared goods are not rivalrous. We usually enjoy a good joke more when we share it with others (Anderson, 1993, p. 145). Similarly, good teachers want to share understanding with other interested people.

The market sphere is also want-regarding:

> It responds to 'effective demand' – desires backed by the ability to pay for things. Commodities are exchanged without regard for the reasons people have for wanting them. . . . Since it offers no means for discriminating among the reasons people have for wanting or providing things, it cannot function as a forum for the justification of principles about the things traded on it. Thus the market provides individual freedom from the value judgments of others. . . . But it provides this freedom at the cost of reducing preferences, from the market's point of view, to mere matters of taste, about which it is pointless to dispute.
>
> (Anderson, 1993, p. 146)

Finally, participants in the market have influence over the provision and exchange of commodities via what Albert Hirschman has called 'exit' and not 'voice'. While the customer can exit, the producer can shrug and tell the customer to take it or leave it, the customer has no voice and so no say in the design of the product, despite efforts to develop student voice or invite customers to engage via social media.

On this view, it is not surprising that we are losing hold of the social meanings of cultural goods, like education or universities. For the market does not admit critical debate. Without a discourse in ideas about what things mean for us, and what they are meant to be for (other than, perhaps, economic growth and 'competitiveness', which fit with market norms) it is not surprising that goods which were socially shared have come to be seen in terms of their value to individuals. The market does not recognise the force of reason, and it does not bring people together in any communicative sense either. Participants in the market have their own ends, which are not directly related to others: the market is the realm of the idiot, the individual divorced from the public world.

Now, if we take the good of higher education and hold it against this theoretical template, can we say that here we have a good that is not amenable to market norms? Firstly, education is a shared good. Knowledge and understanding could not exist unless we agreed on what they were. Education is not impersonal.

After all, a degree from a British university was highly valued precisely because students were allowed a relatively high degree of contact with their tutors. The relation between student and teacher operates on a dialectical basis, where understanding and critical reasoning come about via a hermeneutic process. Learning is not egoistic; since it is a shared good, learning takes place in the context of an open community. The benefits of knowledge are not limited to a purchaser. Society as a whole reaps rewards. Scholarly activity is not want-regarding; the reasons for embarking upon research are always relevant to any conclusions that such research draws. Finally, an academic community has to be characterised by voice and not exit. If, for example, we disagree with the aims or the conclusions of some piece of work: say, the genetic cloning experiments carried out on sheep in the UK, then it is not enough just to not take part in that work, or to resign from the research group. Education and research require justification which can only be found in a freedom of 'voice' and not 'exit'.

But, of course, we can also think of instrumental characteristics of education which do relate to market norms. Academia is a sphere where the market does have a role to play. Education must be firmly placed within (the somewhat nebulous realm of) civil society.

> Civil society includes markets, profit-making firms, nonprofit institutions such as hospitals and schools, professional associations and labor unions, political parties and action groups, and philanthropic and ideal-based organizations. Although the state may regulate and even fund these institutions, individuals pursue their own purposes in them, which are defined by internal institutional ideals and functions rather than by state fiat. And though individuals may engage in market transactions in their non-market institutional – or role-given capacities, their activities are not and should not be comprehensively governed by market norms. The scope of the market is limited by other roles and institutions in civil society.
> (Anderson, 1993, p. 147)

Academics, for instance, pursue understanding, and performance is judged in this field by the standard of understanding which academics have, rather than by external criteria such as the profitability of research. When academics adhere to this ideal or goal of understanding, opportunities for making money can be passed by. However, when professionals, such as teachers, lecturers or researchers sell their services, there is a danger that market norms conflict with their professional norms of excellence: consider the pressures on an examiner to pass weak students whose fees pay for examiners:

> The goods internal to these professions become *partially commodified*. Pluralism does not repudiate such mixed practices. Sphere differentiation should not be confused with complete sphere segregation. The freedom of professionals to sell their services promotes equality of opportunity and

autonomy. Achieving excellence in the professions is a full-time activity. If professionals could not be paid for their work, only independently wealthy people would be able to pursue it.

(Anderson, 1993, p. 147)

So, limiting the market is not so simple as naming spheres that either can or cannot be. Rather, setting boundaries to the market requires a very fine tuning that cannot be done from some kind of Archimedean point. Instead, what is required is a critical debate within the sphere of education on where the limits of the market should lie. Unfortunately, the norms of the market prevent such debate from taking place on a wide-ranging scale; the instrumental reason that dominates the market is hardly oriented towards a critical reflection. The debate, it seems, will have to be foisted onto the realm of education in order to begin to appraise just what it is that education, learning, research and training are for in contemporary society.

Chapter 8

Implications for policy and practice

Here, I examine some of the practical problems associated with a state bureaucracy that is attempting to transform into a market bureaucracy. The details focus on the situation in England, but the broader issues will pertain to any higher education system that moves from an independent situation (that I have tried to characterise as 'publicly orientated') into a state dominated system, and then into a marketised system.

The expansion of the universities, in terms of student numbers, has brought with it the notion that access to higher education is no longer a privilege but a right held by all those capable of benefiting from a university education. This is anachronistic because everyone is potentially capable of benefiting from higher education. It is, in the main, this shift which brings higher education into the realm of schooling. The difference between holding a right to schooling and a right to a university education is that the latter (if we can talk loosely of rights here) must be tied to academic ability. The present agenda to 'widen access' into our universities is misplaced insofar as it forces universities to do the work that schools have failed to do. For instance, classes in remedial grammar and communication are now available in many universities, while compulsory courses in information technology oriented towards transferable skills are pitched below the standard that many undergraduates achieved at school. Widening access to higher education to those who, traditionally, would not have attended university undermines the good of higher education if the students concerned lack the necessary intellectual capabilities. Allowing 'non-conventional' students to participate in higher education is to be welcomed but not to the extent that this infringes what came to be known as the Robbins principle: that 'courses of higher education should be available for all those who are qualified by ability and attainment to pursue them and wish to do so' (Robbins, 1963, p. 8). This applies in equal measure to those students who come from the kind of social background where attending university is considered normal and is, in fact, expected. Many of the difficulties which universities currently face, especially those institutions which tend not to engage in research and instead operate almost exclusively on the basis of teaching undergraduates, stem from problems in schooling which universities, as remedial educational institutions, are being called on to rectify. It makes much more sense to abandon this and to focus instead on resolving problems in schools and further education colleges. There is, however, a role for widening access to universities. Of course, higher education ought not to be the preserve of young, affluent, white men and women. But, the task of widening access to higher learning should not be undertaken at the expense of the quality of education on offer. It is, after all, plausible that universities could, and often do, educate people from all sorts of social class backgrounds while retaining the idea that higher education is about fostering intellectual excellence.

In part we are witnessing the side-effects of higher education expansion alongside under-investment in the universities. Just as soon as the state decided that it should oversee the regulation of the universities' performance in return for public funds it faced problems in planning, and the imposition of a quasi-market attempts to side step those planning problems. The Education Reform Act of 1988 created the Universities Funding Council (UFC) and the Polytechnics and Colleges Funding Council (PCFC); these bodies gave statutory institutional form to the regulation of higher education for the first time (Salter and Tapper, 2000, p. 74). These funding councils were expected to monitor performance in higher education institutions and to specify what these institutions should provide in exchange for state funding. This brought the idea of quality assurance directly into higher education. However, the problem then, which remains now, is how to relate the principle of quality assurance to practice. As Salter and Tapper put it:

> Initially the politicians and bureaucrats had placed faith in performance indicators as the means for establishing the accountability relationship . . . desired between cost and quality (of which the RAE is an outstanding example) but despite the growth of an official industry on the subject in the late 1980s and the early 1990s no consensus emerged on what the key indicators were and how they could best be related to funding. The key shift in direction came with the realization that in its approach to regulation it might be more in the state's interest to focus on the *process* of teaching rather than its *outcomes* in the form of performance indicators. Such a focus allows the state to encroach directly on to the academic territory of knowledge transmission, to argue for its own definitions of standards and to organize its monitoring activities accordingly. Perhaps most importantly, the range of possible state interventions is expanded to include not only funding adjustments but also changes in academic practice.
> (Salter and Tapper, 2000, p. 75)

It should come as no surprise that the regulation of universities, via performance indicators which focus on outputs, has been controversial, since the performance indicators direct the universities' activities rather than merely reflecting the most efficient or effective university.

The popular performance indicators have remained more or less unchanged over two decades. They allow for comparisons to be made across the university sector and include: 'unit costs', that is the expenditure on academic departments per full-time student; the percentage of students who fail to complete their degree course; the percentage of graduates who attain first or upper-second class degrees; the percentage of graduates unemployed or in short-term work six months after graduation; research grants per full-time academic; and the average research ratings across all departments (Johnes and Taylor, 1990, pp. 10–11). As we might expect, the devil is in the detail: the manner in which performance indicators are interpreted is central. However, the indicators are left to speak for themselves and left for prospective students to interpret.

This, though, is not the main concern here. What is worrying is the tendency to steer institutions via performance indicators without holding on to an idea of the purposes of universities. In other words, it is insufficient, in terms of effectiveness, to present performance indicators on university outputs without a clear conception of what universities' outputs ought to be. The prospective student as a potential customer determines the idea of the university. The purposes of the university are, of course, multifarious and many of these purposes are not particularly amenable to measurement in terms of outputs. We cannot measure, for example, an academic ethic cultivated in students and staff, only some of the possible results of such an ethic. So, audit schemes, like the Research Excellence Framework (REF) in the UK, count publications. But, more publications do not equate to 'more academic ethic', especially in the context of the REF. Rather, more publications might point to an instrumental response to the audit at the expense of an academic ethic guided by the participants in the scholarly or scientific community.

While the REF (and the Research Assessment Exercises [RAE] before it) has had a large impact upon academic life in Britain, it is the proposed but ill-defined Teaching Excellence Framework and teaching quality assurance which more closely resembles Foucault's portrayal of education and the process of examinations as a disciplining military camp:

> The superimposition of the power relations and knowledge relations assumes in the examination all its visible brilliance. It is yet another innovation of the classical age that the historians of science have left unexplored. People write the history of experiments on those born blind, on wolf-children or under hypnosis. But who will write the more general, more fluid, but also more determinant history of the 'examination' – its rituals, its methods, its characters and their roles, its play of questions and answers, its systems of marking and classification? For in this slender technique are to be found a whole domain of knowledge, a whole type of power.
>
> (Foucault, 1991, p. 185)

The arrival of the TEF brings with it an examination of the examiners and their exams through a variety of metrics and outputs. The recent history of higher education is mirrored in the ideological struggle played out over quality assurance in teaching. On the one hand, we have the bureaucratic state with its emphasis on the economic ideology of the university – whereby universities take as their purpose a functional role for economic growth. On the other hand, we have the liberal idea of the university – vaguely subscribed to by the majority of academics, though apparently without an inherent logic capable of delivering the goods promised by the economic ideology of higher education.

Quality assurance in teaching was a major theme in the 1991 White Paper, *Higher Education: a New Framework*, which introduced the triumvirate of quality control (internal institutional mechanisms for monitoring and maintaining quality), quality audit (external scrutiny of quality control mechanisms) and quality assessment (external assessment of teaching in institutions). A year later the Higher Education Act 1992 established the new higher education funding councils, which were required to assess the quality of education provided in the institutions they fund (Salter and Tapper, 2000, p. 75). Following the requirements of the 1992 Act the funding councils established the Quality Assessment Committee (QAC), charged with providing the funding councils with the information on quality required. Here was a body specifically established to promote quality assurance, on behalf of the state, in terms of efficiency and management. Now, the 'buffer' of the Higher Education Funding Council which stood between the state and the universities is to go, to be replaced by the Office for Students, which will combine the roles of the funding council, the Office for Fair Access and the Office of the Independent Adjudicator. Stefan Collini noted wryly that the role of the student has indeed transformed from the radical stereotype of the late 1960s into the customer who will ensure good value from feckless academics (Collini, 2016).

Within higher education the CVCP's Jarratt Report of 1985 had inquired into the uses of performance indicators as a means to monitor and assure quality within higher education. However, the Reynolds Report of 1986 on academic standards and quality still hankered after the liberal idea of learning. It argued that:

> To make the statement that 'This system is better than that one' requires an explicit and exclusive determination of the purposes of higher education and a universally-applied blueprint of entry criteria, of teaching and assessment processes, and of classification procedures which would be to adopt an unacceptably extreme position.
> (Salter and Tapper, 2000, p. 76)

The universities' attempts, through the CVCP (now called Universities UK), to challenge a bureaucratic model of quality assurance, were, however, weak. The worry was that without some form of credible self-regulation, the universities would find themselves subjected to external inspection by the state in some form. It was in the light of this that the Higher Education Quality Council (HEQC) was formed in 1992 by a combination of the CVCP, the Committee of Directors of Polytechnics, the Conference of Scottish Centrally Funded Colleges and the Standing Conference of Principals.

So, according to Salter and Tapper, by 1992 we had the HEQC working on quality assurance on behalf of the higher education institutions and the QAC promoting quality assurance on behalf of the state:

> The HEQC, chosen champion of the higher education institutions . . . had the interesting problem of creating a justification for a form of self-regulation which . . . would not be state-sponsored. On the other side, the HEFCs and the Department for Education (DFE), as it became in 1992, having established the statutory legitimation for state involvement in higher education governance, had now to deliver it. It was to be a new type of political contest characterized by competition for the control of as yet unborn concepts and techniques set in the context of the familiar ideological stand-off between the traditional ideal and the economic ideology of education.
>
> (Salter and Tapper, 2000, p. 76)

The tendency was for HEQC to offer guidelines which stressed the importance of autonomy within higher education institutions. Accountability vis-à-vis teaching and learning was to be rendered by audit of institutional quality assurance mechanisms carried out by knowledgeable and impartial peers. In other words, HEQC proposed an internalist solution. The TEF proposes overturning this in part. The Green Paper *Fulfilling Our Potential* (BIS, 2015) suggests that the TEF ought to change higher education providers' behaviour, allowing institutions which are successful in the TEF exercise to raise tuition fees beyond the present £9,000 ceiling and allowing the less successful institutions to make way for new entrants into the higher education sector. The basic idea seems to be to transform the higher education sector into something resembling a contestable market by lowering barriers to entry and exit.

With hindsight it seems obvious that the old regime would not suffice for the state bureaucracy, especially given the lengths it had already gone towards in establishing disciplinary institutions and processes via the higher education funding councils, which were determined to make their mark. Moreover, the established methods for ensuring shared standards throughout higher education, the external examiner system, was coming under increasing pressures: increased workload for examiners, little reward for work done and heightened attention on their activities thanks to the state's focus on quality assurance. The attempt to retain an internalist system of quality assurance soon collapsed to be replaced by a state-mollifying system which placed more emphasis upon external controls:

> When in the summer of 1994 the then Secretary of State [for Education] John Patten invited the CVCP and the SCOP to give greater attention to the 'broad comparability of standards' in higher education, HEQC responded by

setting up the Graduate Standards Programme and, in so doing, announced its intention to move to a new definition of self-regulation where the internal, individual professional definition of standards would be replaced by one which was external and corporately professional.

(Salter and Tapper, 2000, p. 77)

This change in emphasis was compounded by an increasingly systematised organisation of teaching through modularisation, the idea of credit accumulation and transfer (CAT), and relating the curricula to the future employment needs of students. These developments pointed towards a system designed to provide employers with a skilled graduate workforce, where universities faced the tricky task of balancing the requirements of students, who had now apparently acquired a right to a certain threshold of university education, employers who expected a certain level of competence in their new graduate employees and taxpayers, who apparently demanded to pay as little tax as possible in return for a university system which would deliver high rates of economic growth. Of course, all of the connections being made in this scenario are, to some degree, spurious. In the ideological struggle between universities and the state it was the latter which seemed to hold the better cards. So, for instance, while the HEQC engaged in monitoring quality assurance systems, it was the funding councils' QACs which assessed teaching directly through TQA. Moreover, it was the funding councils which held the power of financial sanction over higher education: 'The political range of the HEQC's discourse and hence its ability to influence the governance agenda was therefore limited by the scope of its institutional responsibilities' (Salter and Tapper, 2000, p. 79). And hence the political initiative rested with the funding councils and the state. Now, of course, we see the culmination of this process as the funding council vanishes, removing any semblance of a buffer between the universities and the state.

However, it was not until after a Joint Planning Group set up by the CVCP and the funding councils made its report in 1996 and the Dearing Report of 1997 recommended a single body to police standards in higher education that the Quality Assurance Agency was established. Martin Trow pointed out that:

> The creation of national bodies with common criteria across the board flows naturally from an inability to accept genuine diversity of institutions – of form, function, and standard – in British higher education. Nowhere is this seen more clearly than in the [Dearing] Report's recommendation for yet another national agency, the Quality Assurance Agency. . . . On Dearing's recommendation, this agency would create and manage a 'strengthened external examiner system' to enforce a system of common standards across all institutions and departments. This renewed commitment to a 'gold standard' of 'quality' reminds us of King Canute's firm instructions to the incoming tide. A common standard of performance and achievement does not exist in British higher education today, and has not for many years, if it ever has. . . . The issue is not whether standards in one place are

higher or lower in another, but rather that they are so profoundly different that they cannot be measured against the same yardstick. And that is the essence of mass higher education. It is not that the myriad courses and programmes that are offered in British colleges and universities cannot be assessed, but they can only be assessed against their own criteria, and by people close to them who can know what these criteria are and how they are being pursued.

(Trow, 1998, p. 111)

According to Trow, the QAA was the institutionalisation of a principle appropriate to an elite university system but cannot be made to fit a mass higher education system. So we see here that those who designed the QAA were at once operating with an everyday *lebenswelt* understanding of universities, derived from some normative background conviction of what a university system ought to be like, and attempting to apply this to the mass higher education system of the late twentieth century. Although the QAA was supposed to represent a strengthening of the external examiner system, it is not, in fact, controlled by academics. Despite the fact that the QAA involves examiners or 'academic reviewers' who 'should be academics of high standing and integrity who are sufficiently specialised within degree disciplines', the QAA itself was not directed by academic interests:

> Of its fourteen directors, four are nominated by the representative bodies of the higher education institutions, four by the Funding Councils and six are independent directors representing the interests of the wider community. So in effect the collective responsibility of the academic community is to be defined and implemented by a body it does not control: a significant loss of power by the academic profession.
>
> (Salter and Tapper, 2000, p. 80)

The QAA, then, marked the end of autonomous universities, and the TEF takes the situation even further away from the idea of higher education as a public space, outside of the state. This poses a problem if we subscribe to the democratic view that education concerns itself with the creation of autonomous citizens capable of engaging in a public sphere free from systematic distortion. How can universities develop this sense of autonomy in students if those who teach are not themselves their own legislators in terms of what they teach and how they teach?

The functionary intellectual and the purposes of scholarship

In 'The Present Crisis of the Universities' Zygmunt Bauman questions the role of knowledge and the place of the contemporary university at the centre of society, undertaking functions in terms of legitimating power and shaping people to perform socially assigned roles. Bauman's argument is that the university's authority has been undermined on two fronts. On the one hand, the state has 'has ceded most of the integrative functions it claimed in modern times to forces which it does not control and which are by and large exempt from political process' (Bauman, 1997, p. 48). In short, the contemporary state has given over control to market forces. This has meant that the authority of the universities to generate and disseminate knowledge is being contested by other agencies. In terms of knowledge and those who produce it, reputation is no longer made within the universities and reliant on the judgement of academic peers. Instead, reputations are managed by public relations experts; standards of scholarly significance have reduced in significance (Bauman, 1997, p. 48). We see this, for instance, in situations where scholarly norms have begun to shift as academic journals adopt metrics based on social media tweets and expertise becomes a synonym for media broadcasting experience. Normative standards from outside of universities come to be adopted by those within.

The second front is not unrelated to the first. The university's *sui generis* role in forming cultural values is no longer tenable. Bauman attributes this to the recession of cultural universality. In their role as value-creators, universities compete with other agencies more adept at managing publicity and addressing themselves to consumers of news and information. In terms of developing the capacity to act in the public realm, individuals may be better placed to learn within an advertising agency than a university.

So, within the university system we have witnessed the undermining of the academic community's own judgement, which has been displaced by research ratings decided upon by the state's research councils and based upon bibliometric methods of valuing research. In other words, the funding councils have begun to attempt to measure the productivity of university researchers and have tried to make qualitative assessments of this research based upon publication. Now Lord Stern[1] has conducted an inquiry into the administration of the REF to try to determine whether it offers good value. In teaching too the universities no longer uphold their own scholarly standards. Instead, teaching processes are monitored, supposedly, by the QAA and TEF.

Much has been made of the claim that a university degree confers private economic advantages, largely in terms of future income, to those individuals who hold one. Much research into a comparison of private and social rates of return to higher education has been undertaken (see McMahon, 2009 and McGettigan, 2013 for detail). However, whilst tables which purport to show the private versus the social gains attached to a degree have influenced policy-makers, the data that have been used to construct such private and social added-values are necessarily based on past graduate earnings. Moreover, the notion that social or private rates of return can be readily measured seems doubtful. Whilst private returns can be accounted for through increased salaries, individual enlightenment should be more difficult to rate. Social and public rates of return to higher education will be determined by more nebulous criteria, these could be under-estimated and any rate ascribed to social returns will be more a judgement than a measurement. What all this ignores is how the meaning of a degree has changed and how the meanings of a degree in dentistry and a degree in sociology will have markedly different meanings for both society at large and the individuals who hold these degrees. So, on the one hand, the meaning of a degree shifts over different subject areas, and on the other hand, the meaning of a degree has evidently shifted over time. It is quite plausible to suggest that the arrival of a mass higher education system may not mean a drastic reduction in the quality of degrees, but the private gains attached to graduation will be very different for a 2010s social science graduate when compared to a 1960s social science graduate. Nonetheless, it was this argument that the benefits of a university education accrue in the main to the individual which was used to justify the introduction of and increases in tuition fees and means-tested loans in place of grants for undergraduates. But this argument looks rather frail. If we set aside the problem of economic advantage accruing solely to the individual (whilst some individuals certainly do benefit, there are gains for society more broadly to be had from an educated or trained membership), there are still problems. For instance, a post-industrial economy demands a highly trained workforce. But it is this same technological revolution that demands high-level skills which renders these skills ever more short-lived. Professional training and short, flexible courses become more attractive than a university education as the skills in demand by employers change and update. We see in England, for example, training courses for new teachers moving away from theoretical knowledge provided by universities and replaced with practical skills practised in schools. University student numbers remain high largely because of systemic under-employment (Bauman, 1997, p. 49).

It is just this situation which has forced universities along a path which caters primarily for employers. If a spell at university is attractive to students because it can stave off unemployment or underemployment, then it is hardly surprising that universities, in an era of mass higher education, are so keen to make suggestions of promises around employability and offering experience of 'leadership' to all. Higher education is understood, from the vantage point of the policy-makers, as a lubricant to the labour market, and universities don't seem to mind how they are understood so long as they receive increased funding. The costs involved in this scenario are numerous and they tend to fall on the weakest.

Firstly, individual students, graduates and their families have to shoulder the immediate costs such as university tuition fees and payments to cover the cost of living. Undergraduate students now fund themselves through a combination of parental financial contributions, loans (normally from the Student Loans Company at preferential interest rates – which further benefit more affluent students since this money can be borrowed at a minimal cost and invested at a higher rate of return), part-time work, personal savings or perhaps through a partner's income. The idea that the costs are borne by the individual is problematic. Whilst, in formal terms, loan repayments are subject to graduates' earnings, the reality for those students who have no independent wealth is that they are supported and support themselves through a network of different sources. Frequently, part-time work compromises students' academic work and substantial debts upon graduation are regarded as normal. Although the current funding of undergraduate study is not supposed to discourage students from low-income families, in some respects this is simply impossible. In relation to student funding in the United States of America, Amy Gutmann points out the general fact that:

> One might argue that universities cannot help but discriminate against students from poor families, because the short-term costs of going to college are so great. The costs include not only tuition, room, and board, but also the income forgone from not getting a job. . . . As long as a college education is costly in this sense, students from poor families are less likely to apply to college than equally able students from rich families, even if they have a good chance of getting a full scholarship if admitted and of earning more money after graduation. The greater short-run sacrifices, which are certain, are likely to overwhelm the greater long-run gains, which are only probable.
> (Gutmann, 1999, p. 222)

Gutmann's last point here hints at an important issue which is ignored in the funding formulae. This is simply that students (and their families) from a poorer background will almost certainly have a different attitude towards debt compared to families from higher income brackets. So, regardless of income-related tuition fees and maintenance loans, students from less affluent families could be averse to the thought of borrowing money against the possibility of higher future earnings. Indeed, this seems quite reasonable. The argument that there are future financial rewards to be had from the earning power of a university degree is based on historical evidence under conditions where the meaning of a university education was radically different. Until relatively recently only a small minority of people gained a university degree. These lucky few were usually rewarded with higher earnings, but they had developed a *specialism*. The problem with this idea of a specialism, or an expertise, is that it is a relative quantity. Nowadays more people hold degrees and it is widely suspected by employers, probably quite justifiably, that a university education is not now what it once was. In Britain, the accountancy firm EY and Penguin Books no longer insist on prospective employees holding degrees. The reality of the university experience for many students is often large classes taught by postgraduates, and inadequately stocked libraries. Education, though, is monitored by state (or quasi-state) agencies in order to ensure that standards are kept high. This, of course, has a perverse effect. The quality assurance mechanisms are all pervasive in their effects upon universities. But they are policy tools from Kafka's Castle. Teaching becomes reduced to a method of knowledge delivery. In research, publication, so long as it is with a sufficiently prestigious publisher or journal, is an end in itself. And the academic with a good track-record for bidding successfully for grants from research councils, government departments, industry or the European Union is a sought after commodity, regardless of the quality of his or her teaching and research.

This leads to the second cost-bearer: the universities themselves. Here, the costs can be counted in terms of higher ratios of students to staff, decreased funding in relation to numbers of students, an increased prevalence of short-term contracts for academics, increased administration resulting from teaching quality assessment and a requirement to publish frequent articles thanks to the bibliometric REF. Overall, the costs of higher education expansion, insofar as it has been implemented in a utilitarian fashion, have been detrimental to scholarship and the academic ethic.

There has been concern over the idea of trying to determine levels of scholarship. For example, academics were asked: how much time should be devoted to scholarship? Such a question illustrates a central misconception which underlines a bigger problem. Scholarship is not something that people *do* from time to time in some universities. Rather, it is an attitude, an ethic of working. This, however, is problematic for the state and its agencies, which wish to monitor universities. Scholarship cannot readily be measured, directly at least. It is more an attitude of operating in good faith. It implies diligence in terms of work, and modesty in terms of the results which are claimed from that work. This, unfortunately, opposes the kind of dramaturgical attitudes encouraged by state agencies which seek to measure, rank and record such qualities in a bid to make the academy accountable. However, academics are already accountable to their own communities' standards of scholarship, in much the same way that the scientist has to lay bare his or her work before peers. But, the bibliometric style of the research audit pressurises academics to publish their work in time for the next article count, so undermining scholarly standards. Professor Peter Higgs, the Nobel laureate who discovered the Higgs boson particle, even admitted that he thought he would struggle to get a job in a university nowadays (Aitkenhead, 2013). Academics are rewarded if they can sell their ideas or knowledge to a broad audience. What is implied here is the 'uselessness' of the academic. So, research councils build in to their grant awarding 'impact' criteria that research should be of value to a wider audience than merely other academic researchers working in the same field. This, of course, encourages a scholarly, entrepreneurial attitude amongst some. But the logic of this is to denigrate the worth of scholarship in and for itself, and to encourage the rise of a kind of academic salesman. It engenders the values of the *agora* rather than the *polis*. Scholarship here is valued not according to the internal standards of a scholarly community, but instead in terms of the breadth of appeal that research findings have. We can see here that the intention is to try to break down the perception of the ivory tower and for academics to engage with a broader public. Certainly, this is a good thing. The problem arises when a researcher's audience acquires the role of a consumer and, to be sure, this is implicit in the research councils' methods for allocating funding. Here, Ronald Barnett is insightful:

> Discursively, the university is situated in society more than ever. It takes on an increasing spread of the discourses of the wider society. In so doing, it plays its part in shaping those discourses through all the main activities of the university. The university cannot help but be discursively implicated in society. This discursive implicatedness, this entanglement in society's discourses at once reduces the critical scope available to the university and expands it. . . . Students are expected to show that they can perform in various ways and to be self-reflective and in control of themselves. But the instrumental, the technological and the performative are liable to squeeze out the hermeneutic, the liberal and the contemplative. The possibilities for critical thought are not being extinguished but they are reducing. Critical thought becomes defined by interests in promoting effectiveness, economy and control. Reflection that modifies practices and thinking towards those ends is acceptable, indeed welcome. . . . But the university neither needs to nor should allow the newer definitions of critical thought to be construed and practised in this way. It does not need to do so precisely because there are new demands for self-monitoring, self-critique and self-agency. This spirit of reflexivity could be interpreted through the perspective of instrumental reason, such that self-critique is a means for promoting technological change (understood broadly), or it could be interpreted as a vehicle for emancipatory ends. Higher education, therefore, has a choice: does it sponsor reflexivity for instrumental or for emancipatory ends?
>
> (Barnett, 1997a, p. 44)

To some extent Barnett's prognosis seems slightly naive. Why, for instance, cannot emancipatory ends include instrumental reason? Emancipation as a conceptual category should include, but delimit, instrumentalism. Instrumental and emancipatory ends are not mutually exclusive. Moreover, this reflexivity that Barnett refers to is particularly shallow insofar as it focuses inwards on the self: how can *I* act more effectively in these circumstances, not how can I transform these circumstances? It is a responsive rather than an active form of critical thinking. Barnett recognises this impoverished conception of reflexivity but plays down the width of the gap between instrumental critical thought as a set of techniques to be employed by individuals modifying their actions in the face of heteronomous circumstance and the idea of a culture of critical discourse which is both more broadly construed and values critical discourse in itself. According to Barnett the task of expanding the horizon of this reflexivity beyond an instrumental attitude towards a communicatively rational-critical discourse is possible because this responsive reflexivity is already encouraged. However, we should remain more skeptical. A culture of critical discourse does not logically flow from instrumental reflexivity. Rather, the relationship lies in the other direction. To explain: individuals could, of course, develop this individualised reflexivity under conditions which favour emancipation, but emancipation does not necessarily flow from individuals being encouraged to question their actions and established practices. What seems to be at odds here is an instrumental view of university education set against the discursive conditions under which scholarship can exist and breathe.

This resonates with an argument made by Charles Taylor on politics and deliberation (Taylor, 1980). Here Taylor argues that the central problems of our politics are the primacy of the individual subject and our instrumental orientation in thinking about politics. For Taylor, this conception of politics screens out 'Any view of the political community, its structures and practices, where what is important is the quality of common life they embody' (Taylor, 1980, p. 78). It is precisely this problem we see with universities. Due to the instrumental view that we tend to take on when we think of universities, we screen out the quality of life they embody. Moreover, it is the state's attempt to measure this quality of life that is, in a large part, undermining that which it wishes to sustain. In an attempt to ensure the accountability of academia to the state, which in part foots its bill, the state de-legitimises that which it seeks to hold accountable.

Let's examine this point in more detail. The university has a variety of purposes, but focuses on two central goals. Firstly, people within the university undertake research. Secondly, people within the university teach students. In practice, these activities are distinct. As Karl Jaspers points out, there is no connection between good research and good teaching. Some individuals who have produced groundbreaking findings within the realm of their research find teaching difficult. Similarly, some people make excellent teachers but incompetent researchers (Jaspers, 1960). But, the point here is rather empty. Conceptually, teaching and research are not entirely distinct. For things to be taught, they must first have been researched, though not necessarily by the same individual. So, universities involve teaching and research, or the development and the dissemination of knowledge. Universities also form relationships with local communities. The purposes of universities, though, are not synonymous with their functions. Teaching is undertaken for reasons. For example, one reason might be the education of future holders of office, as Amy Gutmann puts it; in other words, students are educated to prepare them for work. Another reason for teaching might concern the symbolic reproduction of a lifeworld. We are taught, and teach, not only so we can labour more efficiently, but also so that we might pass on the world from one generation to the next, and alleviate the sense of 'throwness' that the uneducated will encounter in going into the world. In this context, teaching loses its instrumental purpose and takes on an educative, caring role, modelled on communicative premises and oriented towards understanding in common. Such a role for teaching is fundamental. Without this communicative mode instrumental teaching would not be possible. Instrumental or strategic action therefore depends on the priority of communicative action. In this example, we can say that teaching for the purposes of understanding must be prior to the training of students in skills. The same can be said for research. Not all research can be recognised as immediately useful. Indeed, the implication of Thomas Kuhn's work on scientific revolutions is that important work that falls outside of the contemporary paradigm will not gain the recognition it deserves (Kuhn, 1970). This is a central problem with the idea of markets in knowledge, or with universities being encouraged to pursue research which will be of value to research users. The beauty of research is that it concerns, to greater and lesser extents, finding something new, the value of which is unknown. This understanding of research, however, clashes with a purposive-rational understanding of research which aims to apply knowledge to a specific end through efficient means.

But new ideas or theories or inventions are also regarded with suspicion and fear. Zygmunt Bauman, for example, points out that Foucault's well-worn connection between the development of scientific discourse and ever-tightening surveillance meant that scientific advances are charged with leading to constraint and dependency. In its broad form, the idea goes back to Rousseau on the corruption caused by the development of the arts and sciences. However, the enthusiasm with which social scientists have taken up Foucault's connection between science and loss of freedom has undermined the claim of universities to social resources and public authority (Bauman, 1997, p. 50).

Now, I am not sure that this point is so widely accepted. After all, we can turn to the justifications for charging tuition fees to undergraduates to illustrate that knowledge or training in skills can lead to a career which brings with it individual well-being. The science parks, bio-technology centres and business incubators which have sprung up around universities also show us that at least some kinds of knowledge are still regarded as beneficial. What we have witnessed is a twist in the chain linking knowledge and well-being. There is, no longer, any assumed link between knowledge-acquisition and moral refinement. What has been connected are some forms of specialist knowledge and individual or institutional earning power.

Referring to higher education expansion in the 1950s and 60s rather than the present, Bauman explains that an attempt was made to justify the legitimacy of the university on grounds of social equity. Opening up universities would distribute the privileges enjoyed by the elite (Bauman, 1997, p. 50). We have seen in the latter half of the twentieth century the expansion of higher education institutions has largely benefited young people from middle class backgrounds, and the benefits are diluted.

Of course, the idea that expansion spreads benefits misses the connection between 'the privilege-bestowing potential and the scarcity of the good. University education did confer privilege as long (and because) it remained elitist; the idea of "universally shared privilege" is blatantly a contradiction in terms' (Bauman, 1997, p. 50). So, what we are left with might be characterised in terms of what Ronald Dore called the qualification-escalation ratchet in *The Diploma Disease*. His illustration of the problem using bus conductors and clerks applies just as well, I would argue, to degrees, degree classifications and higher degrees.

Just look, for instance, at the high numbers of people willing to pay for MBA qualifications, the value of which rests on the (previous) scarcity of the qualification as well as on the skills developed in students on these courses.

> The way the qualification-escalation ratchet works is roughly like this. A bus company may 'normally' require a junior secondary leaving certificate for £5-a week bus conductors and a senior secondary leaving certificate for its £7-a week clerks. But as the number of senior certificate leavers grows far larger than the number of clerkships that are available, some of them decide that £5 a week as a bus conductor is better than nothing at all. The bus company gives them preference. Soon all the available conductor slots are filled by senior certificate holders: a senior certificate has become a necessary qualification for the job.
>
> (Dore, 1976, p. 5)

This problem is apparent in the social sciences today. Look, for example, to the numbers of doctoral students in economics (relatively low numbers) compared with sociology. There are unclaimed studentships in some branches of the natural sciences and engineering. The Arts and Humanities Research Board has no such problem. What we are witnessing is a shift in how knowledge is socially valued. On the one hand, graduates from the 'hard' sciences can command reasonably high starting salaries from private-sector employers. To compete with these salaries, the Wellcome Trust set its studentship stipend at a much higher level than any of the state research councils. On the other hand, many graduates from the arts and humanities believe that higher degrees, which are often self-financed, are more likely to result in securing a good job. In order to make their own graduates more employable, most universities place a heavy emphasis upon key or transferable skills, like working in a team, since this is something that employers have thought their graduate employees lacked. However, the idea of a transferable skill is contested. Is a skill not, for instance, closely related to the context in which it is practised? If a skill can be employed in a variety of different situations then it is likely to not be a skill at all. Not, at least, a specialist skill requiring a university training. It can be called into question whether universities can even teach 'interpersonal skills', for example. The ways in which we relate to others are surely, by and large, a result of much wider processes of socialisation, or perhaps even inherent personality traits. But such a skill is certainly not something which can be delivered in a classroom.

This, however, is an aside. It remains that universities have to re-think their role in the world.

> One obvious strategy is to accept the new rules and play the game accordingly. In practice, this means to submit to the stern criteria of the market: usefulness measured by the presence of 'clearing demand.' To treat the know-how universities may offer as one commodity that still has to fight for a place on overcrowded supermarket shelves. . . . The entitlement of the

knowledge-bearers to claim superiority for their judgments over those of the supply-and-demand game are questioned and assaulted from inside the academia. In a desperate attempt to make a virtue out of the necessity, or to steal the thunder, intellectuals downgraded by the market competition convert into zealous promoters of market criteria in university life. . . . Spiritual leadership is a mirage; the task of the intellectuals is to follow the world out there, not to legislate for the standards of propriety, truth and good taste.

(Bauman, 1997, p. 51)

The alternative academic strategy is to retreat from the populist sphere of the market into the realm of the esoteric. This withdrawal is not always viable. Bauman argues that a country like the United States, densely populated with academic professionals, could and does support such a move. However, both of these strategies abdicate the universities' traditional role as central and autonomous institutions in intellectual work (Bauman, 1997, p. 52). As a possible alternative for the university, Bauman turns to the idea of the intellectual.

The notion of the intellectual in the university

It seems that the university is doomed either to the role of servant of the market or the state, on the one hand, or to become an irrelevance in the face of overwhelming systemic pressures. However, we should not lose sight of the importance of the autonomous university to a democratic society: 'Universities are the main, perhaps the sole, institutional focus for the gathering and self-reproducing and rejuvenating of the forces of any society – and thus their crisis is by necessity also the crisis of intellectual powers in general' (Bauman, 1997, p. 52). What, though, is meant by the intellectual? It is, after all, a contentious term.

Bauman argues that the idea of the intellectual derives its meaning from two assumptions. Firstly, he argues that intellectuals, whether artists, academics, writers or lawyers of distinction share a common attribute. The understanding they hold enables them to act as guardians of truth (although they may very well disagree with each other):

They have a *right*, therefore, to bring the enormous public deference in which they are held on the account of their professional achievements, to bear on their standing in the public matters of general interest and concern: they have the right to speak with authority on questions not directly entailed in their specialist credentials.

(Bauman, 1997, pp. 52–53)

Secondly, and connectedly, taking up a position on issues of public policy

becomes a *duty* of such persons whenever the politicians, the professional managers of the public arena, fail in their care. As a group, the intellectuals hold *responsibility for monitoring and scrutinizing the actions of the appointed wardens of public values; and an obligation* to intervene if they find those actions below standard.

(Bauman, 1997, p. 53)

The intellectual, then, has the ability and the will to transcend his or her own particular interests and specialism to act as the collective conscience: 'Being an intellectual means *performing a peculiar role* in the life of society' (Bauman, 1997, p. 53).

This role, to be sure, has historically been connected with the university and, indeed, other professions such as journalism. Even the intellectual is not completely autonomous though. He or she is not entirely independent from those institutions for which he or she works. As Edward Said notes:

> [G]roups of individuals are aligned with institutions and derive power and authority from those institutions. As the institutions either rise or fall in ascendancy, so too do their organic intellectuals. . . . [T]he question remains as to whether there is or can be anything like an independent, autonomously functioning intellectual, one who is not beholden to, and therefore constrained, by his or her affiliations with universities that pay salaries, political parties that demand loyalty to a party line, think tanks that while they offer freedom to do research perhaps more subtly compromise judgment and restrain the critical voice.
>
> (Said, 1994, pp. 50–51)

I have argued that higher education is an increasingly inhospitable setting for the intellectual: as universities are further bureaucratised, research becomes more specialised and orients itself towards research audits and grants for specific projects or themes from private industry, the state or European Union and the research councils; and teaching becomes dominated by administrative requirements for quality assurance purposes, and even the subject matter of what is taught is influenced by the economic ideology of education. So, can we retain a plausible idea of the intellectual as an individual voice, as the guardian of truth and objectivity? A realistic answer is that an intellectual has always been a rather rare figure. The intellectual, as characterised here, is heroic in her stance against power. However, we should not push this into a caricature:

> To accuse all intellectuals of being sellouts just because they earn their living working in a university or for a newspaper is a coarse and finally meaningless charge. It would be far too indiscriminately cynical to say that the world is so corrupt that everyone ultimately succumbs to mammon. On the other hand, it is scarcely less serious to hold up the intellectual as a perfect ideal, a sort of shining knight who is so pure and so noble as to deflect any suspicion of material interest. . . . The fact is that the intellectual ought neither

to be so uncontroversial and safe a figure as to be just a friendly technician nor should the intellectual try to be a full-time Cassandra, who was not only righteously unpleasant but also unheard.

(Said, 1994, pp. 51–52)

So, for example, Russell Jacoby's *The Last Intellectuals* argued that, in the United States, the non-academic intellectual 'had completely disappeared, leaving no one in that place except a whole bunch of timid and jargon-ridden university dons, to whom no one in the society paid very much attention' (Said, 1994, p. 52). The result of this is that academic intellectuals have retreated into the realms of theoretical exchanges which demand a highly specialised knowledge from the participants. This, of course, infringes Bauman's claim that the intellectual has a duty to engage with the world rather than hide away from it. But we should be wary of the strong claim that the age of the intellectual is passed. Firstly, this overstates the autonomy of the intellectual, who has always been a rare figure anyway. But secondly, it also forces us to think in terms of the intellectual as an individual or a group of people rather than a particular kind of ethic. As Said makes clear, 'the intellectual does not represent a statue-like icon, but an individual vocation, an energy, a stubborn force engaging as a committed and recognisable voice in language and in society with a whole slew of issues, all of them having to do in the end with a combination of enlightenment and emancipation or freedom' (Said, 1994, p. 55).

If the idea of the intellectual is, in fact, a way of acting rather than a dandyish autonomous individual, then the forces ranged against the intellectual are also based around a certain ethic. For Said, the intellectual is threatened by 'professionalism', and the intellectual's response to this should be an amateurism: an activity fuelled by care and attention rather than by profit or personal gain. It seems that in these days of a literal scientisation of politics where public health matters over, for instance, BSE infected meat and genetically modified crops are debated over at a highly technical level by interested specialists from the food industry on the one hand, and environmental pressure groups on the other, the need for the public spirit of the intellectual is urgent. The colonisation of the academic ethic, if it means the withering away of the spirit of the intellectual, may well be a high cost to bear since it involves the demise of rational politics in a democratic sense. The suggestion, then, is that a democratic state ought to pay serious attention to strengthening sources of its own opposition; such a move would be brave but its effects would be democratically dramatic. Universities were intended to protect those who worked within them from external forces; they cannot be improved by simply opening them up to those forces.

Note

1 Nicholas Stern (2016) *Building on Success and Learning from Experience: an Independent Review of the Research Excellence Framework*. Available at https://www.gov.uk/government/uploads/system/uploads/attachment_data/file/541338/ind-16-9-ref-stern-review.pdf

Chapter 9

Towards a modern democratic society

On the concept of corruption, Seumas Miller points out that:

> If the process of corruption proceeds far enough then we no longer have a corrupt official or corruption of an institutional process or institution; we cease to have a person who can properly be described as, say, a judge, or a process that can properly be described as, say, a judicial process – as opposed to proceedings in a kangaroo court. Like a coin that has been bent and defaced beyond recognition, it is no longer a coin; rather it is a piece of scrap metal that can no longer be exchanged for goods.
>
> (Miller, 2011)

A higher education system that has lost sight of its fundamental purpose, or allowed its purpose to be systematically distorted and degraded, bent and defaced, stands in danger of losing its authority. This may well apply to universities which take graduate employment and a consultative model of research (with 'impact') as their central goals and ignore broader epistemic and democratic ends. If authority is power coupled with recognition of legitimacy, then we see in our universities an empirical manifestation of a crisis in educational legitimacy. Corruption is damaging to the good of higher education itself and to matters of sustainability related to education. Miller distinguishes the corrosion of an institution from the corruption of an institution. In the former concept Miller proposes that 'the undermining of institutional processes and/or purposes is not a sufficient condition for institutional corruption. Acts of institutional damage that are not performed by a corruptor and also do not corrupt persons are better characterized as acts of institutional *corrosion*' (Miller, 2011). In the case of corruption, corrupting policy undermines institutional policies and corrupts people working within the institution. There are instances of both corruption and corrosion within contemporary universities which render problematic a rational-reconstructive democratic purpose of the university. By this I mean that an important function of the university is to help foster cultural, cognitive, attitudinal and epistemic conditions which enable a democratic society to flourish.

From the sacred to a profane education

Under the present political conditions, universities are not regarded as an important democratic force which guards against repression. Neither are they, particularly, viewed as institutions which help to create more worldly citizens. Universities are increasingly, however, seen merely as institutions for producing graduates who will be able to function as competent citizens because of the earning power at their command. Those universities more focused on 'widening participation' appear functional in times of labour market expansion, but dysfunctional during periods of increasing unemployment. In terms of research, academics are regarded as consultants, or in the social sciences, as 'think tanks'. This institutional shift can be seen in terms of a move from a sacred to a profane idea of the university (Taylor, 1995). However, at the same time, we ought to be wary of a jeremiad narrative which portrays the structural transformation of the idea of the university in wholly negative terms and looks back in sentimental nostalgia upon some mythical past.

Not so very long ago the university held a special place within the collective social imagination. The university, thanks in part to its priestly origins, was a place for the teaching of universal knowledge. Graduates were men of letters and universities were gatekeepers to many social offices. But when the ancient, revered tradition of the university is invoked we should be wary. While the ancient British universities – Oxford, Cambridge, Edinburgh, Glasgow, St. Andrews and Aberdeen – did constitute something closer to a scholarly community engaged in a timeless conversation within the Great Chain of Being, we should remember that universities today, although they carry the same title, are very different. Peter Scott writes that:

> [U]niversities fulfilled very different purposes from those which are familiar today. They were largely concerned with the training of clergymen and teachers, entwined professions. Their mission, in today's terminology, was to sustain intellectual hegemony, the established Anglican (or Presbyterian) order, not to encourage a progressive science or provide a liberal education. Although members of elite social groups passed through universities, they rarely completed their degrees. The subsidiary mission of the pre-industrial universities was to complete the socialization of future elites, social and political.
>
> (Scott, 1995, p. 12)

In a sense, because most universities in Britain are thoroughly modern, British higher education institutions are trading off the back of a brand image and appealing to an idea which predates the university system. Of course, there would be nothing wrong with this if universities were living up to their own grand ideal, if universities were pursuing their scholarly duties. Amy Gutmann explains that the scholar's responsibility is to maintain autonomous scholarly judgement in the face of influence that may take different forms: 'Financial influences are the most obvious, but not all financial influences are improper' (Gutmann, 1999, p. 178).

Gutmann gives us Louis Pasteur's career as an example. Pasteur often diverted his attention from his work to concentrate on the pressing practical problems of the day. He directed his scientific attention to silk-worm disease, problems in wine-making and beer-brewing and chicken cholera, among other issues. But he did not work as a consultant to silk-worm growers, wine makers, brewers or poultry farmers. Rather, Gutmann tells us, he took a scholarly attitude to his work: he pursued knowledge for the sake of serving society but was independent of the brewers and the rest. He did not confine himself to an ivory tower, but he did not only serve those who could pay for his services. Clearly, if Pasteur took payment from wine producers who, in turn, could interfere with his methods or results, then this would be no more than bribery and would violate Pasteur's scholarly autonomy to exercise his intellectual judgement (Gutmann, 1999, p. 178).

For the most part consulting contracts do not contain such restrictions. But the restriction of research through consultancy can take more a more subtle form. The acceptance, and indeed the encouragement, of academic consultancy leads to a situation where the legitimacy of scholarship is underwritten by new, and less valid, norms. It is the short-termism of a consultancy model of academe, which looks to the immediate future in terms of research impact and fails to employ new academic staff on secure contracts, that marks the coming of the profane, secular university. Gutmann argues that:

> [T]he widespread acceptance of consulting contracts can skew the types of problems that scholars pursue – drawing them away from investigating more serious social problems that have fewer immediate pay-offs or away from equally serious problems that afflict people who cannot afford to hire consultants. Not all types of research contracts interfere with the collective autonomy of scholarship, but many do.
>
> (Gutmann, 1999, pp. 178–179)

And, it can be added, that an academic culture which promotes consultancy, which our current universities certainly do in order, paradoxically, to remain free from the state intervention carried out in the name of accountability, will not be an autonomous academic culture. As such, a scholarly climate which encourages consultancy will be characterised by license rather than liberty and the academy's democratic function is weakened. In this round about way an academic culture which is policed by the state in order to ensure value for money from public services *will not be able to fulfil its public function*. A marketised or a state controlled model of academe fails in its scholarly duty to protect its own and others' freedom as citizens. We require, in short, an autonomous university sector, or some equivalent, if we are to have autonomous citizens. This presupposes an academic community free from the disturbing effects of both state and market where scholarship is legitimated through the academic community itself. This idea has always been latent in our understanding of the university. Some system whereby the scholarly community sanctions academic work which it deems to lack serious scholarship is not, after all, inconceivable; this is how the academy is supposed to work. Of course, this would mean an end to the Stakhanovistic vagaries of crude devices designed to increase the productive efficiency of academics like the Research Excellence Framework. The problem faced, in a nutshell, is that bureaucratic devices designed to legitimate higher education externally through greater levels of accountability have eventually begun to encroach upon the norms internal to the university and started to destroy those features which legitimated the academic world in the past.

The welfare state and autonomy through social rights

In Habermas' theory of the welfare state under conditions of reflexive democracy, decision-making processes are guided by the informally formed public opinion of citizens. This model is designed to curb the paternalism of the welfare state while retaining and, indeed, improving the state's ability to meet people's needs. As it is presently conceived, Habermas argues that the welfare state provides the basis for a humanly dignified existence by providing security in health care, income, housing and education. However, in doing so, the welfare state may undercut the very autonomy it also seeks to promote (Habermas, 1996, p. 407). But the dangers inherent in welfare-state juridification 'that threatens to twist the declared goal of restoring private autonomy into its opposite' (Habermas, 1996, p. 410) do not mean that the welfare state should be scrapped. Instead it ought to be pursued at a 'higher level of reflection' that allows for the taming of the capitalist economic system without undermining the autonomy of citizens. This would involve linking the administration of the welfare state to communicative power in order to ensure its legitimacy. To ensure its effectiveness would require training the administrators to employ mild forms of indirect steering (Habermas, 1996, p. 410). We see here that Habermas regards the legitimacy and the effectiveness of the welfare state as in tension.

In both *Between Facts and Norms* and his essay 'Citizenship and National Identity', Habermas makes mention of T. H. Marshall's division of citizens' rights into the categories of 'civil', 'political' and 'social' rights (Marshall, 1964). Habermas distinguishes between: liberal negative rights which protect the private legal subject; rights of political participation which 'enable the active citizen to take part in democratic processes of opinion- and will-formation' (Habermas, 1996, p. 77 and p. 503); and social rights which grant social security to clients of the welfare state. Now Habermas follows this distinction in order to emphasise a further distinction between an idea of citizenship based upon inclusion and an idea of citizenship oriented towards autonomy:

> [O]nly rights of political participation ground the citizen's reflexive, self-referential legal standing. Negative liberties and social rights can, by contrast, be conferred by a paternalistic authority. In principle, the constitutional

state and the welfare state are possible without democracy . . . these negative and social-rights are still Janus-faced.
(Habermas, 1996, p. 78 and p. 504)

Only through a reflexively constituted welfare-state based on autonomy can a state escape the paternalistic and juridified tendencies of the welfare state which reduce citizenship to the role of a client to administrations that provide benefits. Habermas explains the conceptual difference between civil (liberal), social and political rights:

> From a *functionalist* viewpoint, one can conceive [liberal rights] as institutionalizing a market economy, whereas, from a *normative* viewpoint, they guarantee individual freedoms. Social rights signify, from a *functionalist* viewpoint, the installation of welfare-bureaucracies, whereas, from a *normative* viewpoint, they grant compensatory claims to a just share of social wealth. It is true that both individual freedom and welfare guarantees can be viewed as the legal basis for the social independence that first makes it possible to put political rights into effect. But these are empirical, and not conceptually necessary, relationships. Negative liberties and social rights can just as well facilitate the privatistic retreat from the citizen's role.
> (Habermas, 1996, pp. 504–505)

There seems to be a problem here. While Habermas sees a possibility that social rights and political participation rights are empirically connected, he denies any necessary conceptual connection. Thomas Janoski makes a similar point along Hohfeldian lines:

> [S]ocial . . . rights are different from civil and political rights. Not only are social rights in the private (economic) rather than the public (political) realm, but social rights are 'claims,' rather than 'liberties' like civil rights, or 'powers' like political rights. Thus, citizenship rights differ qua rights.
> (Janoski, 1998, p. 44)

To the extent that political participation does not take place under idealised conditions, however, we could assume a link between *democratic* (rather than, say, populist) participation and well-formulated social rights *of certain kinds*. Of course, here I am thinking of the sorts of social good that enable participants to engage in opinion-forming action. Now the goods required for this will vary between different political actions. But, on the whole, education of some sort will be necessary. An education aided by critical theory would help to bring out such self-reflexivity so as to allow individuals a

> critical awareness of the contingent conditions which make one's own standpoint possible . . . and an awareness of whom and what the knowledge

one produces serves in society.... Such self-reflexivity leads us, in Horkheimer's words, to become aware of 'the motives of thought', and is constituent of individual and collective autonomy.

(Benhabib, 1986, p. 281)

The rational-reconstructive role of the universities

Habermas argues that deliberative politics depends on the connections between institutionalised will-formation at the formal level and informal opinion-formation. Regulated procedures must be supplemented with informal communication (Habermas, 1996, p. 308). An era of social media and smart phones calls into question the quality of informal communication through newspapers and magazines now largely funded by online advertising and the click-bait articles that drive revenue. However, these technological developments also raise questions about the quality of communication that emanates through and from universities in the form of the qualities of students, graduates and academics and the research they produce.

It is crucial to remember that Habermas' theory combines a proceduralist understanding of decision-making alongside the more nebulous idea of informal public-opinion formation. This corresponds, to some extent, with Nancy Fraser's idea of strong and weak public spheres. Now, universities ought to occupy an important place within this framework because they feed in to both strong and weak publics. Higher education, in other words, impacts on decision-making within formal structures through expert advice and the formal training universities provide for future office holders. However, universities also feed in to informal public-opinion formation through a general cultivation of particular ideas at particular points in time which become influential, like, for instance, the impact that monetarist economics had on public opinion in the 1980s. Ideas too 'trickle down': they flow from university departments and exert an influence on the informal public sphere. They do this, however, in more or less formal and informal settings. With regard to formal, constitutional opinion- and will-formation deliberation is procedurally regulated. With informal opinion- and will-formation, the general public sphere is more suited to 'struggles for recognition', which can then feed in to the procedurally regulated formal system. The two settings, informal and formal, act and react upon one another:

> Only after a public 'struggle for recognition' can the contested interest positions be taken up by the responsible political authorities, put on the parliamentary agenda, discussed, and, if need be, worked into legislative proposals and binding decisions. And only the *regulation* of a newly defined criminal offense or the *implementation* of a social program intervenes in the sphere of private life and changes formal responsibilities and existing practices.
>
> (Habermas, 1996, p. 314)

Autonomous private and public action, however, will be dependent upon liberal, political and social rights. For instance, functionalists like Durkheim and Talcott Parsons place part of the burden of ensuring autonomy upon educational institutions, as Habermas explains:

> [I]n discussing the development of civil society as the social basis for public and inclusive processes of opinion- and will-formation among voluntarily associated citizens, Parsons stresses the significance of equalizing educational opportunities or, more generally, uncoupling cultural knowledge from class structures. . . . With this concept of an 'educational revolution' Parsons also touches on the political-cultural conditions for a responsive political public sphere.
>
> (Habermas, 1996, p. 76)

Despite the expanded (both in terms of student numbers and institutions) higher education system we have today in Britain, this uncoupling of cultural knowledge and class structure has failed to take place. As long as education remains, for the most part, tied to job and earning prospects, then autonomy can only count in a liberal-economic sense. Even so, higher education fails on this front because of problems of qualification credentialism (or 'grade inflation') and the fact that a university degree, because it grants a certain social status (still), is a *positional* good as well as a straightforward investment good. We can, though, conceive of higher education as an autonomy conferring social good which will undergird political, social and liberal rights. Such a higher education system would have to orient itself towards more than the skills requested by employers' organisations and a consultancy research model, although it could do this too – it just would not be its primary role. The academy would have to act as an independent, critical voice free from state coercion and financial interests which might impinge upon its academic freedom. The university system (and those involved in scholarship within it), in other words, requires its own set of liberal, political and social rights. If scholarship, and, by association, higher education, in Britain is to retain the value that it holds (sometimes) in an international market setting, then it will have to be protected against government infringements, allowed to take part freely in opinion-forming processes and offered state assistance to take part in such opinion-formation when this possibility is blocked. Now, if this is impossible in the universities we currently have, then we should pare down the system to a more manageable size where financial pressures would be less acute. This would, in some ways, mean a return to a higher education system which is not artificially unified, but where different institutions play to their strengths. Some would be involved in what would probably be held to be lower status activities like 'widening participation', while others would lead the field in international research in particular subject areas. Such a system would come under attack for being elitist and re-introducing a kind of class divide between different universities. But we should not kid ourselves. This divide between ex-polytechnics and 'old' universities remains anyway, by and large. It can be seen in quality assurance proposals which assure us that 'beacon' institutions with a well-established reputation for high quality teaching provision will be policed with a 'lighter touch'. It is also evident when we look at the cash sums made available for research where the same dozen or so universities receive the lion's share of research money.

University education then, and academic freedom, can be argued to be a social right for those in certain circumstances. Just as welfare benefits and payments are made available for those who require them to take up a role as fully autonomous citizens, universities can provide high-level education to those who qualify for it academically, where qualifying is a judgement made by academics within universities and not disturbed by state determined performance indicators tied to finance. Universities, in other words, are fundamentally social institutions which undergird public participation. Universities' primary duty is to serve the good of democracy while their secondary function is to the state or the economy.

However, before we can make this argument convincingly we have to turn to a problem in Habermas' schema of civil, political and social rights and their link to autonomy and the legitimacy of democratic procedures. In any process of democratic opinion-formation, material inequality which threatens the ability to participate will create political inequalities between citizens. Citizenship requires both private and public forms of autonomy, which are, in Habermas' view, co-original and reciprocally presuppose each other. Kevin Olson explains that public reason and autonomy require discursive competency among citizens and this entails basic civil liberties in order to participate in deliberation. But the private freedoms that citizens allow each other must also be deliberated through public discourse. This means that public deliberation needs to be securely institutionalised in order that a legitimate system of laws can be developed to ensure private freedom and autonomy (Olson, 2006, p. 102).

Autonomy, then, in a private and public sense, provided through a system of social rights, has to be empirically realised under conditions of democratic legitimacy. While civil and political rights have a mutual, 'internal' relation to each other, so that one justifies the other, social rights stand apart from this co-dependent relationship:

> Social rights, in contrast, are not part of this idealized mutual implication. They are contingent and subsidiary, dependent upon the complex empirical relations between autonomy, on the one hand, and income distribution, class, status, personal abilities, and other factors that influence autonomy's development, on the other. Social rights can thus be justified *only* if material or social deprivation produces systematic inequalities in the worth of civil or political liberties. They serve as functional adjuncts for the achievement of autonomy, and thus do not have the free-standing status of civil and political rights.
> (Olson, 2006, p. 104)

But, if Habermas' model of discursive democracy is to move us away from a paternalistic welfare state, then these social rights also have to be deliberatively legitimated. Civil, political and social rights would all be subject to an ongoing deliberative process of constitution formation within which our understandings of the requirements for equal participation would be undergoing constant refinement and re-evaluation. The process has echoes of Oscar Wilde's quip that socialism takes up too many evenings.

The tension here is clear. At the same time Habermas wants to give social rights a compensatory role in discursive democracy – those who lack autonomy will be entitled to the appropriate social rights – while participants in deliberation will also determine these appropriate social rights. The interlocutors require these social rights to function as competent participants, but this means that incompetent participants (without legitimate social rights) have to legitimise concrete social rights. As Olson puts it, social rights are required, on Habermas' view, only if citizen autonomy is insufficient to enable equal participation in political processes. The problem is that in a deliberatively constituted welfare state, these people who require social rights have to be able to articulate their social right requirements and describe the sorts of structural changes to the welfare state that would enhance their autonomy up to a point of equality (Olson, 2006, p. 120).

A circularity is involved here because those whose public participation is likely to be most impaired are also those who would benefit most from appropriate social rights. It seems that this idea of private and public autonomy backed by social rights is problematic. The needs and interests of marginalised people could be systematically excluded from discourse, so perpetuating political and economic inequality.

Olson attempts to side step this problem by invoking what he terms a 'bootstrapping' argument which stresses the temporal and the dialectical character of constitutional reform:

> Social rights . . . would develop in a dialectical process in which political discourse becomes more substantively equal through on-going processes of critique and correction. To get such processes off the ground, a minimal interpretation of autonomy would have to be enshrined in the constitution, providing guidelines for the development of civil, political, and later, social rights. In its most basic form, this set of rights would have to guarantee sufficient capabilities and freedoms to put marginalized people on the road to full autonomy. Once such a preliminary constitution had been established, better and more adequate interpretations of social rights could be developed in an on-going process of public dialogue and constitutional reform.
> (Olson, 2006, p. 121)

Now, once we envisage the relation between autonomy and rights in this developmental sense, we can break out of the circularity that might be read into

Habermas' argument. But this is not yet the end of the matter because, in order for this bootstrapping argument to work, we require some acceptable way of beginning the process. In other words, how should we all agree upon a minimal interpretation of autonomy which would give voice to those presently disadvantaged citizens? Olson argues that it has to be possible to begin to speak on behalf of the marginalised without their voice: social rights could be justified without equal participation in the public use of reason (Olson, 2006, p. 122). He suggests that a rational-reconstructive social science can provide the basis for the process for constitutional reform. For Olson, rational-reconstructive sciences should guide reform, speaking on behalf of those without the capacities to yet participate on equal terms:

> This kind of science would try to determine what capabilities are needed for fair and equal democratic participation, identifying inequalities in their distribution. It would provide a kind of expert assistance in the development of legislation about social rights, picking up the slack for the democratic process's failure to represent all citizens' interests. This proposal asks those who *are* autonomous to discern the needs of those who are not. Individuals capable of viewing the world from another person's perspective would try to infer or approximate the kinds of social rights required by those less fortunate.
>
> (Olson, 2006, p. 122)

There are, at least, two problems with this. On the one hand, it brings us back to a paternalistic grounding of autonomy that is set against the spirit of discursive democracy. On the other hand, we ought to be wary of regarding social science as an autonomous tool capable of the task, given the present context of functional scholarship which tends to, and is encouraged to, pander to business and the state. We might say that universities should be well-placed to carry out this role, but their present performative role as status seeking and conferring institutions makes them weak candidates. Elizabeth Anderson points out that isolated elites are not well-placed to look out for the disadvantaged:

> Constant personal contact across social divisions enhances the personal knowledge elites have of the disadvantaged, making knowledge of their interests and circumstances more salient. Constant interaction across divisional lines in contexts where cooperation is required enhances elite intergroup competence to learn about and heed relevant first- and second-person knowledge. Constant pressure to heed the second-person claims of the disadvantaged helps entrench their perspectives practically in elite decision making. In these ways, an elite that is socially integrated across lines of disadvantage is more qualified to perform its functions than a socially insular elite drawn overwhelmingly from the ranks of the multiply advantaged.

If segregation makes an elite ignorant and incompetent, then integration makes it more knowledgeable and competent.

(Anderson, 2007, p. 611)

Habermas' critical theory seeks to justify substantive rights intersubjectively. To replace this, at the outset, with a monological, social scientific privileged position displays, perhaps, a certain arrogance or naïveté. The extent to which this is the case, I think, depends on the form that social scientific research takes and the context within which it takes place. A recognition of the sensitivity of such a social scientific task would guard against the worst excesses involved in attributing the requirements for autonomy to disadvantaged groups or individuals. Olson recognises his suggestion that social science plays this rational-reconstructive role is somewhat problematic, but he remains, on the whole optimistic: 'Recent advances in social science, particularly a new sensitivity to the pitfalls of interpretation and representation, would make it possible to avoid some of the paternalism inherent in this model. In addition, it is likely that the forms of public autonomy needed in a society would be fairly universal' (Olson, 2006, p. 123). But, of course, though the 'forms of public autonomy' might be 'fairly universal', this fails to help because what is at issue here is the manner in which the means to autonomy are distributed and disputes over recognising this distribution.

The difficulty here lies in a slightly naïve attitude towards a juridified university. Recently, Fantuzzo has drawn Max Weber to the attention of philosophy of education. He presents a careful reading of Weber's work and its dual tendency to take up a critical stance to both charismatic and bureaucratic domination. In opposition to a superficial reading of Weber, he shows us that both the rule of man (charisma) and the rule of law (bureaucracy) involve domination:

> [I]t may seem as though charismatic domination is the preferable choice over bureaucratic domination. For instance, consider an oft-quoted line from Weber's *Protestant Ethic* (2003): 'No one knows who will live in this cage in the future, or whether at the end of this tremendous development entirely new prophets will arise, or, if neither, mechanized petrification, embellished with a sort of convulsive self- importance' (p. 182). Reading such a line, we may cheer for the 'new prophets' and boo the 'mechanized petrification'. Yet both forms of domination are undesirable from the standpoint of self-determination. Their commands are both heteronymous: You must be this way.
>
> (Fantuzzo, 2015, p. 50)

Both charisma and bureaucracy lead away from autonomy and towards becoming dominated; non-domination points away from a credentialist 'patent of education' and also from charismatic education where the purpose is to elicit charismatic capacities and develop heroism. And yet, Fantuzzo points out, this domination is something taught. Our education system is inclined towards a bureaucratic form of education: rote drills, exams and the 'patent of education'. Charismatic education involves challenges to be overcome in order to elicit charismatic capacities the educator assumes to be latent in the student (Fantuzzo, 2015, p. 51).

Take a simple example. Adult illiteracy is a barrier to autonomy in many ways, and literacy might be one form of 'fairly universal autonomy'. A person's inability to read will mean he has few formal qualifications, and probably, therefore, has an unskilled, manual job which is poorly paid, if he has a job at all. This person will probably shirk formal public participation and cope privately with his inability to read, even to the extent that he refuses to enrol for adult literacy classes if they are made available in a convenient form. In this example illiteracy is a barrier to autonomy, but a further barrier will be the likely unwillingness to admit publicly to a lack of autonomy. The most sensitive social scientific research will experience great difficulties in identifying this type of person and his lack of autonomy. Moreover, this lack of autonomy cannot be remedied straightforwardly. Even if I can identify all of the illiterate adults in my local community and teach them to read, an extremely difficult task in its own right, rectifying the illiteracy will not endow these people with autonomy because damage has already been done by the previous effects of that illiteracy. In short, although adult illiteracy will mean a lack of autonomy, remedying this illiteracy will not render such people autonomous because they have already been socialised into a role of adult illiterate. Although he can now read this person has other new barriers to autonomy which remain hidden behind illiteracy. For example, if he has been unemployed for a lengthy period he will probably still find it very difficult to find work; if he has no formal qualifications he will have difficulty getting any which will increase his autonomy; if he has never engaged in political communication he will probably still continue to consider his arguments as unworthy of attention. This is not to say that teaching adults to read is a waste of time, far from it, but it is to suggest that even those things which more obviously hamper our autonomy are difficult to remedy from the observer's perspective. From the participant's perspective, an articulate but illiterate adult could explain the multifarious ways in which he lacks authority, but not all of those who cannot read will be articulate enough to do this, and not all will be willing to come forward.

In part, the problem with specifying social rights from the point of view of the observer pertains to the nature of social rights relative to civil and political rights. Civil and political rights can be, more readily, formulated generally and judicially applied appropriately. Social rights, however, are more tangible. Their material and substantive nature means that they have to be specifically designed to fit the situation in hand and, assuming a lack of non-autonomous participants in the process of autonomy building, leaves these social rights more open to the paternalism which Habermas sought to avoid. At the same time, calls for social rights, because they are conceived substantively, could become no more than a (possibly infinite) wish list, unless we draw some kind of minimum threshold for autonomy. The problem with this, however, is that the minimum threshold will itself be socially contingent. It is near on impossible, in other words, to arrive at an autonomous conception of autonomy.

The further problem remains of employing social science to plug this gap in autonomy, given the current climate within which universities operate. After all, what we have been examining is, in part, the ways in which universities (including departments within social science) manifestly fail to be autonomous themselves. Olson's idea of 'bootstrapping' depends on an autonomous – or an as close as possible to autonomous – starting point. For him, social science and critical theory themselves pass this test. And, of course, there are elements of autonomy in academe, and, moreover, the university is still, probably, one of the few remaining institutions capable of the job Olson sets. However, we ought to be wary. I think there is a prior task here of ensuring that universities and the various departments within them are guided by autonomously set values and norms rather than bureaucratically steered by performance targets or determined by some notion of demand in an academic market.

I wish to conceive of a university education as a social right for all who qualify for it according to relevant academic criteria. This does not seem so utopian since it is what a mass higher education system promises. It does, however, beg the question of what constitutes relevant academic criteria. Some answers to this seem obvious. For example, academics should decide whether candidates for courses are adequately qualified. By and large, academics still make this decision but admissions tutors are pressurised, in varying degrees in different subject areas and in different universities, by state determined aims to recruit students from socio-economic backgrounds which, traditionally, have had little or no contact with university education. The pressure to 'widen participation' (since it is linked to financial incentives) can, in some circumstances, outweigh other considerations, such as, for example, a putative student's ability to write in clear, declarative prose. The net result is that some institutions, and these tend to be those which have trouble in attracting research income, are forced to enrol students who then have to be taught to write to an acceptable standard. The task of the university, in this instance, then overlaps with that of the school, and this transforms the normative standards of academe. My point is that external influences on admissions policies, in this instance, have consequences internal to the academy which are much more broad in their effects than merely altering the intake to the student body. This is only one example. It remains, however, that the statement that all who qualify for a university education according to the academy's own judgements should receive a university place begins to appear more complex than it does at first glance when we consider the function of the university and how this purpose can be so easily altered. The central point is one of academic freedom. In this instance, academic freedom is required in order to make judgements on qualifications. It seems self-evident that if universities, and the people within them, are to preserve civilization, to offer a critical standpoint and to come up with new ideas which enhance the quality of our lives, then they require academic freedom. It is this which should be institutionalised as a social right because without it we are left with mere ideology.

The policy intended to widen the range of backgrounds from which students tend to be drawn ends up changing, and possibly devaluing, the experience of studying at university. Neither higher education, nor further education, should be seen as a ground for rectifying past pedagogical (or, more likely, broader social) mistakes. It seems evident that it is wasteful to use universities to teach basic, mundane, perfunctory subject matter.

Widening participation in higher education is about more than merely increasing the official statistics relating to those who take up university places. Widening participation in higher education requires a prior effort to bring these new students to an appropriate educational level, though this prior effort could take place in universities themselves. This would, however, require university degrees to be redesigned with this in mind and, accordingly, academics would have to be trained to meet these new requirements. It would be more efficient and more effective to meet the demand for more basic levels of education at earlier educational levels where appropriately trained and experienced staff already exist. Moreover, we should not miss the point that there is a deep connection between academic freedom to research and the academic freedom to teach. Similarly, we can think of the university (and its members) as an institution which, among other things, helps to create citizens (through teaching) and acts as a kind of citizen (through the published research it provides). These are connected through their appeal to a common scholarly tradition. And one of the ways in which this scholarly tradition is kept alive is through the recruitment of new members to the academy. This recruitment is one way in which academic freedom to teach and to research are connected, for the university has to replenish itself. Some of the students it teaches will go on to become politicians, some will be journalists, some will be arms traders, but some will go on to become university lecturers. Some of those who are at one time formally taught and who engage with scholarly research as students become the teachers who engage with scholarly research as researchers themselves. An idea of the university couched in instrumental terms looks to the present and the future and neglects its tradition. In this idea we return to Charles Taylor's conception of secularisation. The instrumental university, oriented towards the (knowledge) economy, locates itself purely in profane time.

Chapter 10

Concluding remarks
Communicative rationality and the cultural impoverishment of the university

Universities hold a valuable role. As sources of democratic legitimacy they can help support the public sphere in times of trouble. They are imperfect, obviously, and in times of peril they collapse under the weight of tyranny. But they offer protection from populist politics and from short-term political considerations. However, I have attempted to argue that their democratic value is draining away. The contemporary university under the kind of market conditions we see in Britain, especially England, Australia, New Zealand, many parts of the USA and Canada is the frequent victim of social processes which have led to what Jürgen Habermas termed the colonisation of the lifeworld. Though universities differ in terms of their character, age, size, specialisms and reputations, I have tried to argue that a 'new' managerialism, often encouraged by the state, has left universities in a parlous condition. It is not simply that the physical institutions that we call universities, and those who work and sometimes live within them, are coming under increasing stresses, more than this (because it is more insidious and less avoidable) it is what it means to be a university which is under attack. There is a danger that the reasons why we value universities will disappear from view: people with epistemic resources can hold power accountable.

There is, perhaps, nothing particularly new in this idea, though the pressures under which academe is now burdened are more intense than when Weber spoke of the proletarianisation of the academic and Veblen attacked the business ethic of salesmanship at work in American universities. Theodor Adorno pointed to an impoverished idea of scholarship too:

> Today, now that the better-paid office-boss has replaced the scholar, the lack of intelligence is not only celebrated as the virtue of the unassuming, well-adjusted team-member, but is institutionalized in the structure of the research process, which recognizes individual spontaneity only as a coefficient of friction. There is something intrinsically small-minded about the antithesis of high-flown inspiration and solid research-work. Thoughts do not arrive out of thin air, but – even when their actual appearance is unexpected – have been crystallizing in long-drawn-out underground processes. The suddenness of what research technicians patronizingly refer to

as intuition marks the eruption of living experience through the hardened crust of *communis opinio*; it is the sustained opposition to the latter – not the privileged moments of inspiration – which permits the unregimented mind that contact with the essence of things which the interposition of an over-inflated apparatus so often relentlessly sabotages.

(Adorno, 1976, p. 253)[1]

The bureaucratic devices put in place in market-oriented universities in order to assure teaching and research are of an acceptable quality (to the state and the consumers of these services) steer universities purposefully towards just such a mechanistic conception of scholarship and higher learning.

I have tried to grasp the situation through Habermas' thesis of communicative reason, and related ideas, and attempted to demonstrate how it applies to the academy. I want to conclude by examining firstly, the idea of communicative rationality and attempt to demonstrate how it is normatively instituted in the academic community. Secondly, I want to explain the idea of the colonisation of the lifeworld and show some of the forms this colonisation takes within contemporary universities. Thirdly, I shall explicate the idea of cultural impoverishment and relate this to academe.

The argument which runs throughout this work is that the worth of universities and the things they do hinge upon the legitimacy of universities. It is over the question of legitimacy that ideals clash. The state attempts to legitimate universities and their (sometimes expensive) activities through managerial mechanisms and metrics that steer universities in certain directions. This functions as a kind of external check on universities which is designed to provide legitimacy. Unfortunately, I have argued, it is these same external steering mechanisms which, in fact, undermine the legitimacy of universities.

John Rawls writes, at the very beginning of *A Theory of Justice*, that:

> Justice is the first virtue of social institutions, as truth is of systems of thought. A theory however elegant and economical must be rejected or revised if it is untrue; likewise laws and institutions no matter how efficient and well-arranged must be reformed or abolished if they are unjust. . . . The only thing that permits us to acquiesce in an erroneous theory is the lack of a better one; analogously, an injustice is tolerable only when it is necessary to avoid an even greater injustice. Being first virtues of human activities, truth and justice are uncompromising.
>
> (Rawls, 1973, pp. 3–4)

In these propositions Rawls is expressing our intuitions about justice, and it is these intuitions that he wishes to account for, if they are sound. Justice, of course, is one of those tricky issues: a concept that remains rather porous and capable of taking on many meanings. Whilst Rawls seeks to establish a conception of justice through the *a priori*stic reasoning of a hypothetical social contract, Habermas adopts a somewhat similar approach, though he drops, or intends to drop at least, the *a priori* elements:

> [Habermas] sees matters of justice as determined by what would be agreed to by the parties involved in an act of collective decision, under what he describes as conditions of ideal speech or communication: these conditions are meant to ensure that everyone has the same rights and opportunities of speech, that there are no distorting differences of power and influence, and that the culture is one of radical questioning. A consequence of envisaging the relevant contract in this way is of course that Habermas leaves himself unable to tell how the parties would in fact decide. Thus this contractarian approach does not have the methodological attractions of [Rawls'] alternative.
>
> (Kukathas and Pettit, 1990, p. 33)

This is entirely debatable. While the contractarian approach Rawls adopts in *A Theory of Justice* seeks to deliver a rational conception of distributive justice which yields substantive results, Habermas' tack gives us a procedural conception of justice. This might not tell us what participants in the 'contract', or rather in the process of argumentation, to employ a more Habermasian turn of phrase, will actually say or do, but it does give substantive results (of a different type) and it does, therefore, hold methodological attractions which I intend to demonstrate. Moreover, the aspects of Rawls' work which are often deemed methodological attractions are, in fact, methodologically problematic, as Hegel pointed out with regard to Kant. Seyla Benhabib summarises this argument against such 'state of nature' theories:

> [I]f a theory begins by resorting to counterfactual abstraction, then the theorist must possess criteria in light of which certain aspects of the human condition are ignored while others are included in the initial abstraction. But any such criteria will themselves be normative, for they will depend on what the theorist considers essential or inessential aspects of human nature. ... The initial counterfactual abstraction from which the theorist proceeds does not justify, but merely illustrates, the concept of human nature and reason that he subscribes to.
>
> (Benhabib, 1986, p. 25)

It is just this sort of counterfactual abstraction which Habermas attempts to avoid in his theory of communicative action, but to do so he locates his theory at a highly abstracted and formal level. I have also attempted to avoid such counterfactual abstraction by tracing an outline of the empirical situation in which students and academics find themselves in contemporary universities.

Critical theory and emancipatory cognitive interests

A sketch of critical theory and its relations to epistemology will be necessary. Since the thesis examines those organisations (the universities) which institutionalise knowledge (though they are not alone in this role), epistemology, or at least critical theory's orientation to epistemology, is important. Critical theory and the 'Frankfurt School' include figures such as Horkheimer, Adorno and Marcuse and also later theorists such as Habermas, Wellmer and Honneth. According to Raymond Geuss there are three theses which distinguish the Frankfurt School's critical theory. Firstly, critical theory guides human action towards enlightenment insofar as it allows agents to determine their real interests. In this respect critical theory is inherently emancipatory. Secondly, critical theory is a form of knowledge in itself; it has cognitive content. And thirdly, critical theory is reflective, as opposed to (positivist) science's tendency to objectification. As Geuss puts it:

> A critical theory, then, is a reflective theory which gives agents a kind of knowledge inherently productive of enlightenment and emancipation. In Frankfurt usage a 'positivist' is a person who holds: (a) that an empiricist account of natural science is adequate, and (b) that all cognition must have essentially the same cognitive structure as natural science. If all theories in natural science have an 'objectifying' structure then to assert that all cognition has the structure of natural science is to assert that all cognition is 'objectifying' cognition. So positivism can be seen as the 'denial of reflection,' i.e. as a denial that theories could be both reflective and cognitive. . . . The very heart of the critical theory of society is its criticism of ideology. Their ideology is what prevents the agents in the society from correctly perceiving their true situation and real interests; if they are to free themselves from social repression, the agents must rid themselves of ideological illusion.
> (Geuss, 1981, pp. 2–3)

Now, Geuss' account points to an oppositional relation between critical theory and science, but this is not the case. For, as Seyla Benhabib explains:

> [U]nlike positivism and analytical philosophy, critical theory neither considers valid knowledge the monopoly of the sciences alone, nor does it seek to analyze the foundations of the sciences exclusively. Critical social theory seeks a collaboration between philosophy and the social sciences in particular which goes beyond epistemological critique. It might be worthwhile to dwell on this for a moment, for it is one of the most misunderstood aspects of critical theory in Anglo-American philosophy. The image of the relationship between philosophy and science as presented by Richard Rorty, for example, is exclusively the epistemological one of analyzing the foundation of the sciences. Critical theory, by contrast, proceeds to an immanent

critique of the sciences. The distinction between an epistemological and an immanent critique is the following: whereas in the first mode, only the conceptual foundations of the sciences and their knowledge claims are analyzed, the second approach aids in the development of new scientific theories, conceptualizations, and verification procedures, thus actively collaborating with them.

(Benhabib, 1986, p. 280)

And this is the case with Habermas' understanding of critical theory. He criticises the 'objectivism' of the sciences (or, rather, of modern positivism and its scientism) and of classical philosophy. Under this illusory view the world appears as a 'universe of facts whose law-like connection can be grasped descriptively. In truth, however, knowledge of the apparently objective world of facts has its transcendental basis in the prescientific world. The possible objects of scientific analysis are constituted a priori in the self-evidence of our primary life-world' (Habermas, 1978, p. 304 and see also McCarthy, 1989, pp. 57–58). As McCarthy writes, as soon as this objectivist illusion is 'dispelled and theoretical statements are understood in relation to prior frames of reference in the lifeworld, their connection with interests that guide knowledge becomes apparent' (McCarthy, 1989, p. 57).

According to Habermas, processes of inquiry fall into three categories. Firstly, empirical-analytic sciences, which include natural and social sciences insofar as they aim at uncovering nomological knowledge. Secondly, we have the historical-hermeneutic sciences, which include the humanities, the historical and the social sciences insofar as these aim at interpretive understanding. Lastly, there are the critically oriented sciences, which include psycho-analysis, critical social theory and critical, reflective philosophy. These three categories are each connected with a particular cognitive interest. The empirical-analytic sciences have a technical cognitive interest, the hermeneutic sciences incorporate a practical interest, and the critically oriented sciences incorporate an emancipatory cognitive interest. These cognitive interests are 'general cognitive strategies' which guide the various modes of inquiry (McCarthy, 1989, p. 58). But these cognitive interests cannot simply be eliminated in order to arrive at objective knowledge, for they are invariant and fundamental. McCarthy explains that 'although the sciences must preserve their objectivity in the face of particular interests, the conditions of possibility of the very objectivity that they seek to preserve include fundamental cognitive interests' (McCarthy, 1989, p. 58). For in this view, there is no view from nowhere.

The rise of professionalism in the universities

This is relevant precisely because the managerial hold over higher education demands control and visible effects upon the object of its attention – 'bang for bucks'. In clearer parlance, those who fund universities require their money to have a direct effect over the world – preferably one which benefits them in some manner. There is, in short, a worrying tendency towards valorising technical cognitive interests in higher education. It is as if all forms of cognitive interest are encompassed within the technical form.

This is evident, I think, in recent syllabus amendments in universities which increasingly refer to employability and the 'delivery of transferable skills' to students in order to prepare them for employment. This could, however, be no more than a passing fad since a rigid set of skills is unlikely to be flexible enough to keep pace with employers' demands from their staff. An argument could be made, for instance, that nurturing creativity and imagination, encouraging a broadened democratic horizon, would be more likely to provide better economic prospects for students than a set of supposedly transferable skills, which are, interestingly, frequently taught devoid of any real practical context – something that seems to conflict with the sense in which the term skill is usually employed in everyday life. Technical interests, however, lie behind the popularity of university courses in computer science and business studies, nursing and teaching. Employers value the technical knowledge ('powerful knowledge' means knowledge holds use-value rather than intrinsic value) involved and so students are induced to follow these courses. Moreover, technical interests are responsible for the increasingly consultative, and applied, form which academic research takes. All this is exacerbated by state policies (and the tacitly sanctioned practices) which encourage such instrumental attitudes. For instance, it comes as no surprise that students opt to 'read' in subject areas which offer scope for employment when they, and their parents, are paying university tuition fees and a combination of student loans, part-time employment and overdraft facilities provide for living expenses. This form of (lack of) student finance is justified in terms of the private returns which accrue to individuals with a university degree.[2] This logic is left unquestioned by many within the universities because higher education has been inadequately financed, given the number of students involved, for the last thirty years or so. Private finance from students was seen as a way of loosening the ties with the ever decreasing, yet increasingly regulated, state funding mainly from what was called the Higher Education Funding Council for England (HEFCE) – Scottish, Welsh and Northern Irish higher education budgets are now part of those devolved powers which are distributed through separate bureaucratic mechanisms – and now to be administered by the Office for Students in England. In terms of scholarship, the Research Assessment Exercise (RAE) or Research Excellence Framework (REF), which is held every five or six years, has had a powerful effect on academic culture. The last decade has witnessed a growth in supply of academic journals which function to provide academics with an opportunity to publish in order to meet the metric requirements of the RAE/REF. Further, an expectation is held by university managers that academics publish sufficient work within the REF time span regardless of the quality of the work put forward for publication. This has had a profound effect upon the kind of work that academics undertake to research: there is little time for books, for instance, or the same article might be written from four different angles. Similarly, the effects of the Quality Assurance Agency's (QAA) attempts at Teaching Quality Assessment (TQA) and now the Teaching Excellence Framework (TEF), which looks as though it will harvest graduate salaries from the Inland Revenue directly, will tend towards a standardisation of curricula in British universities as courses and teaching methods become more bureaucratically regulated. This shows up a tendency towards common course structures and 'benchmarking' which, in turn, undermines autonomy in higher education at many levels: the university loses institutional freedom to set its own curriculum, individual teachers lose the autonomy to connect their teaching with their research interests, the academic community loses its hold over what constitutes valid teaching material and, finally, the student loses the freedom to engage actively with the object of study. Ted Tapper and Brian Salter write that while current policies

> may not mean the emergence of a national curriculum as such, the clear thrust is towards an agreed modular degree structure with threshold standards that will permit credit transfer. In effect this is a national curriculum by another label. It relieves the universities of one pressure (the visitations incurred by TQAs), but imposes upon them more constraining demands.
> (Tapper and Salter, 1998, p. 31)

In summary then, what I have attempted to sketch out here is that universities, once they became conceived as a system of 'mass' higher education under the control of the state, have been changed from the outside, and from within. In a nutshell, externally conceived procedures, intended to inject instrumental accountability into the system, begin to alter what universities do and what I have referred to as their purpose: chiefly to cultivate our humanity, to appeal to ideas of truth, objectivity and beauty in an age when the validity of such categories are called into question. At the same time the internal norms of the university have altered. An increasing differentiation of value spheres within the academy involves a loss of the binds which once tied the various elements of the university together. Between and within disciplines the self-understanding of what it means to be an academic splits, which aids the development of autonomous subsystems of purposive rational action. A dialectical relationship exists between societal and cultural rationalisation.

An analysis of this process in terms of critical theory is particularly apt for several reasons. Firstly, critical theory takes as its aim the release of those emancipatory potentials that lie latent in the present. This chimes with the aim of fostering autonomous individuals within universities. Secondly, as I noted in the introduction, Habermas' critical theory, which now relies on a notion of communicative rationality, has parallels in the idea of the academic community and the academic ethic. Thirdly, our public institutions are being eroded by an impoverished and one-sided rationalism which ought to be supplanted by a richer mode of reason. Since critical theory has always been, at least, about the illumination of ideology, it should have a self-interested claim on the future direction of philosophy, the humanities and the natural and social sciences insofar as these are instituted within universities.

Models of rationality

The Theory of Communicative Action was published in German in 1981 (volume two in 1987) and marks Habermas' shift in theoretical strategy from the epistemologically rooted idea of cognitive interests, presented most comprehensively in his *Knowledge and Human Interests*, to a critical social theory grounded in the theory of language and the 'general presuppositions of communication'. As Habermas explains it:

> I prefer to speak of general presuppositions of communicative action because I take the type of action aimed at reaching understanding to be fundamental. Thus I start from the assumption . . . that other forms of social action – for example, conflict, competition, strategic action in general – are derivatives of action oriented to reaching understanding.
> (Habermas, 1979, p. 1)

So, Habermas contrasts strategic with communicative rationality, and these mirror the distinction drawn between system and lifeworld (Dryzek, 1995, p. 101). I will explain these concepts in turn because they play an important role in Habermas' theoretical framework and are, moreover, important for my purposes in examining the recent experiences of the universities.

Strategic rationality, according to Stephen K. White, is the dominant 'conception of practical reason in social science. This conception is most explicitly embraced by those who consider themselves rational choice theorists' (White, 1989, p. 10). Under this banner we see particular models of action and rationality: action is intentional, self-interested behaviour in an objectivated world. Rational action is conceptualised in terms of the efficiency of means to ends (White, 1989, p. 10).

As White points out, however, self-interested behaviour is not conceptually necessary to the strategic model of action. In practical terms though, it is an assumption which rational choice theorists usually add in to their frame because self-interest seems a straightforwardly universalisable motivation. Nonetheless, it remains that strategic and prudential actions are not one and the same thing. The conclusions which rational choice theorists draw are important because they illuminate the sort of collective action which can be expected if individuals conform to a purely strategic rationality. In this respect, they help to answer the Hobbesian problem of how purely strategic agents can come to agree upon a set of collective arrangements which are good for all. As White phrases the question: '[T]o what degree can we account for cooperative as well as the conflictual dimension in political life without any appeal to motivations which are not exclusively self-interested and to some moral sense of rationality?' (White, 1989, p. 11). His point, of course, is that a solely strategic model of rationality has a normative significance as well as the explanatory powers which rational choice theorists claim.

The problem with working with a purely strategic, or instrumental, mode of rationality is that it has difficulty in accounting for how such strategically rational actors provide themselves with public, or collective, goods (goods which, because they cannot be withheld from one individual without withholding them from all, must be supplied communally), or even goods which are neither purely public nor purely privately consumed. The paradigm example in political theory hinges on providing a just set of political arrangements. White explains the emptiness of the rational-choice theorist's account of voting:

> The difficulty involved with cooperative action to provide collective goods revolves around the results of a rational actor's calculations as to whether the costs of participating in such action outweigh the benefits. For example, in regard to voting, it appears that a rational individual would decide not to vote, for the simple reason that the cost in time and effort of that act is far too high when measured against the benefit of having his party win, once he considers the likelihood that his one vote will make the difference between his party winning or losing. By not voting, the individual does not measurably change the probability of the collective good (his party in office) being supplied: if his party loses, it would have done so even if he had . . . voted; if it wins, he gets the benefit of the collective good without any cost, that is, as a free rider.
>
> (White, 1989, p. 12)

The good of a just set of political arrangements requires participation and participation requires moral commitment. Moral commitment can be supplied through a higher education that demands engagement in an atmosphere of civility.

Higher education as an instrumental private good

Of course, many people in representative democracies do still vote, but there are growing concerns that not enough do. I introduce this idea, however, to show up some similarities in the arguments for various methods of providing and funding higher education. Recently, this has meant a question of where the balance lies between financing universities through, on the one hand, tuition fees paid by students (and their families) and research contracts with private industry and the state and, on the other hand, the state raising funds through general taxation and distributing these via the higher education funding and research councils.

Decisions taken on how university education ought to be funded have focused upon the extent to which a degree benefits the individual graduate, or whether the benefits accrue more generally to society. If the former holds then a degree can be conceived as a private good; if the latter holds then a university education must be a public good, even if not purely in the technical sense – obviously, social benefits are derived from the existence of higher education, but these are not the same as the benefits which accrue to the individual graduate. Attempts to calculate the individual and the social returns on higher education simply miss one of the main points of higher education: namely, that university education is part of civil society, the (immanent) service it can provide in terms of scientific advancement, cultural gains and moral refinement cannot be reduced to the financial calculus of cost-benefit analysis (Cohen & Arato, 1994, pp. 37–41). Despite this, the claim that the benefits of a university education largely accrue to the individual graduate was used to justify the policy of tuition fees being charged to undergraduates and a system of student loans that replaced Local Education Authority maintenance grants. Even under the same logic the subtleties were missed: for instance, individual benefits will accrue at varying rates to graduates of varying universities in varying subject areas, while different gains are distributed along gender, ethnic and social class lines. Moreover, the financial benefits that graduates are said to gain from possessing a degree will be considerably lessened under a system whereby between a third and a half of all young people graduate with some kind of higher education qualification. In Britain, the supposedly elite Russell Group of universities has been arguing since that group's inception for uncapped tuition fees, along the lines of the fee system employed by universities in the United States, that is differential rates of tuition fees across various universities set by these institutions themselves, in order to compete in an international higher education market place. These institutions' managers and vice-chancellors argue that they are currently hampered from competing effectively on the global level because of a lack of sufficient state funding. That such a differential fee structure will emerge is inevitable given that recent and current governments have been so keen to relieve the public purse through measures such as public/private partnership arrangements. The loans system, however, merely pushes the funding problem into the future and onto the next generation.

The benefits accruing to the individual graduate, however, cannot be calculated in terms of future individual income alone, if at all. As Elie Kedourie puts it, 'The methods, the ethos, the established traditions, the particular intellectual style, the quality of mind which a university and its teachers preserve, nurture and transmit – these are what count' (Kedourie, 1989, p. 11). Of course, it is precisely these factors which refuse to fit into a strategically oriented rationality. We might argue over the extent to which such qualities survive in the current university system, but it remains that they are not quantifiable and cannot be crudely assessed in terms of a private return. To put it another way, if we regard the function of the university in terms of, firstly (though not in any order of importance), material reproduction and, secondly, symbolic reproduction, then we might have a chance at calculating the returns on the former, but this would render the latter invisible. Put bluntly, higher education cannot be conceived as a private investment good alone, though sometimes it functions in this way. A university education, and indeed all education worthy of the name, functions to support and ameliorate our civilization.[3] How it does this is necessarily open to debate, but the fact that this is the central purpose of education from a normative perspective makes education a public good as much as a just set of political arrangements. Indeed, we might well say that it is a necessary part of just political arrangements. The very fact that a higher education is, for the most part, considered a private investment good shows us that a strategic form of rationality is coming to dominate this sphere. This is, however (and unfortunately), an empirical point. It is not to say that our universities should be considered in this narrow way. It is, after all, another empirical point when we say that universities and the scholarship that often goes on within them have, on the whole, contributed positively to the world. This is obviously not to say that only good things come from the university, but that learning and societal development allow for increased individual autonomy which contributes to the commonwealth of society in terms of a democratic gain.

Communicative reason

A communicative model of rationality makes room for the aspects dropped by strategic rationality in the foregoing discussion. In other words, communicative rationality is intended to illuminate one-sided or foreshortened conceptions of reason and the pathologies of modernity. Stephen K. White explains that the main issue in Habermas' thought is the idea of an incomplete project of the Enlightenment. Habermas is trying to demonstrate that instrumental or strategic rationality is a one-sided conception of reason. This is the Arendtian critique of the rise of the social expressed in different terms. For Habermas, Weber's theory of rationalisation therefore demonstrates a threat to human emancipation (White, 1989, p. 25).

Communicative action is that where actors are oriented towards coming to an understanding, where this understanding is motivated by no more than the force of the better argument. Such a process has built into it a rationality, but it does not take a strategic form, which is determined by the efficiency of means to ends. Rather, Habermas claims that:

> [T]he speech acts of communicatively competent actors conform to a set of rules, some of which establish the criteria of communicative rationality. What Habermas calls 'rational-reconstruction' is the task of rendering what is a universal competence or implicit know-how into a set of explicit rules; in this case he is reconstructing 'formal-pragmatic' rules.
>
> (White, 1989, p. 28)

So, for instance, someone who is engaged in communicative action, in performing a speech act, raises certain discursively redeemable validity claims. This means that a person who participates in a process aimed at reaching understanding must raise the following validity claims:

> The speaker must choose a comprehensible [*verständlich*] expression so that speaker and hearer can understand one another. The speaker must have the intention of communicating a true [*wahr*] proposition . . . so that the hearer can share the knowledge of the speaker. The speaker must want to express his intentions truthfully [*wahrhaftig*] so that the hearer can believe the utterance of the speaker (can trust him). Finally, the speaker must choose an utterance that is right [*richtig*] so that the hearer can accept the utterance and speaker and hearer can agree with one another in the utterance with respect to a recognized normative background. Moreover, communicative action can continue undisturbed only as long as participants suppose that the validity claims they reciprocally raise are justified. The goal of coming to an understanding [*Verständigung*] is to bring about an agreement [*Einverständnis*] that terminates in the intersubjective mutuality of reciprocal understanding, shared knowledge, mutual trust, and accord with one another.
>
> (Habermas, 1979, pp. 2–3)

Communicative rationality, then, refers to the process of coming to an understanding or agreement, and thus coordinating action, through employing validity claims oriented to truth, rightness and sincerity (that is, cognitive, normative and aesthetic validity claims), whereas non-social instrumental or social strategic purposive rationality [*Zweckrationalität*] takes as its telos a form of mastery over the world. To relate this to the university we can say that the academic community, in an ideal form, appeals to a communicative rationale, rather than a strategic one. Even though in the concrete settings of universities academics often display a strategic rationality (insofar as there is a career structure to climb, courses to be administered efficiently, research grant applications to be made, periods of sabbatical to be secured and metrics to be chased), the action of what academics research and teach is informed by open debate throughout the academic community. Policy-makers have attempted to generate a balanced set of metrics in order to keep the central goals of the university in view. However, this still allows the democratic horizon to drop out of sight. Although individual academics compete with one another, this does not mean that scholarship relates most closely to a strategic mode of action. What it does mean, however, is that in practice it is difficult to distinguish between strategic and communicative action. How, the question must be, can we decide whether people, academics in this instance, are operating according to a mode orientated towards reaching understanding in their actions or according to more instrumental motives? In everyday life these forms of action must overlap. As Stephen K. White notes in relation to criticisms which Fred Dallmayr has levelled at Habermas: 'the more you scratch at the surface of communicative action, the more it begins to resemble strategic action' (White, 1989, p. 46). There is a problem here of adequately separating an orientation to consensus from an instrumental orientation. This, it is suggested, arises because both strategic and communicative action are teleological; the difference lies in their having different goals. Habermas says as much:

> [T]he teleological structure is fundamental to all concepts of action. Concepts of social action are distinguished, however, according to how they specify the coordination among the goal-directed actions of different participants. . . . In all cases the teleological structure of action is presupposed, inasmuch as the capacity for goal-setting and goal-directed action is ascribed to actors, as well as interest in carrying out their plans of action. But only the strategic model rests content with an explication of the features of action oriented directly to success. . . . In the case of communicative action the interpretive accomplishments on which cooperative processes of interpretation are based represent the mechanism for coordinating action; communicative action is not exhausted by the act of reaching understanding in an interpretive manner.
>
> (Habermas, 1991, p. 101)

All action is teleological in some sense, otherwise it would cease to be action and merely be some kind of inadvertent twitch. Similarly, reason has to be teleological if we are to be able to distinguish between, for instance, good and bad reasons. This does not make all reason or all action instrumental. For language, as White puts it, 'is not simply an instrument in Habermas's account but also a pre-existing context' (White, 1989, p. 47). This idea of the linguistic context, or the lifeworld [*Lebenswelt*], takes us a little further on this question, because we can look to the context within which action takes place rather than simply looking at the actions of individuals. To be clear, I mentioned that it could be impossible to determine whether a scholar was acting in a communicative (and scholarly) manner or was simply orientated towards personal career success, for example, in a strategic way. Fortunately, we do not have to be pushed to make this judgement. We can examine instead the contextual background within which academics work, and this is what I have tried to do in preceding chapters. The contextual background will, of course, vary between different disciplines and different universities, though insofar as it is meaningful to speak of the university and of higher education, we should be able to paint in broad strokes.

Norms of 'narrow civility' ensure undistorted communication within formal publics (Estlund, 2008, chapter X, *passim*), while 'wide civility' is appropriate within informal publics. One way of understanding the university is as a public that educates in understanding the appropriateness of both wide and narrow civility. There is interesting scope here for research in deliberative democracy and education.

System and lifeworld

Habermas takes the idea of the social lifeworld from the phenomenology of Alfred Schutz. Habermas writes that:

> Subjects acting communicatively always come to an understanding in the horizon of a lifeworld. Their lifeworld is formed from more or less diffuse, always unproblematic, background convictions. This lifeworld background serves as a source of situation definitions that are presupposed by participants as unproblematic. . . . The lifeworld also stores the interpretive work of preceding generations. It is the conservative counterweight to the risk of disagreement that arises with every actual process of reaching understanding; for communicative actors can achieve an understanding only by way of taking yes/no positions on criticizable validity claims. The relation between these weights changes with the decentration of worldviews. The more the worldview that furnishes the cultural stock of knowledge is decentred, the less the need for understanding is covered in advance by an interpreted lifeworld immune from critique, and the more this need has to be met by the interpretive accomplishments of the participants themselves.
> (Habermas, 1991, p. 70)

The lifeworld presents us with a backdrop stock of knowledge, a store of cultural recipes, as Schutz put it, which is always already at hand for actors to draw on. Habermas, however, develops the idea of what he terms the 'rationalized lifeworld'. Here the lifeworld takes on a sense of reflexivity. The conditions of modernity gives us less in the way of unproblematic traditional knowledge to draw on as knowledge comes to be specialised, through a cultural rationalisation, along cognitive, normative and aesthetic lines. Simultaneously, growing system complexity at the level of societal rationalisation leads to the development of communicative short-cuts as the steering media of money and power replace the need for understanding between participants in discourse. This eventually results in an 'uncoupling' of system and lifeworld. Habermas explains that:

> Everyday communicative practice is . . . embedded in a lifeworld context defined by cultural tradition, legitimate orders, and socialized individuals. Interpretive performances draw upon and advance consensus. The rationality potential of mutual understanding in language is actualized to the extent that motive and value generalization progress and the zones of what is unproblematic shrink. The growing pressure for rationality that a problematic lifeworld exerts upon the mechanism of mutual understanding increases the need for achieved consensus, and this increases the expenditure of interpretive energies and the risk of dissensus. It is these demands and dangers that can be headed off by media of communication. The way these media function differs according to whether they focus consensus

formation in language through specializing in certain aspects of validity and hierarchizing processes of agreement, or whether they uncouple action coordination from consensus formation in language altogether, and neutralize it with respect to the alternatives of agreement or failed agreement.
(Habermas, 1992a, pp. 182–183)

The lifeworld begins to fail to keep up with the complex demands asked of it. The power of tradition to legitimate practices, for instance, weakens. In order to deal with this situation, systemic 'steering media' short-circuit the need for understanding. Take the academic community as an example of a rationalised lifeworld. Especially in a mass higher education sector, we could conceive of agreements to be increasingly difficult to reach. One instance might be the replacement of democratic governance of universities by academics with managers specialised in administration; another example would be the idea of peer review of research. It would be a burdensome task to judge the worth of all academic research via communicative means and, therefore, alternative arrangements are made, in this case the bibliometric REF exercises or a Teaching Excellence Framework that looks as though it will measure teaching quality based on graduate employment outcomes. These metrics operate as steering media and bypass the need for any consensus within a community of scholars. Habermas explains this uncoupling of subsystems from the rationalised lifeworld:

> The transfer of action coordination from language over to steering media means an uncoupling of interaction from lifeworld contexts. Media such as money and power attach to empirical ties; they encode a purposive-rational attitude towards calculable amounts of value and make it possible to exert generalized, strategic influence on the decisions of other participants while bypassing processes of consensus-oriented communication. Inasmuch as they do not merely simplify linguistic communication, but replace it with symbolic generalization of rewards and punishments, the lifeworld contexts in which processes of reaching understanding are always embedded are devalued in favour of media-steered interactions; the lifeworld is no longer needed for the coordination of action.
> (Habermas, 1992a, p. 183)

This is what Habermas refers to as a 'technicization of the lifeworld', and the results, when related to the sphere of the university, are a far cry from Veblen's idea of idle curiosity or from Nietzsche's claim to be a 'friend of lento' (Nietzsche, 1997, p. 5).[4] Media-steered subsystems thus distort the sphere of intellectual inquiry resulting in the production of ideology; 'the subjective inconspicuousness of systemic constraints that instrumentalise a communicatively structured lifeworld takes on the character of deception, of objectively false consciousness' (Habermas, 1992a, p. 187).

The colonisation of the lifeworld

Such deformations of the lifeworld are, then, systemically induced as the media-steered subsystems (the economy and bureaucratic administration are the most obvious of these – money and power are the media themselves) first split off from their lifeworld context and then react back upon it. A functionalist rationality – that is, where a 'system becomes more rational as its complexity increases . . . as its range of adaptation to environmental changes is enhanced' – enhances the capacity for material reproduction (White, 1989, p. 104). However:

> The specific problem Habermas wants to illuminate is how the development of capitalism, with its differentiated subsystems of economy and administration, can be understood both as an evolutionary advance from a systems perspective, but also as a phenomenon which methodically undermines the processes by which a rationalized lifeworld is reproduced.
> (White, 1989, pp. 104–105)

The same structural differentiation of value spheres which makes possible the rationalised lifeworld eventually leads to a reification, on the one hand, which is to say that the medium of money and the subsystem of the economy become the dominant steering mechanisms of sociation, and on the other hand, there results a cultural impoverishment, a growing differentiation of value spheres which leads to a desolation, an epistemic alienation: understanding becomes possible only for experts in their own specific fields. This dual thesis mirrors Weber's idea that rationalisation results both in the iron cage of bureaucratisation and the loss of magic, or disenchantment, resulting from processes of modernisation.

Reification, for Habermas, takes the form of a 'colonisation of the lifeworld' which begins when the media of money and power begin to displace communicatively structured sociation in terms of cultural transmission, social integration and socialisation. While action coordinated discursively makes possible understanding, action steered by the media of money or power takes on an objectivating attitude and an orientation to success (White, 1989, p. 110). Habermas, since he wants to hold on to the possibility of a rationalised lifeworld that is communicatively structured, wants to point to a boundary line beyond which mediatisation intended to enhance material reproduction will create pathological side-effects which threaten symbolic reproduction of the lifeworld, in other words our ways of sociating, our democratic practices and how we come to understand our lives. This threat to symbolic reproduction will have a deleterious effect on our abilities to take up critical positions to events in the world around us. These processes are shown up in the manner that individuals increasingly become private consumers and clients of the welfare state rather than citizens capable of privately and publicly autonomous action. For instance, the student as a customer of the university's higher education no longer has the same orientation towards acting and building the world because she comes to regard herself as a skill set for appropriate labour markets. As Stephen K. White explains:

> Habermas is claiming, then, that the pathologies specific to contemporary capitalism arise as the media of money and power increasingly infiltrate spheres of social life in which traditions and knowledge are transferred, in which normative bonds are intersubjectively established, and in which responsible persons are formed.
> (White, 1989, p. 110)

One form of colonisation that Habermas sketches is the phenomenon of 'juridification', that is, increases in formal law within the welfare state. This tends to force citizenship into a private, rather than a public, category. Citizens thus increasingly orient themselves towards the state in terms of a strategically rational attitude. In short, private citizens become consumers of state services, and state services become private goods (Habermas, 1992a, p. 350). Of course, not all formal law results in juridification, as Habermas' later work in the field of legal theory goes to great pains to point out. Law has both freedom-guaranteeing and freedom-reducing aspects. In the light of this, Habermas draws a distinction between 'regulative' and 'constitutive' law (Habermas, 1992a, p. 366). The former connects to already existing institutions within the lifeworld. The latter, however, follows the imperatives of economic or bureaucratic systems and, therefore, takes on a colonising role. The steering mechanisms intended to render universities accountable to state funding function as constitutive law, shifting the academic norms and displacing democratic values and a public orientation. The broad culture that supports the legitimacy of the democratic state is undermined.

Cultural impoverishment relates to the idea of a loss of meaning in the modern world, equivalent to Weber's concept of disenchantment. It is the result of a structurally differentiated lifeworld that has gone beyond its own limits of self-understanding. Here, expert cultures split-off from everyday practice, which results in a reduced opportunity for communicatively structured action since understanding is no longer available to all. Expert cultures, then, take on a functional role, and we see as much in the increasingly consultative role of social science research, for instance. What we have is a situation where cultural impoverishment or desolation acts as a catalyst for processes of colonisation and the end point of which will be either an over-regulation of individuals and a smothering of their capacities to act autonomously, or a form of anomie where understanding (and associated critical capacities) other than a functional recognition of, and response to, systemic imperatives will be removed from the range of possibilities available to individuals.

Habermas suggests that one possible avenue for a critical research programme to follow relates to the development of legal theory along discursively oriented lines. One reason for this is that law connects system and lifeworld insofar as it is both regulative and constitutive of actions. However, there is equally good reason to see these pathological processes at work in our education system, and education also binds system and lifeworld together. We can regard the education which is offered up to citizens and future citizens as a kind of hinge which links together our abilities to become the authors of our own laws with the technical knowledge required for material reproduction. Indeed, Habermas has already commented on the tendency towards instrumental reason in universities (Habermas, 1987, 1994). He criticises a one-sidedly instrumental idea of the university which looks solely towards the production and transmission of technically exploitable knowledge. Rather, there are (at least) three further responsibilities connected to the university. Firstly, equipping graduates with the 'extrafunctional abilities' not contained within professional knowledge and skills. Here, he is referring to 'those attributes and attitudes relevant to the pursuit of a professional career', such as leadership skills and capability of exercising official authority. Habermas writes that 'Of course, the university certainly does not produce the virtues of these unwritten professional standards, but the pattern of its socialization processes must at least be in harmony with them' (Habermas, 1987, p. 2). This, however, differs markedly from today's universities in Britain, at least. Here and now universities attempt to force such capabilities into a written form and make them part of the curriculum in response to state requirements that universities cater to the demands – which are often ill-thought through and short-termist – of employers. Secondly, universities are responsible for transmitting, fostering and developing the cultural tradition of society. And thirdly, 'the university has always fulfilled a task that is not easy to define; today we would say that it forms the political consciousness of its students. For too long, the consciousness that took shape at German universities was apolitical. It was a singular mixture of inwardness . . . and of loyalty to state authority' (Habermas, 1987, p. 3).

This apolitical culture within the universities which Habermas laments is all too evident today. It takes the form of a depoliticised student body, inwardly oriented towards issues of identity, but also a professionalised conception of the academic whose research is functional and consultative in its nature. The university is no longer constituted by people, but by administration through rules and steered by metrics. The culture that emerges from this is catalysed by a populist social media and is deeply damaging for democratic politics. Hopefully, the lack of critical perspective available in increasingly instrumental universities will not have such disastrous consequences as fascism, the concern that remains in the background of Habermas' work. However, at a time when education is considered to play an important role in enabling social mobility and equality of opportunity, it is strikingly odd that the form that this education takes is increasingly oriented to the economy at the expense of democratic politics.

The ideas of the university

> Institutions are forms of objective spirit. An institution remains capable of functioning only as long as it embodies in living form the idea inherent in it. As soon as the spirit leaves it, an institution rigidifies into something purely mechanical, as an organism without a soul decomposes into dead matter.
> (Habermas, 1994, p. 101)

Cardinal Newman in *The Idea of the University*, first published in 1873, argues that the purpose of the university is the enlargement of the mind, something which serves to raise the intellectual cultural tone. His comments demonstrate, I think, that this notion of the instrumental university is in no way recent. Newman pointed out that universities are generally considered merely as places for acquiring knowledge.

> Knowledge then is the indispensable condition of expansion of mind, and the instrument of attaining to it; this cannot be denied, it is ever to be insisted upon; I begin with it as a first principle; however, the very truth of it carries men too far, and confirms to them the notion that it is the whole of the matter. A narrow mind is thought to be that which contains little knowledge; and an enlarged mind, that which holds a great deal. . . . And yet this notion is, I conceive, a mistake . . . the end of a Liberal Education is not mere knowledge, or knowledge considered in its matter.
> (Newman, 1976, pp. 115–117)

Enlargement of mind is, for Newman, not only the knowledge that is taught, but also the attitude we take on in acquiring it.

> The enlargement consists, not merely in the passive reception into the mind of a number of ideas hitherto unknown to it, but in the mind's energetic and simultaneous action upon and towards and among those new ideas, which are rushing in upon it . . . it is a making the objects of our knowledge subjectively our own, or, to use a familiar word, it is a digestion of what we receive, into the substance of our previous state of thought; and without this no enlargement is said to follow. . . . It is not the mere addition to our knowledge that is the illumination; but the locomotion, the movement onwards, of that mental centre, to which both what we know, and what we are learning, the accumulating mass of our acquirements, gravitates. And therefore a truly great intellect . . . is one which takes a connected view of old and new, past and present, far and near, and which has an insight into the influence of all these on one another; without which there is no whole, and no centre. It possesses the knowledge, not only of things, but also of their mutual and true relations; knowledge, not merely considered as acquirement, but as philosophy.
> (Newman, 1976, pp. 120–121)

An education, then, is more than the facts, facts, facts demanded by Mr Gradgrind's utilitarian pedagogy, more than the delivery of learning materials via the internet, and more than a system of accreditation where threshold competences have to be demonstrated by the student to the teacher and by the teacher to the state institutions that police the education system. Newman's idea of the university is based upon an institution which preserves and transmits knowledge. It takes elite teaching to be the primary focus of the university, and it does so because Newman's university is derived from a Christian mediaeval tradition (connecting the elite and the elect) where the emphasis is on cultivating the character of an elite in line with the traditional authority of the Church (Halsey, 1992, pp. 24–25). Newman's idea harked back to the origins of mediaeval universities engaged in vocational training for ecclesiastical office.

An alternative, and more modern, idea of the university originates in Germany in the form of the research university. This idea was exported to the United States and found its institutional expression at the likes of Johns Hopkins and in the University of Chicago (Halsey, 1992, p. 39). According to Thorstein Veblen, writing from Chicago in 1918, the

> single distinguishing function unique to the university was the pursuit of knowledge, not for profit nor indeed for any utilitarian purpose but simply to satisfy idle curiosity. The university of the future, he [Veblen] thought, made this the only unquestioned duty incumbent on the university. He recognized, of course, that the advancement of higher learning involved two lines of work, distinct but closely bound together – scientific inquiry and the instruction of students. . . . [However] the work of teaching properly belonged in the university only in so far as it facilitated the pursuit of new knowledge in science and scholarship. It had an appropriate place only in so far as it trained each rising generation of scholars and scientists for the further pursuit of knowledge. Training for other purposes was necessarily of a different kind and was best done elsewhere.
> (Halsey, 1992, p. 41)

Whilst it is the quest for knowledge which is central to Veblen's idea of the university, this is pursuit of knowledge for its own sake, not for the purposes of application. For Veblen, the university was a place suited to the idle curiosity of the student, inappropriate to the ethic of business salesmanship. Thus, the research university that he has in mind finds no equivalent in contemporary British universities, where the business ethic has been forced on faculties by state policy. Research, Veblen argues, should not be undertaken in search of profit, or any other utilitarian purpose, but only to satisfy our curiosity.

With Newman we have the idea of the teaching university; in Veblen we find the research university. One opens up a critique of the kind of training in skills which universities have moved towards; the other points to the dangers of a commercialised research culture in the universities. Of course, universities reflect the culture they inhabit just as they attempt to define and shape that culture. However, part of the problem is that as our universities have opened up, ceased to educate only an elite group of students and begun to engage in research on behalf of industry and the state, they have also become prone to be shaped by the culture outside of their walls and less able to determine cultural standards. The university no longer stands at the apex of a cultural hierarchy. The result is that it has become less plausible to speak of an idea of the university. The foundational idea of the university disintegrates in the face of the differentiation of value spheres and increased system complexity which characterise modernity. The modern university, properly speaking, can have no idea or, at least, no unifying idea. Habermas explains that Max Weber's theory of the development of bureaucracy demonstrates that organisations no longer embody ideas (Habermas, 1994, p. 102). This renders Jasper's claim impotent that only those who embody the idea of the university can think and act appropriately for the university.

On such a reading of Weber a rationalised, modern university is too highly culturally differentiated and unable to direct increasingly autonomous subsystems to hold on to a unifying idea. In other words, colonisation of the lifeworld and cultural impoverishment spell the end of the idea of the university. Once this is recognised we can see that the possibility of resurrecting the idea of the university will be no mean feat. Habermas argues that university expansion after 1945, alongside the increasing separation of teaching from research in the universities, makes a functionalist interpretation of change in higher education compelling. Expansion of the universities in the twentieth century, in line with general patterns of modernisation, helped to create well-known ideologies of growth and economic development, social mobility and meritocracy – all fostered through higher education and academic research. Rather than renew the idea of the university for new times, science, scholarship and education became functionally autonomous and dropped the need for normative validity in the self-understanding of the universities' scientists and students. Functional autopoiesis replaced normative autonomy as systemic mechanisms began to steer university administration in the direction of technically usable knowledge and professional qualifications that emphasise technical skill (Habermas, 1994, p. 106).

But this, I think, is based upon a one-sidedly functionalist appropriation of Weber which leads inexorably towards disenchantment and the iron cage: remember that, for Weber, rational-legal authority stands alongside traditional and charismatic authority and the picture begins to look less austere. After all, in our universities the ideas of truth, rightness and authenticity do still hold sway. In science, scholarship, learning and teaching in the university students, researchers and lecturers appeal to unifying ideas – or, at least, they could be said to hold on to a certain commonality in their self-interpretations as members of the university. And, insofar as they do, they appeal to an academic ethic, a style of conduct appropriate to the idea of the university. These ideas, or common self-interpretations, may be transgressed, they may be set aside for pragmatic reasons, and this might well be done on an increasingly frequent basis, but it remains that within the lifeworldly horizon of the university we can still speak of the relevance of a normative model of the university. The alienation of academics and students comes from the conflict between the way the normative idea clashes with the lived experience. Habermas suggests that scholarly and scientific productivity may well depend on a bundling of functions within the university. Research productivity, he suggests, is likely to depend on general education, preparation for future academic professionals and the formation of public opinion (Habermas, 1994, p. 107). This would be so because it is the university as a communication community that generates the diverse opinions and inquisitive dispositions that support new connections between old ideas.

Moreover, the fact remains that we still have institutions which we refer to as universities, where academics work and train, students are examined for degrees and public opinion forms around theoretical and empirical research. To the extent that universities act in ways which make them recognisable as universities, the idea of the university must still remain, even if it is fading. But, certainly, we can at least claim relevance for the idea of the university if we can appeal to it as a kind of critical yardstick and a template against which to judge policy and practice, rather than an unrealistic model to emulate. It is only with a normative ideal in mind that we can see problems connected to democratic legitimacy and pathologies of education modelled on status, success and inflamed *amour propre*. The question we must bear in mind is how far the university allows for the kind of free inquiry that enables genuine progress (rather than merely measurable output) in knowledge and understanding.

Just as we find Newman to be critical of any conception of university teaching as the delivery of modules of information and Veblen to be critical of a university research culture steered by commercial attitudes, it is in Humboldt's idea of the university that we find that some of the other current problems facing higher learning and scholarship are addressed. Humboldt is concerned with how scholarship and science can be institutionalised without protection from the church. Unprotected, the universities lie at the mercy of the state and the market, where both have an overwhelming interest in the applications of scientific and scholarly work, rather than the work itself (Habermas, 1994, p. 108).

Humboldt, in other words, wants to preserve the early liberal idea of the quarantine model of the university: 'Just as the liberal principle [under early capitalism] delimited a realm of economic activity separate from the state, so too the university was conceived as possessing an institutional autonomy that must be preserved at all costs from external interference' (Smith, 1991, p. 194). However, as Humboldt realised, university autonomy could not be secured through privatising the university and separating it from the state, for institutions of science and scholarship had to be protected from both political interference via the state and social imperatives via the market. What was required was a *Kulturstaat* where the state would guarantee the university an internally unlimited freedom to conduct itself as a university. It was the state rather than the market which would offer universities autonomy because of the

> beneficial consequences that the unifying, totalizing power of science and scholarship institutionalized as research would necessarily have. If scientific and scholarly work were left to the inner dynamics of the research process, and if the principle of 'regarding science as something that has not yet been and never will be completely discovered' were maintained, then . . . the moral culture, indeed the whole spiritual life of the nation would come to be concentrated in the institutions of higher learning.
> (Habermas, 1994, p. 109)

An autonomous university offers tangible gains. One such gain is the reproduction of the capacity for action in terms of democratic authority. This is even more obvious in a climate of uncertainty, where we, as citizens, are left with little real choice but to trust in science or, more specifically, to trust in the caricature of science which is presented to us through television, newspapers, social media and popular science books. That trust would be better placed in an academic rather than a commercial science. For, unfortunately, a time has now been reached when so much confusion reigns over the idea of science that we can speak of different scientific orientations. Allow a reductionist example to illustrate the point: we have scientists in laboratories working for giant pharmaceutical corporations alongside scientists in lecture halls within universities. But we live in an age of surfaces, and the scientist in the former will, on average, have more to show. Her salary will, in all likelihood, be higher, her laboratory equipment will be newer, her work, however, is still scientific. The university scientist is relatively poorly rewarded, yet it is this scientist bound by the academic ethic who ought to elicit our trust. The values of truth, morality and trust are rewarded by social status no longer. Instead, we collectively trust in commercial interests and their application of science and then worry about the after-effects later. The point, however, is that scientists and scholars are defined not only by what they do, but also how they do it. The ethical conduct of the scientist or scholar is as essential to her identity as her job title, employer, work done or qualifications already gained. Gradually, however, the requirement of a style of conduct is being replaced by a system of branding designed to indicate competence to an outside world composed of potential customers.

Humboldt's view could not have been more different. As Tony Smith puts it:

> In this view the mission of the universities was to provide a solid grounding in the traditional faculties. Philosophy was looked upon as the centerpiece, integrating the content of the other faculties into one coherent view. An individual having undergone training in this Universitas litterarum

would possess the moral and aesthetic sensibility and wide-ranging learning required for enlightened autonomy.

(Smith, 1991, p. 195)

Within Humboldt's idea theory was related directly to praxis. But this relationship was not the one that exists between practice and a training in skills[5] or technique because the university was insulated from the need for material production:

> Scientists in the universities engaged in what was called 'natural philosophy,' the goal of which was the discovery of ultimate metaphysical truths regarding the universe. These men had no concern whatsoever for the practical application of their theories. Conversely, the practical men in the shop had little use for theory. They regarded traditional lore and the lessons of experience as sufficient in their search for profit. These techniques of production were rules of thumb passed from generation to generation without formal instruction. Around the turn of the twentieth century all this changed. The centuries-long split between science and the useful arts was overcome. Science became a direct means of capital accumulation through the application of discoveries in physics and chemistry to the processes of commodity production.
>
> (Smith, 1991, p. 195)

This process did not restrict itself to the natural sciences; the twentieth century saw the growth in the instrumental application of social sciences through new management and administrative sciences. This is clearly seen in the development of business studies as an academic discipline. Not only do business schools in our universities attract money via private research contracts and fees from overseas and MBA students, but business studies is acquiring the kind of integrative function which philosophy once held for Humboldt. The importance of commercial awareness, for instance, and skills required for business, become part of all aspects of the university curriculum at all levels. These tendencies are pushed forward by the actions of state bureaucracies: the research councils require the research students they fund to be trained in (transferable) research skills and methodology, for example. Business and research-method skills have the unifying role that belonged to philosophy. But these skills are not up to the job assigned to them because they cannot, so long as they are presented as skills, integrate the critical function at the core of academic discipline and this inadequate integrative capacity splits apart the conceptual unity of teaching and research. This is not to suggest that business is not a legitimate object of study but, rather, that it is in this field that some of the tendencies I point to are most apparent.

In Humboldt's romantic idea of the university, philosophy plays a special role. Philosophy here is a unifying power capable of unifying cultural tradition, socialisation and social integration. Habermas explains that philosophy was structured encyclopedically, in the round, to help bring about unity in terms of differentiated sub-disciplines. Philosophy was a reflexive form of culture itself and its Platonic form was intended to bring together scholarly research with the acquisition of a general education in order to develop the ethical character of the scholar-researcher and unify science and scholarship with a general project of enlightenment. Such a conception of philosophy clashes with a modern idea of esoterica, which is partially attributable to steering that encourages ever-greater specialisation in the name of progress (Habermas, 1994, pp. 110–111). The task for philosophy, then, was to act as a unifying force.

In these capacities philosophy is, no doubt, overburdened. What is being proposed amounts to philosophy replacing the integrative role of religion: reason replaces faith in tying together highly specialised and differentiated ways of thinking. Philosophy's task aims at unifying. It seeks to unify research and teaching, the scientific and scholarly disciplines, science and scholarship with general education, and science and scholarship with enlightenment. In the Humboldtian idea of the university philosophy rises up to acquire leadership over other schools, because all academics must be rooted in philosophy. This idea remains instituted in the universities insofar as the majority of doctoral candidates are examined as Doctors of Philosophy. However, the degree title disguises the fact that the kind of work done varies dramatically between different academic departments. Moreover, there has been a recent growth in the development of professionally oriented doctoral courses, such as Doctorates of Education, where taught courses are supplemented with professional experience and a shorter dissertation. However, this is an aside. The notion that philosophy should be elevated to the status required by Humboldt flies in the face of the reality of university structures. Philosophy departments, in terms of teaching and research, have lost their strength. On the one hand, student demand has fallen for philosophy, in general terms (though we can still point to the popularity of an Oxford PPE degree). By and large, the idea that a degree in the classics or philosophy leads to a career in the civil service or the BBC has passed. Students have become, and have, over the years, been instructed to become, much more instrumental in their choice of degree subject. And even this instrumentalism is one sided because it looks to employment as the dominant end purpose of a university education. Governments and employers recently bemoan the lack of skills in graduates without pausing to consider that the problem could be that universities are not well-suited to providing skills specifically for the workplace. In terms of research, philosophy has suffered because of the tacit requirement that research is useful and can be disseminated to user groups. The language that permeates the bureaucracies concerned with teaching and research is anathema to philosophy, which has reacted by turning in on itself. Rather than holding out the potential of integrating the separation of value spheres associated with increasing cultural differentiation, philosophy has specialised itself in a celebration of esoterica. Of course, esoteric debate between experts is inevitable. What is required is a concerted effort to encourage the disparate expert spheres to engage in dialogue with one another. This does happen through interdisciplinary research programmes and more flexible degree courses which allow credit-transfer. While this looks like a step in the right direction on the surface, this flexibility does not allow complete autonomy. Collaboration may be encouraged in research but it is still, by and large, purposive-rational research oriented towards the functionalism of state policy-making or private commercial interests. What is required is a more thorough self-reflection in science and scholarship, which would allow for and highlight connections between research and the lifeworld in terms of culture, traditions and the enlightenment of the public sphere (Habermas, 1994, p. 118).

The cultural impoverishment brought about by cultural rationalisation is, however, unlikely to be reversed by a naïve faith in self-reflection, especially when such reflexivity is hardly encouraged by the steering media in operation within the university system. It was unrealistic, Habermas himself reflects, to assume reflexivity in the logic of research itself where that research is highly differentiated into separate disciplines oriented towards objectivism. Only crisis moments lead to paradigm changes, but these are quasi-naturalistic rather than properly reflexive. However, where reflection on fundamental issues is established, this tends to settle into simply yet another discipline alongside others (Habermas, 1994, p. 119). Philosophy of education, for instance, merely stands as another optional module that the student might choose, or the academic might specialise in.

Cultural enrichment through reflection in science and scholarship is no automatic fix. The idea of the university is outmoded precisely because ideas and institutions have lost their integrative force in the face of increasing system complexity. Autonomous specialised subsystems form which have precisely one function and one mode of activity. It is this complexity that makes all talk of integrative ideas sound absurd.

But, this systems theory perspective takes a generalisation and applies it across all domains of action. Whilst we can see that the economy is steered by money and state administration guided by power, it is not so straightforwardly obvious that these subsystems are entirely autonomous (from one another if nothing else); neither is it obvious that no domain of action is governed by normative concerns or organised along principles informed by a unifying idea in the way that science and scholarship are actions undertaken within an academic ethic. Systems theory, which describes so well the removal of systems from democratic control, tells us that each area of social action must increasingly specialise into sets of subsystems uncoupled from one another and subject to steering media. At no point does it reflect on the appropriateness of such steering media, or the implications for differentiation and specialisation (Habermas, 1994, p. 121). For instance, if commercially viable research institutes and think tanks were to detach from the university and science and scholarship, will their independence be sustainable? They may well be financially sustainable, but their activities may not be sufficient in terms of the knowledge they generate. Think of how polling organisations have faced problems when they fail to predict election results. It's not long before academics are rushed into TV studios to explain why the polls got it wrong.

Modernisation, for Habermas, cannot be equated straightforwardly with specialisation of autonomous subsystems because some forms of life are dependent on an idea that is preserved at the level of the lifeworld. In the case of the university, Habermas argues, functional differentiation has occurred within the institution. It can be added that this has given rise to alternative sources of epistemic authority with respect to some of the functions of the university.

According to Talcott Parsons, the higher education system has four functions which it seeks to fulfil simultaneously. Firstly, there is the function of research and the connected matter of training new scientists and scholars. Secondly, there is the function of academic preparation for the professions and the production of technically usable knowledge. Thirdly, there is the function of general education. Finally, the university functions to contribute to intellectual enlightenment and cultural self-understanding. Now, in the United States, the higher education system is highly differentiated into separate kinds of institution: graduate schools, professional schools and colleges which, broadly, orient themselves, in varying degrees, towards the first three functions. The fourth function of the university is carried out by academics in their public capacity as intellectuals and, to be sure, through the process of enlightenment students engage with in the course of their education and the self-understanding academics develop in their work. In Britain the differentiation of the higher education system has been much less sure-footed. This is partly because the British system is so overwhelmingly dominated by the Newman idea institutionalised in universities like Oxford, Cambridge, St. Andrews and Durham. Differentiation in a system which holds the weight of such tradition will, inevitably, be resisted in places. Hence, we see in Britain ideas of the university competing with one another – some functions of the university tend to be employed in post-1992 universities, such as professional training and general education, while other universities (like, for instance, Imperial College or the University of Warwick) are geared towards the development of science and scholarship and the production of technically usable knowledge. Other universities, such as Oxford and Cambridge, focus on a general education. This analysis is, of course, too reductionist in its outlook; all universities bundle the functions together, but it is still plausible to speak of different types of university. This, however, is rather anachronistic because the idea of the university has been held on to for its unifying potential. The problem arises when universities specialise in a particular conception of the university to the exclusion of other legitimate functions because this limits the possibility of critical self-reflection and enlightenment. If we think, for instance, of science and scholarship and the relations between science and scholarship, morality and art, then the functions of these cultural value spheres produce what were once grasped as unities: research and training, science, scholarship and general education, science, scholarship and enlightenment and, indeed, the unity of science and scholarship themselves (Habermas, 1994, pp. 121–122).

So, when we come across references to 'research universities' and 'teaching universities' or universities which specialise in the production of knowledge for industry or the state we ought to be wary. The university, if it is anything, is a unifying force which cuts against the grain of cultural rationalisation. At once the university is a place where we come across highly specialist knowledge, but, at the same time, an institutionalisation of understanding between fields of specialist knowledge. If the university has an overriding idea it pertains to the reintegration of value spheres. It is the (often all too latent) potential to integrate knowledge of science and scholarship, morality and art that is the university's greatest strength in the context of the modern world, for this ability is instituted nowhere else. From a normative perspective the university can unify or balance competing categories: efficacy with civility, labour with work, steering media with norms and values. The reintegration of value spheres – a cultural enrichment – makes possible the recoupling of system and lifeworld. However, this is only conceivable in a process of enlightenment institutionalised along the lines of communicative reason.

The dualism of either state or market control (or freedom) for the university misses this point so long as it allows an unravelling of the bundle of functions of the university. It is only through a spirit of publicness that the university can hold on to its purposes. Otherwise the idea of the university gets steered towards instrumental goals of professional training and the production of technically usable (and therefore commodified) knowledge. But this is the problem with anchoring the university in an idea, for ideas blow in the wind:

> The ingenious thing about the old idea of the university was that it was supposed to be grounded in something more stable: the permanently differentiated scientific process itself. But if science can no longer be used to anchor ideas in this way, because the multiplicity of the disciplines no longer leaves room for the totalizing power of either an all-encompassing philosophical fundamental science or even a reflective form of material critique of science and scholarship that would emerge from the disciplines themselves, on what could an integrative self-understanding of the corporate body of the university be based?
>
> (Habermas, 1994, p. 123)

The only answer, for Habermas, lies in communication and language itself: 'it is the communicative forms of scientific and scholarly argumentation that hold university learning processes in their various functions together' (Habermas, 1994, p. 124). In short, the quest for truth is rooted in public argumentation and cannot be regarded as a steering medium of a specialised subsystem. Neither can the quest for truth be substituted by other steering media in a bid to offer universities which offer good value for money in terms of inputs and outputs. The university, if it is to hold its value, cannot leave behind the democratic horizon of a unifying lifeworld, but this poses a problem because the true value of both the university and higher education lie in their integrative potential. This is needed more than ever but it remains essentially immeasurable.

Summary

I have tried to argue that the idea of the university has a unique democratic value that is worth holding on to especially in times of political turmoil. Too often, our contemporary culture democracy is populist and short-termist and politics is reduced to a Schumpeterian battle between elites. Our newspapers and television channels are changing beyond recognition because of technological developments in social media. This charge is not new. Horkheimer and Adorno and John Dewey all made these claims. There is a tendency for contemporary politics, the media industries and experts in sales and marketing to appeal to our emotions as part of their sales techniques (Dewey, 2012). Rousseau pointed to education as a possible antidote. But education is now caught up in the same game. Axel Honneth points out that, for Dewey, the deviation in the press from

> the ideal of objective, informative and sociologically enlightening reporting is so harmful and fatal because it essentially prevents the formation of a public in the first place. In [Dewey's] view that would require that a group of people, brought together by the interdependence of their individual actions, reach an understanding about the 'consequences' of their 'associated activities' and thus about which of these they take to be desirable. Only if such a communicative understanding about the consequences of their associated action in the group comes about can we speak of the 'We' of the public.
> (Honneth, 2014, p. 273)

Cultural markets need a democratic counterweight which is largely absent in an atomised society. A public sphere focused on branding and glamour is not public at all where *amour propre* is inflamed. Rousseau argued that education's purpose was to dampen this tendency, but instead we have universities that sell the prospect of status and success through an entertaining student experience in return for debt. Accountability has lost its democratic aspect and instead means that state-funded institutions should be steered by targets in a quasi-market. Public institutions, however, have a democratic role in holding the state to account. They cannot perform this duty properly under market conditions.

The dominant 'polities of justification' all tend towards an economic form. These ignore calls for equality and authority. Instrumental learning fits with these economic polities, but does not sustain an outward orientation towards others or commitment to a public good involving moral duty (which appears as a cost to the individual). Moreover, the purposes of universities cannot support a 'fidelity of deference' towards the state and instead rely on a 'fidelity of reason'. In other words, the 'state service' of higher education is contracted out. This way of thinking shows the absurdity of a state imposed market for higher education, for the university's public purposes are not conducted for the state but for democracy itself. Knowledge cannot, in the last analysis, be privatised since for something to be known means it must be justified to others, and if something is publicly justified then – much like Wittgenstein argued with regard to language – it cannot be private. Part of the public understanding of the university is that it ought to subscribe to rational debate in science and scholarship. These activities inform the state and the public. As much as universities can provide evidential support for state policies, they can also criticise the policies of states or big business. The rationality involved cannot exclude anyone who participates through reasoned debate.

In Britain, a good deal of the controversy around policy change has been about headline tuition fee levels. However, much of the technical funding analysis has ignored the educational impact of cost-sharing, assuming that funding modes are ethically neutral. Dworkinian hypothetical insurance markets and Rawlsian veils of ignorance approach questions of distributive justice from a direction where impartiality is intended to ensure fairness. But, impartiality also creates a kind of moral myopia where the social meanings of goods become blurry. I have argued that goods are often sustained by their traditional social meanings and markets often threaten that sustainability. Part of the glue that holds universities together in an academic community across institutions and across languages and national borders is trust and cooperation. But competition and instrumental reason dissolve trust. Perhaps what is needed is a constitutional guarantee for universities in return for their democratic commitments. If universities take their public role seriously they need to curtail their trade in social status rather than autonomy. Students and educators are told they need to aspire for success, but aspiration to success is no more than the inflamed *amour propre* that Rousseau insisted education should transcend.

I argued that authority is commonly seen in terms of obedience to power, something the democrat is usually keen to limit, but it really holds a deeper meaning related to action and making the world. On this view, education is ultimately concerned with passing on the ability to act and re-make the world in the light of changing circumstances. The democratic burden on educators here is high and involves considerable trust, from students and from the rest of the community. Education prepares participants to act in the world by providing knowledge, self-confidence, virtues and skills. All of these combine into a 'language of action' that goes well beyond attributes for the labour market. But regimes intended to set educational standards are fixated on one utilitarian dimension related to life rather than the world. The upshot is that consumers of higher education do not acquire authority and educators are ill-equipped to deliver the good that students demand. Trusting relations between student and teacher are fractured in a higher education context where students report back on whether they are satisfied with their university experiences. It's perhaps relevant, and certainly interesting, that 'satisfaction' originally related to performing an act for a priestly authority to atone for sin.

I argued that liberal notions of the citizen are passive and limited, while the republican citizen participates. Higher education sets its sights too low when it regards citizenship in rights-bearing or basic Schumpeterian terms of choosing the right leaders. To sustain a viable democratic society citizens should be educated as if they are to be leaders, that is as if they are to assume authority, with thoughtful outward-oriented attitudes based on rational-critical attitudes. Universities can only provide such rational-critical graduates, however, if academics and students have the freedom to criticise. Market-based policies tend to pander to power.

The surveillance of state-funded services has generated instrumental rationality in a sphere intended to cultivate action. Higher education carries a heavy responsibility if it is to cultivate the capacity for action, but when understood on instrumental lines this responsibility starts to sound like weaving straw into gold because of the prohibitive costs of investment for technical training in high technology and financial industries. I suggested that training has become mistaken for education because of the loss of the world. If education is meant to reproduce the authority to sustain the world, then we can say that education only became training because of a previous failure in education that is further compounded by policies that misconstrue universities. Policies need to be redrawn that fully take into account the role of universities in supporting legitimate authority, not just by educating graduates but by seriously criticising states. If the democratic state is saintly, then the universities must operate as the devil's advocate.

I claimed that market systems often impoverish the goods they distribute. Instrumental reason spreads misinformation that disrupts the public sphere. The efficiency gains that are intended to be brought about through market competition can readily evaporate through corruption of the good distributed. In this situation attention falls on keeping up appearances of the good, and this generates problems of sincerity that undermine trust and authority but hold out some weak promise of success. This also explains the considerable resources expended by educational institutions on branding and advertising.

The siren call that led to new universities in the twentieth century was the causal link drawn between knowledge gains and economic growth. However, I think the expansion of higher education for economic gain has transformed higher education into further schooling. Alongside this inefficiency the purposes of universities in reproducing authority for the future have melted into air. The development of quality assurance and benchmarking in helping to coordinate the system hindered academic freedom in teaching and reduced academics to a functional role where judgement has pared down and conditions became ripe for grade inflation. The intellectual rewards of work within universities were diluted and the result has been the alienation of many academics and students. Higher education thus became stultifying rather than emancipatory.

The crisis in universities, therefore, goes beyond exploitative tuition fees and indebtedness, or alienating employment for junior academics, or too many graduates with skills unsuited to contemporary labour markets or the over production of over-specialised research published in esoteric and expensive journals. These are all symptoms of the malady that policy-makers are more or less keen to treat. However, the policy remedies that are designed to steer universities, academics and students in functional directions only serve to further undermine academic authority. The policy problem relates to the liberal state's difficulty in invoking social rights to support autonomy while trying to specify the content of those social rights. The solution to this problem in terms of higher education has been to open up the social right to the market place to let 'the market' determine the content. This, however, is the wrong arms-length prescription because the democratic state has to open itself up to rational-critical debate in order to sustain its own future. This explains why a focus on status, branding, consumer information sets, a balanced score-card of targets are all market-oriented mistakes. Rather than regard higher education policies towards universities in purely economic terms, we need to reconceive of universities as institutions that help to sustain democratic authority by supporting public reason over and between generations. Such a move would also serve to address much discontent with the political system too.

Notes

1 This text is an excerpt from Max Horkheimer and Theodor W. Adorno (2002) *Dialectic of Enlightenment: Philosophical Fragments*, Standford, CA: Stanford University Press.
2 It is frequently claimed that a university degree substantially increases an individual's lifetime earnings, and this claim is invoked to justify increased (or differential) tuition fee levels for students. It is pointed out less often that the 'rate of return to the highest education started to fall in most countries in the 1970s'. A. H. Halsey (1992) *Decline of Donnish Dominion: The British Academic Professions in the Twentieth Century*, Clarendon Press: Oxford, p. 9.
3 This is from Thorstein Veblen, for whom 'the possibility of a university was rooted in universal human nature as "the instinct of workmanship" and the impulse to "Idle Curiosity". These impulses, he held, gave rise to esoteric knowledge in all known civilizations and therefore to a custodial function for 'a select body of adepts or specialists – scientists, scholars, savants, clerks, priests, shamans, medicine men. The particular organization of highly valued knowledge varies from one society to another but always makes up the central substance of the civilization in which it is found' (Halsey, 1992, p. 40).
4 Nietzsche signs off his preface with a telling comment: 'A book like this, a problem like this, is in no hurry; we both, I just as much as my book, are friends of *lento*. It is not for nothing that I have been a philologist, perhaps I am a philologist still, that is to say, a teacher of slow reading: – in the end I also write slowly. . . . For philology is that venerable art which demands of its votaries one thing above all: to go aside, to take time, to become still, to become slow – it is a goldsmith's art and connoisseurship of the *word* which has nothing but delicate, cautious work to do and achieves nothing if it does not achieve it *lento*'. When we stress efficiency it's too easy to lose sight of the value of doing things carefully.
5 For Humboldt, teaching and learning are subordinate to the progress of science and scholarship. However, teaching is still important here insofar as it allows the community of scientists and scholars to replenish itself from a pool of successors.

Bibliography

Theodor W. Adorno (1976) 'Sociology and Empirical Research' in Paul Connerton, ed., *Critical Sociology: Selected Readings*, Harmondsworth: Penguin Books.
Decca Aitkenhead (2013) 'Peter Higgs Interview' *The Guardian*, 6th December. Available at https://www.theguardian.com/science/2013/dec/06/peter-higgs-interview-underlying-incompetence
George A. Akerlof (1970) 'The Market for "Lemons": Quality, Uncertainty, and the Market Mechanism' *The Quarterly Journal of Economics*, Vol. 84, No. 3, pp. 488–500.
Elizabeth Anderson (1993) *Value in Ethics and Economics*, Cambridge, MA: Harvard University Press.
Elizabeth Anderson (2007) 'Fair Opportunity in Education: A Democratic Equality Perspective' *Ethics*, Vol. 117, pp. 595–622.
Hannah Arendt (1993) *Between Past and Future*, London: Penguin.
Hannah Arendt (1998) *The Human Condition*, London: University of Chicago Press.
Aristotle (1981) *The Politics*, translated by T. A. Sinclair, London: Penguin.
James Arthur (2010) *Of Good Character: Exploration of Virtues and Values in 3–25 Year Olds*, Exeter: Imprint Academic.
Annette Baier (1986) 'Trust and Antitrust' *Ethics*, Vol. 96, pp. 231–260.
Michael Barber, Katelyn Donnely and Saad Rizvi (2013) *An Avalanche is Coming: Higher Education and the Revolution Ahead*, London: Institute for Public Policy Research.
Ronald Barnett (1997a) *Higher Education: A Critical Business*, Buckingham: SRHE and Open University Press.
Ronald Barnett (1997b) 'Still Breathing . . . Are Universities on their Deathbeds?' *The Times Higher Educational Supplement*, May 30th 1997.
Roland Barthes (1989) 'To the Seminar' in *The Rustle of Language*, Los Angeles, CA: University of California Press.
Mauro Basaure (2011) 'An Interview with Luc Boltanski: Criticism and the Expansion of Knowledge' *European Journal of Social Theory*, Vol. 14, No. 3, pp. 361–381.
Zygmunt Bauman (1997) 'The Present Crisis of the Universities' in J. Brzezinski and L. Nowak, eds., *Poznan Studies in the Philosophy of the Sciences and the Humanities: The Idea of the University*, Amsterdam: Rodopi.
Seyla Benhabib (1986) *Critique, Norm, and Utopia: A Study of the Foundations of Critical Theory*, New York: Colombia University Press.
Seyla Benhabib (2003) *The Reluctant Modernism of Hannah Arendt*, Oxford: Rowan & Littlefield.
John Berger (1972) *Ways of Seeing*, London: Penguin.

Richard J. Bernstein (2012) 'The Normative Core of the Public Sphere' *Political Theory*, Vol. 40, No. 6, pp. 767–778.
BIS (2011) *Students at the Heart of the System*, Cm 8122, London: HMSO.
BIS (2014) *Improving the Student Learning Experience – A National Assessment*, BIS Research Paper No. 169. Available at https://www.gov.uk/government/uploads/system/uploads/attachment_data/file/311288/bis-14-700-improving-the-student-learning-experience.pdf last, accessed 17.09.14.
BIS (2015) *Fulfilling Our Potential: Teaching Excellence, Social Mobility and Student Choice*, Cm 9141, London: BIS.
BIS (2016) *Success as a Knowledge Economy*, Cm 9258, London: BIS.
Luc Boltanski and Laurent Thevenot (2006) *On Justification: Economies of Worth*, Princeton, NJ: Princeton University Press.
Paul Bou-Habib (2010) 'Who Should Pay for Higher Education?' *Journal of Philosophy of Education*, Vol. 44, No. 4, pp. 479–495.
Roger Brown (2011) *Higher Education and the Market*, London: Routledge.
Allen Buchanan (1985) *Ethics, Efficiency, and the Market*, Oxford: Clarendon Press.
Craig Calhoun (2006) 'The University and the Public Good' *Thesis Eleven*, Vol. 84, No. 1, pp. 7–43.
Craig Calhoun (2009) 'Academic Freedom: Public Knowledge and the Structural Transformation of the University' *Social Research*, Vol. 76, No. 2, pp. 561–598.
Craig Calhoun (2012) *The Roots of Radicalism: Tradition, the Public Sphere, and Nineteenth-Century Social Movements*, London: University of Chicago Press.
Eamonn Callan (1997) *Creating Citizens: Political Education and Liberal Democracy*, Oxford: Clarendon Press.
Stanley Cavell (2011) 'The Uncanniness of the Ordinary' in Sterling M. McMurrin, ed., *The Tanner Lectures on Human Values VIII*, Cambridge: Cambridge University Press.
John Clarke and Janet Newman (1997) *The Managerial State*, London: Sage.
Jean L. Cohen and Andrew Arato (1994) *Civil Society and Political Theory*, London: MIT Press.
Ben Colburn and Hugh Lazenby (2016) 'Hypothetical Insurance and Higher Education' *Journal of Philosophy of Education*. doi: 10.1111/1467-9752.12163
Stefan Collini (2012) *What Are Universities For?* London: Penguin.
Stefan Collini (2016) 'Who Are the Spongers Now?' *London Review of Books*, Vol. 38, No. 2. Available at http://www.lrb.co.uk/v38/n02/stefan-collini/who-are-the-spongers-now.
Alan Cribb and Sharon Gewirtz (2013) 'The Hollowed-out University? A Critical Analysis of Changing Institutional and Academic Norms in UK Higher Education', *Discourse: Studies in the Cultural Politics of Education*, Vol. 34, No. 3, pp. 338–350.
Michael Darby and Eli Karni (1973) 'Free Competition and the Optimal Amount of Fraud' *Journal of Law and Economics*, Vol. 16, No. 1, pp. 67–88.
Andrew Delbanco (2012) *College: What It Was, Is and Should Be*, Princeton, NJ: Princeton University Press.
John Dewey (2012) *The Public and Its Problems*, University Park, PA: Pennsylvania State University Press.
Ronald Dore (1976) *The Diploma Disease: Education, Qualification and Development*, London: George Allen & Unwin.
Avihay Dorfman and Alon Harel (2013) 'The Case Against Privatization' *Philosophy & Public Affairs*, Vol. 41, No. 1, pp. 67–102.
John S. Dryzek (1995) 'Critical Theory as a Research Program' in Stephen K. White, ed., *The Cambridge Companion to Habermas*, Cambridge: Cambridge University Press.

Uwe Dulleck, Rudolf Kerschbamer and Matthias Sutter (2011) 'The Economics of Credence Goods: An Experiment on the Role of Liability, Verifiability, Reputation, and Competition' *American Economic Review*, Vol. 101, No. 2, pp. 526–555.
Jon Elster (2015) 'Obscurantism and Academic Freedom' in A. Bilgrami and J. R. Cole, eds., *Who's Afraid of Academic Freedom?* New York: Columbia University Press.
David M. Estlund (2008) *Democratic Authority: A Philosophical Framework*, Princeton, NJ: Princeton University Press.
Nigel Fairclough (1994) 'Conversationalization of Public Discourse and the Authority of the Consumer' in R. Keat et al., eds., *The Authority of the Consumer*, London: Routledge.
John Fantuzzo (2015) 'A Course between Bureaucracy and Charisma: A Pedagogical Reading of Max Weber's Social Theory' *Journal of Philosophy of Education*, Vol. 49, No. 1, pp. 45–64.
Alessandro Ferrara (2014) *The Democratic Horizon: Hyperpluralism and the Renewal of Political Liberalism*, Cambridge: Cambridge University Press.
Michel Foucault (1991) *Discipline and Punish: The Birth of the Prison*, translated by Alan Sheridan, Harmondsworth: Penguin Books.
Nancy Fraser (2013) 'A Triple Movement? Parsing the Politics of Crisis after Polanyi' *New Left Review*, Vol. 81, May–June, pp. 119–132.
Oliver Fulton (1994) 'Consuming Education' in Russell Keat et al., eds., *The Authority of the Consumer*, London: Routledge.
Raymond Geuss (1981) *The Idea of a Critical Theory: Habermas and the Frankfurt School*, Cambridge: Cambridge University Press.
Peter Goldstone and Donald Tunnell (1975) 'A Critique of the Command Theory of Authority', *Educational Theory*, Vol. 25, No. 2, pp. 131–138.
Michael G. Gottsegen (1994) *The Political Thought of Hannah Arendt*, Albany: State University of New York Press.
John Gray (1992) *The Moral Foundations of Market Institutions*, London: The IEA Health and Welfare Unit.
Amy Gutmann (1996) 'What's the Use of Going to School? The Problem of Education in Utilitarianism and Rights Theories', in Amartya Sen and Bernard Williams, eds., *Utilitarianism and Beyond*, Cambridge: Cambridge University Press.
Amy Gutmann (1999) *Democratic Education*, Princeton, NJ: Princeton University Press.
Jürgen Habermas (1978) *Knowledge and Human Interests*, translated by Jeremy Shapiro, London: Heinemann Educational Books.
Jürgen Habermas (1979) 'What Is Universal Pragmatics?' in Jürgen Habermas, ed., *Communication and the Evolution of Society*, London: Heinemann Educational Books.
Jürgen Habermas (1987) *Toward a Rational Society*, Cambridge: Polity Press.
Jürgen Habermas (1989) *The New Conservatism*, Cambridge: Polity Press.
Jürgen Habermas (1991 & 1992a) *The Theory of Communicative Action*, two volumes, Cambridge: Polity Press.
Jürgen Habermas (1992b) *The Structural Transformation of the Public Sphere: An Inquiry into a Category of Bourgeois Society*, Cambridge: Polity Press.
Jürgen Habermas (1994) 'The Idea of the University: Learning Processes' in Jürgen Habermas, ed., *The New Conservatism: Cultural Criticism and the Historians' Debate*, translated by Shierry Weber Nicholsen, Cambridge: Polity Press.
Jürgen Habermas (1996) *Between Facts and Norms: Contributions to a Discourse Theory of Law and Democracy*, translated by William Rehg, Cambridge: Polity Press.
A. H. Halsey (1992) *Decline of Donnish Dominion: The British Academic Professions in the Twentieth Century*, Oxford: Clarendon Press.

Katherine Hawley (2014) 'Trust, Distrust and Commitment' *Nous*, Vol. 48, No. 1, pp. 1–20.
Joseph Heath (2006) 'The Benefits of Cooperation' *Philosophy & Public Affairs*, Vol. 34, No. 4, pp. 313–351.
P. Herbst (1973) 'Work, Labour, and University Education' in R. S. Peters, ed., *The Philosophy of Education*, Oxford: Oxford University Press.
John Holmwood (2011) 'The Idea of a Public University' in John Holmwood, ed., *A Manifesto for the Public University*, London: Bloomsbury.
John Holmwood (2012) 'Markets Versus Publics: The New Battleground of Higher Education' *Harvard International Review*. Available at http://hir.harvard.edu/youth-on-firemarkets-versus-publics/
Axel Honneth (2012a) *Reification: A New Look at an Old Idea*, Oxford: Oxford University Press.
Axel Honneth (2012b) *The I in We: Studies in the Theory of Recognition*, Cambridge: Polity Press.
Axel Honneth (2014) *Freedom's Right: The Social Foundations of Democratic Life*, New York: Columbia University Press.
Axel Honneth (2015) 'Education and the Democratic Public Sphere: A Neglected Chapter of Political Philosophy' in Jonas Jakobsen and Odin Lysaker, eds., *Recognition and Freedom: Axel Honneth's Political Thought*, Leiden: Brill.
Michael Ignatieff (1995) 'The Myth of Citizenship' in Ronald Beiner, ed., *Theorizing Citizenship*, Albany: State University of New York Press.
Jonas Jakobsen and Odin Lysaker (2015) *Recognition and Freedom: Axel Honneth's Political Thought*, Leiden: Brill.
Thomas Janoski (1998) *Citizenship and Civil Society: A Framework of Rights and Obligations in Liberal, Traditional, and Social Democratic Regimes*, Cambridge: Cambridge University Press.
Karl Jaspers (1960) *The Idea of the University*, London: Peter Owen.
Sharon Jessop (2012) 'Education for Citizenship and "Ethical Life": An Exploration of the Hegelian Concepts of *Bildung* and *Sittlichkeit*' *Journal of Philosophy of Education*, Vol. 46, No. 2, pp. 287–302.
Jill Johnes and Jim Taylor (1990) *Performance Indicators in Higher Education*, Buckingham: The Society for Research into Higher Education and Open University Press.
Russell Keat (1993) 'The Moral Boundaries of the Market' in Colin Crouch and David Marquand, eds., *Ethics and Markets*, Oxford: Blackwell Publishers.
Elie Kedourie (1989) *Perestroika in the Universities*, London: The IEA Health and Welfare Unit.
R. Kneller, M. Mongeon, J. Cope, C. Garner and P. Ternouth (2014) 'Industry-University Collaborations in Canada, Japan, the UK and USA – With Emphasis on Publication Freedom and Managing the Intellectual Property Lock-Up Problem' *PLoS ONE*, Vol. 9, No. 3.
Zdenko Kodelja (2013) 'Authority, the Autonomy of the University, and Neoliberal Politics' *Educational Theory*, Vol. 63, No. 3, pp. 317–330.
Thomas S. Kuhn (1970) *The Structure of Scientific Revolutions*, 2nd ed., Chicago: University of Chicago Press.
Chandran Kukathas and Philip Pettit (1990) *Rawls: A Theory of Justice and Its Critics*, Cambridge: Polity Press.
Thomas McCarthy (1989) *The Critical Theory of Jürgen Habermas*, Cambridge: Polity Press.
Eric Macfarlane (1993) *Education 16–19: In Transition*, London: Routledge.
Andrew McGettigan (2013) *The Great University Gamble*, London: Pluto Press.
Walter W. McMahon (2009) *Higher Learning, Greater Good: The Private and Social Benefits of Higher Education*, Baltimore: Johns Hopkins University Press.

Simon Marginson (2006) 'Putting "Public" Back into the Public University' *Thesis Eleven*, Vol. 84, pp. 44–59.
David Marquand (2015) *Mammon's Kingdom: An Essay on Britain, Now*, London: Penguin.
T. H. Marshall (1964) *Class, Citizenship and Social Development*, Chicago: University of Chicago Press.
Christopher Martin (2016) 'Should Students Have to Borrow? Autonomy, Wellbeing and Student Debt' *Journal of Philosophy of Education*, in press.
Karl Marx (1977) 'Economic and Philosophical Manuscripts' in David McLellan, ed., *Karl Marx: Selected Writings*, Oxford: Oxford University Press.
William F. May (2001) *Beleaguered Rulers: The Public Obligation of the Professional*, Louiseville: Westminster John Knox.
John Stuart Mill (2006) *On Liberty*, London: Penguin.
David Miller (2001) *Principles of Social Justice*, London: Harvard University Press.
Seumas Miller (Spring 2011 Edition) 'Corruption', in Edward N. Zalta, ed., *The Stanford Encyclopedia of Philosophy*. Available at http://plato.stanford.edu/archives/spr2011/entries/corruption/
Nicholas Mirzoeff (2015) *How to See the World*, London: Penguin.
Philip Moriarty (2011) 'Science as a Public Good' in J. Holmwood, ed., *A Manifesto for the Public University*, London: Bloomsbury.
Emily C. Nacol (2011) 'The Risks of Political Authority: Trust, Knowledge and Political Agency in Locke's *Second Treatise*' *Political Studies*, Vol. 59, pp. 580–595.
Christopher Newfield (2008) *Unmaking the Public University: The Forty-Year Assault on the Middle Classes*, London: Harvard University Press.
John Henry Newman (1976) *The Idea of a University: Defined and Illustrated*, Oxford: Clarendon Press.
Friedrich Nietzsche (1997) *Daybreak: Thoughts on the Prejudices of Morality*, translated by R. J. Hollingdale, Cambridge: Cambridge University Press.
Martha Nussbaum (1997) *Cultivating Humanity: A Classical Defense of Reform in Liberal Education*, London: Harvard University Press.
Martha Nussbaum (2010) *Not for Profit: Why Democracy Needs the Humanities*, Princeton, NJ: Princeton University Press.
Michael Oakeshott (1991) *Rationalism in Politics and Other Essays*, Indianapolis: Liberty Press.
Kevin Olson (2006) *Reflexive Democracy*, Cambridge, MA: MIT Press.
Collin O'Neil (2012) 'Lying, Trust, and Gratitude' *Philosophy & Public Affairs*, Vol. 40, No. 4, pp. 301–333.
John O'Neill (1998) *The Market: Ethics, Knowledge and Politics*, London: Routledge.
Onora O'Neill (2002) *A Question of Trust*, Cambridge: Cambridge University Press.
R. S. Peters and Peter Winch (1967) 'Authority' in A. Quinton, ed., *Political Philosophy*, Oxford: Oxford University Press.
Michael Polanyi (1998) *Personal Knowledge: Towards a Post-Critical Philosophy*, London: Routledge.
John Rawls (1973) *A Theory of Justice*, Oxford: Oxford University Press.
John Rawls (2006) *Political Liberalism*, New York: Columbia University Press.
Robbins Report (1963) *Higher Education*, Cm. 2154, London: HMSO.
Alan Ryan (1999) *Liberal Anxieties and Liberal Education*, London: Profile Books.
Desmond Ryan (1998) 'The Thatcher Government's Attack on Higher Education in Historical Perspective' *New Left Review*, Vol. 227, pp. 3–32.

Edward W. Said (1994) *Representations of the Intellectual: The 1993 Reith Lectures*, London: Vintage.
Brian Salter and Ted Tapper (2000) 'The Politics of Governance in Higher Education: The Case of Quality Assurance' *Political Studies*, Vol. 48, No. 1, pp. 66–87.
Michael Sandel (2012) *What Money Can't Buy: The Moral Limits of Markets*, London: Allen Lane.
Peter Scott (1995) *The Meanings of Mass Higher Education*, Buckingham: The Society for Research into Higher Education & Open University Press.
Amartya Sen (1977) 'Rational Fools' *Philosophy & Public Affairs*, Vol. 6, No. 4, pp. 317–344.
Edward Shils (1997) 'The Academic Ethic' in E. Shils, ed., *The Calling of Education: The Academic Ethic and Other Essays on Higher Education*, London: University of Chicago Press.
David Neil Silk (1976) 'Aspects of the Concept of Authority in Education' *Educational Theory*, Vol. 26, No. 3, pp. 271–278.
Georg Simmel (1990) *The Philosophy of Money*, London: Routledge.
Tony Smith (1991) *The Role of Ethics in Social Theory*, New York: State University of New York Press.
Woodruff D. Smith (2010) *Public Universities and the Public Sphere*, New York, NY: Palgrave Macmillan.
Paul Standish (2005) 'Towards an Economy of Higher Education' *Critical Quarterly*, Vol. 47, Nos. 1–2, pp. 53–71.
Ted Tapper and Brian Salter (1998) 'The Dearing Report and the Maintenance of Academic Standards: Towards a New Academic Corporatism' *Higher Education Quarterly*, Vol. 52, No. 1, pp. 22–34.
Charles Taylor (1980) 'The Philosophy of the Social Sciences' in M. Richter, ed., *Political Theory and Political Education*, Princeton, NJ: Princeton University Press.
Charles Taylor (1981) 'Growth, Legitimacy and the Modern Identity' *Praxis International*, Vol. 1, No. 2, pp. 111–125.
Charles Taylor (1995) 'Liberal Politics and the Public Sphere' in Amitai Etzioni, ed., *New Communitarian Thinking: Persons, Virtues, Institutions, and Communities*, London: University Press of Virginia.
Alain Touraine (1995) *Critique of Modernity*, Oxford: Basil Blackwell.
Alain Touraine (1997) *What is Democracy?* Oxford: Westview Press.
Martin Trow (1998) 'The Dearing Report: A Transatlantic View' *Higher Education Quarterly*, Vol. 52, No. 1, pp. 93–117.
Jeremy Waldron (1995) 'The Wisdom of the Multitude: Some Reflections on Book 3, Chapter 11 of Aristotle's *Politics*' *Political Theory*, Vol. 23, No. 4, pp. 563–584.
Jeremy Waldron (2014) 'Accountability: Fundamental to Democracy' NYU School of Law, Public Law Research Paper No. 14–13. Available at SSRN http://ssrn.com/abstract=2410812 or http://dx.doi.org/10.2139/ssrn.2410812
Michael Walzer (1980) 'Political Decision-Making and Political Education' in Melvin Richter, ed., *Political Theory and Political Education*, Princeton, NJ: Princeton University Press.
Michael Walzer (1983) *Spheres of Justice*, Oxford: Blackwell Publishers.
Max Weber (1991) 'Bureaucracy' in H. H. Gerth and C. Wright Mills, eds., *From Max Weber: Essays in Sociology*, London: Routledge.
Morgan White (2013) 'Higher Education and Problems of Citizenship Formation' *Journal of Philosophy of Education*, Vol. 47, No. 1, pp. 112–127.
Stephen K. White (1989) *The Recent Work of Jürgen Habermas*, Cambridge: Cambridge University Press.

Bernard Williams (1994) *Shame and Necessity*, London: University of California Press.
Joanna Williams (2013) *Consuming Higher Education: Why Learning Can't Be Bought*, London: Bloomsbury.
Raymond Williams (1988) *Keywords: A Vocabulary of Culture and Society*, London: Fontana Press.
Max Weber (2003) *The Protestant Ethic and the Spirit of Capitalism*, translated by T. Parsons, Mineola, NY: Dover Publications.
Robert Paul Wolff (1969) *The Ideal of the University*, Boston: Beacon Press.
Robert Paul Wolff (1998) *In Defense of Anarchism*, London: University of California Press.

Index

academic authority 51–5, 57–61
academic freedom 12, 17–18, 19, 30, 74–7, 140, 146
academic lifeworld 17
academic preparation 173
accountability 18–19, 64–5, 80, 119, 175–6
Adorno, Theodor W. 31, 147–8, 175
adult illiteracy 144
agent accountability 18
Akerlof, George A. 55
alternative economy 25
American Association of University Professors 17
American University of Malta 41
Anderson, Elizabeth 111–14, 142–3
apolitical culture 164
appeals to fairness 50
Arendt, Hannah 9, 10, 12, 48, 49, 67, 73, 79, 81, 85
aristoi 66
Aristotle 3, 31, 65, 66, 68
Arts and Humanities Research Board 129
attitudes 19–20
auctoritas 61
Augustine of Hippo, Saint 23
Austin, John 51
Australia 92
authority: academic authority 51–5; accountability and 64–5; as *auctoritas* 61; command theory of 50–1; *de facto* authority 50; *de jure* authority 50–1, 61; expert authority 55; obedience and 61–2; obedience to power and 176; state authority 50; trust and 58–9, 62
autonomy 136–8, 140–2, 145, 178

Baier, Annette 58
Barnett, Ronald 71–2, 110, 126
Bauman, Zygmunt 10, 121–2, 128, 130–1
Benhabib, Seyla 149, 150–1
Bentham, Jeremy 3
Berger, John 16–17
Bernstein, Basil 72
Between Facts and Norms (Habermas) 136
Bildung 66
Blair Government 100
Blair, Tony 92
blocked exchanges 107, 108
Böckenförde theorem 4
Boltanski, Luc 21–2
bootstrapping argument 141–2, 145
Bossuet, Jacques-Bénigne 23, 26
Bou-Habib, Paul 35–6
Bourdieu, Pierre 21
Brown, Roger 53, 56
Browne Report 22
Buchanan, Allen 97–9
bureaucracy 167

calculation insight 93–4
Calhoun, Craig 14, 17, 47
Callan, Eamonn 66–7
Calvino, Italo 2
catallactic bias 41, 43–4
Cavell, Stanley 33
charismatic authority 167
charismatic education 143–4
charity 23
citizenship: academic freedom and democratic 74–7; Aristotelian idea of 66; autonomy and 140; civil rights 69; and education 65–9; higher education and 6, 63–77; liberal and republican varieties of 63–4; oriented towards autonomy 136–7; Platonic version of 66; political rights 69; republican citizen 67–8; social rights 69
'Citizenship and National Identity' (Habermas) 136

civic engagement 48
'civic polity' 23
civic privatism 80
civic virtue 63, 65–6
civil rights 68, 69, 136–7, 144
civil society 113
Clarke, John 78
classical liberalism 24
closed economies 24–6
Colburn, Ben 37–40
collective judgement 31–2
Collini, Stefan 5
colonisation of the lifeworld 92, 146, 162–4
command theory of law 51
commodification 102–3
common good 23, 58
communicative action 158–9
communicative rationality 41, 154–5, 157
communicative reason 157–9, 174
competition 21
complex equality 103–7
consent 50
conservatism 66
consultancy 135
consumer-accountability 19
consumer satisfaction 83
conversationalization 102–3
cooperation 43–7
corruption: concept of 133; of democracy and education 92–114; individualistic attitudes 32
costs 123–4
'cost-sharing' policies 35–6
counterpublics 14
credence goods 56–7, 60, 61–2
credit accumulation and transfer (CAT) 120
Cribb, Alan 11
'The Crisis in Education' (Arendt) 81
critical theory: emancipatory cognitive interests and 150–1; of Habermas 66, 150–1, 153–4
cultural impoverishment 163, 172

Dearing Report 120
debt 124
de facto authority 50
degrees 122–3
de jure authority 50, 61
deliberative democracy 12–13
deliberative politics 138
democracy: accountability and 18–19, 64–5; corruption of education and 92–114; deliberative democracy 12–13; education and 3–4; epistemic authority and 6; impact of policy changes on 7; language of 9; problems with contemporary democracy 9–14; public trust and 6; role of universities 6, 35–48; technocracy and 18–19
Democratic Authority (Estlund) 41
'democratic horizon' 11
'democratic play' 66–7
desert island auction thought experiment 37
Dewey, John 3, 17, 66, 175
Diderot, Denis 2
distributive justice 36, 103–7
distrust 59, 61
doctrine of the wisdom of the multitude 31–2
'domestic polity' 23
Dorfman, Avihay 26–9, 31
'double transformation' 42
Dulleck, Uwe 56
Durkheim, Émile 3, 139
Dutch-disease 47
Dworkin, Ronald 37, 176

economies of scale cooperation 44–5
economies of worth 6, 21–2
education: *Bildung* and 66; charismatic education 143–4; citizenship and 6, 63–77; citizenship and university education 69–74; civil society and 113; corruption of democracy and 92–114; costs of higher education expansion, 125, 128–9; cultural impoverishment in 6; democracy and 3–4; drawing the boundaries of the market 102–3; drift from democratic education 81–5; functions of 173; funding 35–40, 123–4; higher education as instrumental private good 155–7; inhospitable setting for the intellectual 131–2; instrumentalisation of 80; as lubricant to labour market 123; marketisation of 6, 43, 53, 60–1; market norms and the good of higher education 111–14; markets in educational context 100–1; purposes of 88–91, 165–6, 175; from the sacred to a profane education 134–6; social and public rates of return to 122–3; technical skills and lifelong learning 85–91; university education as a social right 145–6; value of 53–4
Education Reform Act 100, 116
efficacy 109
efficiency 97–100

Elster, Jon 12
emancipatory cognitive interests 150–1
embarrassment 48
England 7
Enlightenment 14
epistemic authority 57
equality of opportunity 37
Estlund, David 5, 41
exchange-value conception of higher education 26–9
exclusive goods 112
expert authority 55

Fairclough, Norman 102–3
fairness argument 36
Fantuzzo, John 143–4
Ferrara, Alessandro 11
fidelity by reason 27, 175–6
fidelity of deference 27–9, 30, 175–6
forensic accountability 18
Foucault, Michel 117, 128
'Frankfurt School' 150
Fraser, Nancy 14, 42–3, 138
Fulfilling Our Potential Green Paper 119
Fulton, Oliver 97
functionary intellectual 121–30
Further and Higher Education Act 100

gains from trade cooperation 44
general education 173
general taxation 35–40
Geuss, Raymond 150
Gewirtz, Sharon 11
gift relationship 25
Goldstone, Peter 51
Gottsegen, Michael G. 67–8
graduate tax system 38–9
Gray, John 93–4
Grayling, A. C. 31
Great Depression 42
Gutmann, Amy 65, 73–4, 90, 124, 134–5

Habermas, Jürgen: call for more self-reflexive university 90–1; 'Citizenship and National Identity' 136; collective political imagination 10; colonisation of the lifeworld 92, 146, 162–4; communicative action 157–8; communicative reason 157–9; critical theory 66, 150–1, 153–4; *Between Facts and Norms* 136; formation of deliberative politics 138–9; idea of the social lifeworld 160–1; justice 149; *Knowledge and Human Interests* 154; models of rationality 154–5; modernisation 173; portrayal of public sphere 13–14; publicity and 17; role of philosophy 171; role of universities 4, 31, 168, 174; schema of civil, political and social rights 136–7, 140; social rights 141; structural transformation of public sphere 14–15, 47; *The Structural Transformation of the Public Sphere* 13; substantive rights 143; *The Theory of Communicative Action* 154; welfare-state juridification 136–7
Hardin, Russell 59
Harel, Alon 26–9, 31
Harvard University 93
Havel, Vaclav 9
Hawley, Katherine 58–60, 61
Hayek, Friedrich 95
Heath, Joseph 43–7
Hegel, Georg W. F. 66
Heidegger, Martin 33
Herbst, P. 82–5
Higgs, Peter 125
Higher Education Academy (HEA) 54–5, 79, 96
Higher Education Act 118
Higher Education: a New Framework White Paper 118
Higher Education Funding Councils 101, 118–20, 152
Higher Education Institutions (HEIs) 5
Higher Education Quality Council (HEQC) 118–19
Hirschman, Albert 112
Hobbes, Thomas 23, 26, 46, 50, 51
'hollowed-out' university 11
Holmwood, John 5
Honneth, Axel 3, 24, 33, 150, 175
Horkheimer, Max 150, 175
Humboldt, Alexander von 168–70
Hume, David 46

ideal speech situation 4–5
The Idea of the University (Newman) 165
Ignatieff, Michael 63, 65
Improving the Student Learning Experience – a national assessment BIS report 55
incentive argument 36
income contingent state-backed loan 39–40
individualistic attitudes 32
'individual learning accounts' 100
'industrial polity' 23
inefficiency 97
informal opinion-formation 138

informal public-opinion formation 138
information transmission mechanisms 44
'inspired polity' 23
Institute for Learning and Teaching 79
institutionalised will-formation 138
instrumental reason 164
instrumental values 26–7, 29–33, 53–4
intellectual 130–2
intellectual property management 45–6
isonomy 67

Jacoby, Russell 132
Jarratt Report 118
Jaspers, Karl 127, 167
Johns Hopkins University 166
judging 20
juridification 136–7, 163
just property acquisition 59
justice 148–9
justification: economies of worth 21–2; for expansion of universities 41–2; 'polities' of 23–4, 175; stations of discursive justification 22–3
On Justification: Economies of Worth (Boltanski & Thevenot) 21, 23

Kant, Immanuel 3, 15, 24
Keat, Russell 102, 108
Kedourie, Elie 156
Kelsen, Hans 51
Kerschbamer, Rudolf 56
'key skills' 67
kite mark 57
Kluge, Alexander 14
Kneller, R. 45–6
knowing 20
knowledge 72, 86, 90, 152, 165–6, 176
Knowledge and Human Interests (Habermas) 154
knowledge economy 87–8
Kodelja, Zdenko 57
Kuhn, Thomas 128

Lambert Agreement 46
The Last Intellectuals (Jacoby) 132
Lazenby, Hugh 37–40
learning 82, 85–91
'learning society' 87–8
legitimacy 65, 80, 128, 136, 148–9
legitimation crisis 10, 12, 21
liberalism 66
On Liberty (Mill) 18, 32
lifelong learning 85–91, 100

lifeworld: colonisation of the lifeworld 92, 146, 162–4; idea of the social lifeworld 160–1
Lijphart, Arend 9
'liquid modernity' 9
Locke, John 24, 46, 50, 58, 59, 68

Major Government 100
Major, John 92
Malta 41
Marcuse, Herbert 150
market discourses 102–3
market mechanisms 11, 92, 97
market norms 111–14
'market polity' 23–4
market sphere 112
market systems 93–4
marketisation 43, 53, 60–1, 100–1
Marquand, David 11, 36
Marshall, T. H. 136
Martin, Christopher 40
Marx, Karl 95, 103
McCarthy, Thomas 151
'meritocracy' 73
Mill, John Stuart 3, 18, 30, 66
Miller, David 24
Miller, Seumas 133
Million+ Group 26, 34
Mirzoeff, Nicholas 12
Mises, Ludwig von 93
modern identity 108–1110
modernisation 173
money 103–7
'The Moral Boundaries of the Market' (Keat) 102

'narrow civility' 159
Negt, Oskar 14
New College of the Humanities 31
New Deal 42
New Labour Government 44
New School for Social Research 17–18
New Zealand 92
Newfield, Christopher 5, 45
Newman, Janet 78
Newman, John Henry 165, 166, 168, 173
94 Group 26
Nussbaum, Martha 5

Oakeshott, Michael 3, 31, 52, 66, 83
obedience 61–2
oikos 15
Olson, Kevin 140–3

O'Neill, John 95–6
O'Neill, Onora 34, 61
open competition 93
open economies 24–6
optimality 97–100

Paretian efficiency 97
Paretian optimality 97–100
Parsons, Talcott 139, 173
participation 50, 65, 141, 146
participatory democracy 66
partnerships 6, 54–5, 61
Pasteur, Louis 135
payment arrangements 35–40
Peirce, C. S. 4
performance indicators 117
Perpetual Peace (Kant) 15
Peters, R. S. 57
philosophy 170–2
Plato 3, 66
plurality 23
Polanyi, Karl 42
Polanyi, Michael 87
polis 15, 24, 32
Political Liberalism (Rawls) 20
political literacy 13
political republicanism 24
political rights 69, 136–7, 140–1, 144
political theory 3–4
Politics (Aristotle) 31
'polity of fame' 23
Polytechnics and Colleges Funding Council (PCFC) 116
populism 10
post-experience goods 56–7, 61
practical knowledge 86
pragmatism 66
preference satisfaction 40–1
'The Present Crisis of the Universities' (Bauman) 121–2
price mechanism 6
Principles of Social Justice (Miller) 24
private rates of return 122–3
privatisation: case against 26–9; competitive behaviour and 21; instrumental approach to 26–7; instrumental values and privatised universities 29–33; rise of the social and 78–81; types of 78; of universities 6, 29–34
profane education 134–6
professionalism 151–4
promotion 103
property relations 68

Protestant Ethic (Weber) 143
pseudo-aristoi 66
public 21
public attitudes 19–20
public discourse 102
public goods 1–2, 26–7
public opinion 30
public policy 130–1
public rates of return 122–3
public reason 6–7, 15, 140, 178
public space 85
public sphere: attitudes 19–20; competitive behaviour and 47–8; as realm of appearances 12; recognition 138–9; as relational 13–14; structural transformation of 13, 14–15, 47; universities and 6, 9–20
public trust 6
publicity 15, 16

qualification inflation 6
Quality Assessment Committee (QAC) 118, 120–1
quality assurance 116, 118–19
Quality Assurance Agency (QAA) 55, 79, 96, 122, 153
quality assurance mechanisms 82

Rammell, Bill 54
Ramsden, Paul 54
rational choice theory 36–7
rationalism 153–4
rationality 154–5
rational-legal authority 167
Rawls, John 20, 35, 50, 148–9, 176
reason 15
recognition 24, 33, 138–9
'Regrets on my Old Dressing Gown' (Diderot) 2
reification 24, 33–4, 162–3
representative democracy 64
republican citizen 67–8
research 45, 80–1, 84–5, 113, 125–7, 135, 173
Research Assessment Exercises (RAE) 117, 152–3
Research Excellence Framework (REF) 18, 29, 96, 117, 122, 136, 152–3
research university 166–7, 174
Reynolds Report 118
risk management 58
risk pooling cooperation 44
Rorty, Richard 150

Rousseau, Jean-Jacques 3, 23, 46, 50, 66, 175
Russell Group 26, 34, 156
Ryan, Desmond 92, 101, 110–11

sacred education 134–6
Said, Edward 133
Saint-Simon, Henri de 23
Salter, Brian 153
Samuelson, Paul 1
Sandel, Michael 104
scholarship 121–30, 147–8
schooling 4, 65, 79, 90
Schutz, Alfred 160
science 4
Scott, Peter 88–9, 134
sectional interest groups 34
security 50
self-binding cooperative mechanisms 44–6
self-rule 68–9
Sen, Amartya 36
shame 48
shirking 46
Simmel, Georg 106–7
skills 67, 87
social contract 63–4
social contract theory 58
social goods 105–6
social knowledge 88
social rates of return 122–3
social rights 7, 69, 136–7, 140–1, 144–5, 178
social status 46–7
Spheres of Justice (Walzer) 24, 104
'spheres' of life 105
standards 119
Standish, Paul 24–5, 30
state authority 50
'state of nature' theories 149
state sovereignty 26–7, 29
status 6
strategic rationality 154–5
Strauss, Leo 31
street lamps 2
strong public spheres 138
The Structural Transformation of the Public Sphere (Habermas) 13
student loans system 22
student partnership 6, 54–5, 61
student representation 55
'Students as Partners in the Curriculum' project 55
Students at the Heart of the System White Paper 22
Students' Union (NUS) 55

'subaltern publics' 14
Sunflowers (Van Gogh) 105
superiority 98
Sutter, Matthias 56
syllabus amendments 152
systems theory perspective 172

Tapper, Ted 153
Taylor, Charles 108–9, 127
teaching 124–5, 127–8
Teaching Excellence Framework (TEF) 82, 96, 117, 121, 122, 153
Teaching Quality Assessment (TQA) 120, 153
teaching university 166
technical knowledge 86, 106, 152
technical skills 85–91
technically exploitable knowledge 90, 173
technocracy 18–19
technology 13, 175
Thatcher, Margaret 92
The Theory of Communicative Action (Habermas) 154
A Theory of Justice (Rawls) 148–9
Thévenot, Laurent 21–2
thinking 20
Tokyo University 93
Touraine, Alain 9, 80
transparency 33–4
Trow, Martin 120
trust 58–9, 62, 176
tuition fee levels 176
Tunnell, Donald 51

United Kingdom 7, 54, 79, 92
universities: academic freedom 12, 17–18, 19, 30, 74–7, 140, 146; apolitical culture within 164; business ethic of salesmanship at work in 147; call for more self-reflexive 90–1; central goals 127–8; changing meaning of 110–11; citizenship and university education 69–74; closed and open economies of higher education 24–6; collaborative arrangements between industry and 45–6; colonisation of university lifeworld 81–5; constant crisis of 9; consultancy model of academe 135; costs of expansion 125; crisis in 177–8; debate surrounding marketisation of 43; democratic role for 19–20; economies of worth and 24; education at 5; first duty 54; function of 173; higher education as instrumental private

good 155–7; 'hollowed-out' university 11; ideas of 165–75; imposition of market mechanisms on 92; instrumental values and 29–33; justification for expansion of 41–2; language of 9; legitimacy of 65, 80, 128, 148–9; as lubricant to labour market 123; notion of the intellectual in 130–2; payment arrangements 35–40; privatisation of 29–34; publicity and 33–4; public sphere and 6, 9–20; purposes of 2–5, 88–91, 165–6; rational-reconstructive role of 138–46; research university 166–7, 174; rise of professionalism in 151–4; role in democracy 6, 35–48; role in sustaining a democratic culture 6; role of 'communicative' rationality 41; role of philosophy 170–2; from the sacred to a profane education 134–6; structural transformation of 16–18; syllabus amendments in 152; teaching university 166; university education as a social right 145–6; as utilitarian knowledge factory 90–1; virtues required 32–3
Universities Funding Council (UFC) 116
Universities UK 118
university governance: policy changes 6; student partnership 6, 54–5, 61
University of Chicago 166
University of Phoenix 93
University of Wolverhampton 93
unrestricted communication community 4–5
use-value of commodities 112

value for money 64–5
Van Gogh, Vincent 105
Veblen, Thorstein 11, 70, 147, 166
'vicarious decision-making' 66–7
virtue 72
vocationalism 79–80

Waldron, Jeremy 18, 31, 32
Walzer, Michael 24, 66–7, 73, 103–6, 108
Ways of Seeing (Berger) 16
weak public spheres. 138
Weber, Max 143, 147, 167
welfare state 7, 42, 70, 136–8
welfare-state juridification 136–7, 163
Wellmer, Albrecht 150
White, Stephen K. 154–5, 159, 163
Williams, Bernard 48
Williams, Joanna 5
Winch, Peter 51
Wittgenstein, Ludwig 176
Wolff, Robert Paul 50–1
work 6, 82–5
worldliness 72